The 6th/5th century B C E Greek m‹ the most celebrated lyricist of antiq paean to the heroic athlete, and are choral songs of acclamation, the gl .... or triumph at a variety of Panhellenic restivals including the Olympic Games. His other poems, collected in thirteen books, are largely lost or fragmentary – except for the Paeans – but were devoted to the praise of gods and heroes. Yet Pindar, though still respected, is now considered a difficult poet and is sometimes dismissed as a reactionary, celebrating an aristocratic world that was passing and that deserved to pass.

In this wide-ranging introduction, Richard Stoneman shows that Pindar's works, even where they seem obscure, follow a logic of their own and reward further study. An unmatched craftsman with words, and witness to a profoundly religious sensibility, he is a poet who takes modern readers to the heart of Greek ideas about the gods, fleeting human achievement and mortality. The author examines questions of performance and genre; patronage; imagery; and reception, from Horace to the twentieth century.

RICHARD STONEMAN is Honorary Visiting Professor in Classics at the University of Exeter and editor of the Understanding Classics series. His many books include *Pindar: Odes and Fragments* (1997), *Land of Lost Gods: The Search for Classical Greece* (I.B.Tauris, 2010), *Legends of Alexander the Great* (I.B.Tauris, 2011) and *The Book of Alexander the Great: A Life of the Conqueror* (I.B.Tauris, 2011).

In this wide-ranging and stimulating treatment, Richard Stoneman offers a richly detailed and imaginative survey of Pindar's poetry as well as a very welcome foray into his influence on the European lyric tradition from the Renaissance to Romanticism. The book provides a passionate and at the same time very accessible introduction to a difficult subject and will be of undoubted interest not only to undergraduate students but also, more generally, to readers attracted to one of the greatest poets of antiquity.

—Giambattista D'Alessio, Professor of Greek
Language and Literature, King's College London

UNDERSTANDING CLASSICS

EDITOR: RICHARD STONEMAN (UNIVERSITY OF EXETER)

When the great Roman poets of the Augustan Age – Ovid, Virgil and Horace – composed their odes, love poetry and lyrical verse, could they have imagined that their works would one day form a cornerstone of Western civilization, or serve as the basis of study for generations of schoolchildren learning Latin? Could Aeschylus or Euripides have envisaged the remarkable popularity of contemporary stagings of their tragedies? The legacy and continuing resonance of Homer's *Iliad* and *Odyssey* – Greek poetical epics written many millennia ago – again testify to the capacity of the classics to cross the divide of thousands of years and speak powerfully and relevantly to audiences quite different from those to which they were originally addressed.

Understanding Classics is a specially commissioned series which aims to introduce the outstanding authors and thinkers of antiquity to a wide audience of appreciative modern readers, whether undergraduate students of classics, literature, philosophy and ancient history or generalists interested in the classical world. Each volume – written by leading figures internationally – will examine the historical significance of the writer or writers in question; their social, political and cultural contexts; their use of language, literature and mythology; extracts from their major works; and their reception in later European literature, art, music and culture. *Understanding Classics* will build a library of readable, authoritative introductions offering fresh and elegant surveys of the greatest literatures, philosophies and poetries of the ancient world.

UNDERSTANDING CLASSICS

Aristophanes and Greek Comedy	JEFFREY S. RUSTEN *Cornell University*
Augustine	DENNIS E. TROUT *Tufts University*
Cicero	GESINE MANUWALD *University College London*
Euripides	ISABELLE TORRANCE *University of Notre Dame*
Eusebius	AARON P. JOHNSON *Lee University, Tennessee*
Homer	JONATHAN S. BURGESS *University of Toronto*
Latin Love Poetry	DENISE MCCOSKEY & ZARA TORLONE *Miami University, Ohio*
Martial	LINDSAY WATSON & PATRICIA WATSON *University of Sydney*
Ovid	CAROLE E. NEWLANDS *University of Wisconsin, Madison*
Pindar	RICHARD STONEMAN *University of Exeter*
Plutarch	MARK BECK *University of North Carolina, Chapel Hill*
The Poets of Alexandria	SUSAN A. STEPHENS *Stanford University*
Roman Comedy	DAVID CHRISTENSON *University of Arizona*
Sappho	PAGE DUBOIS *University of California, Berkeley*
Seneca	CHRISTOPHER STAR *Middlebury College*
Sophocles	STEPHEN ESPOSITO *Boston University*
Tacitus	VICTORIA EMMA PAGÁN *University of Florida*
Virgil	ALISON KEITH *University of Toronto*

PINDAR

Richard Stoneman

UNDERSTANDING CLASSICS SERIES EDITOR:
RICHARD STONEMAN

I.B. TAURIS
LONDON · NEW YORK

Published in 2014 by I.B.Tauris & Co Ltd
6 Salem Road, London W2 4BU
175 Fifth Avenue, New York NY 10010
www.ibtauris.com

Distributed in the United States and Canada Exclusively by Palgrave Macmillan
175 Fifth Avenue, New York NY 10010

Copyright © 2014 Richard Stoneman

The right of Richard Stoneman to be identified as the author of this work has been
asserted by him in accordance with the Copyright, Designs and Patents Act 1988.

All rights reserved. Except for brief quotations in a review, this book, or any part
thereof, may not be reproduced, stored in or introduced into a retrieval system, or
transmitted, in any form or by any means, electronic, mechanical, photocopying,
recording or otherwise, without the prior written permission of the publisher.

Every attempt has been made to gain permission for the use of the images
in this book. Any omissions will be rectified in future editions.

ISBN: 978 1 78076 184 8 (HB)
          978 1 78076 185 5 (PB)

A full CIP record for this book is available from the British Library
A full CIP record is available from the Library of Congress

Library of Congress Catalog Card Number: available

Text design, typesetting and eBook versions by Tetragon, London

Printed and bound in Great Britain by T.J. International, Padstow, Cornwall

CONTENTS

To Richard Seaford,
who always gives me a new angle on Greek poetry

Illustrations

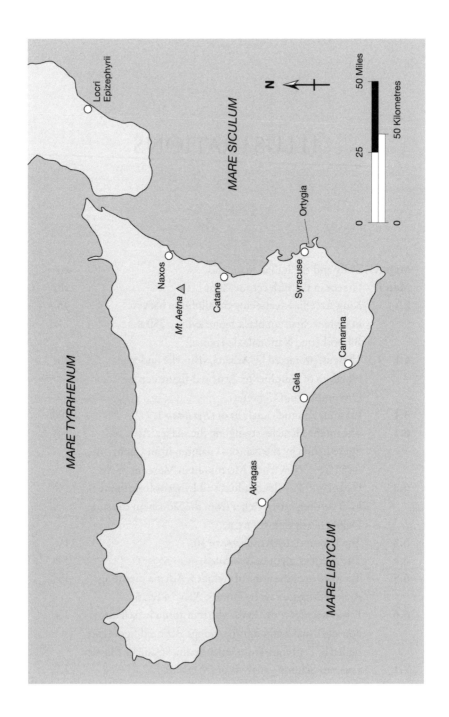

Map A Sicily and the Italian mainland.

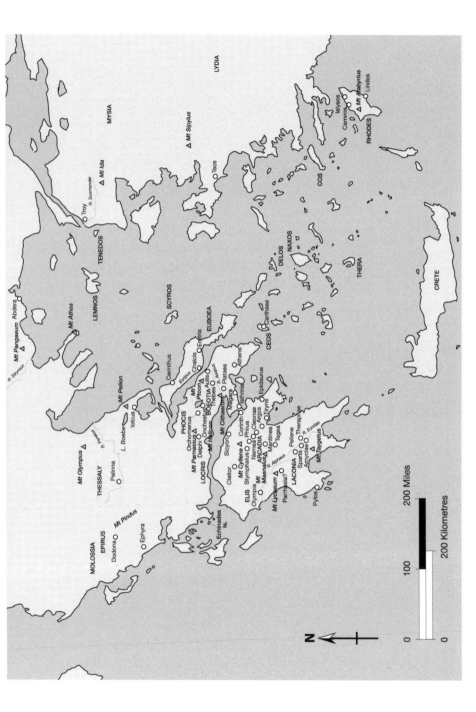

Map B   Greece in the fifth century BCE.

PREFACE

THE AIM OF THE SERIES in which this book appears is to introduce the major writers of Greek and Roman antiquity for the benefit of students and readers at any level who would like a first orientation on these writers. Such readers may or may not have access to the original languages, and the books are designed to be usable by both categories of reader. Most classical authors have a long afterlife, and the work they produced is of vital importance for the understanding of later literatures; consequently, these books also aim to give guidance to the substantial 'reception-history' of their authors. In addition, the books set out the problems in approaching the author in question and the sometimes fraught scholarly debates that make it hard to see the wood for the trees.

Pindar has been particularly bedevilled by interpretative debates, as set out in Chapter 1 of this book. My aim has been to enable readers to discover for themselves (even through the medium of translation) what makes him a great poet and why writers have often turned to him for inspiration. It is a presentation of Pindar in his time, which tries to make use of the recent advances in rhetorical understanding of his poetry to show how he adapts himself to his purposes in any given poem. I never cease to enjoy Pindar for his language and his radiant evocation of a world lost to us, and I hope to show something of this in my discussions.

The book draws on my earlier re-edition of Geoffrey S. Conway's translation of Pindar for the Everyman series (1997), which has been out of print for some years. I first studied Pindar in the 1970s with Hugh Lloyd-Jones, and I remain grateful for the enthusiasm and the rigour that he brought to the study of the poet as well as to the direction of my work. More recently, the Exeter University Classics Department has provided a haven for my scholarly pursuits, and I have found that, among a companionable set of colleagues, Richard Seaford remains as good a friend as when we were graduate students together in the 1970s: to him this book is dedicated.

Pindar the Poet

Ye pow'rs o'er all the flowery meads
Where deep Cephisus rolls his lucid tide
Allotted to preside,
And haunt the plains renown'd for beauteous steeds,
Queens of Orchomenus the fair,
And sacred guardians of the ancient line
Of Minyas divine,
Hear, O ye Graces, and regard my prayer!
All that's sweet and pleasing here
Mortals from your hands receive:
Splendor ye and fame confer,
Genius, wit and beauty give.
Nor, without your shining train
Ever on th'ethereal plain
In harmonious measures move
The celestial choirs above:
When the figur'd dance they lead,
Or the nectar'd banquet spread.
But with thrones immortal grac'd,
And by Pythian Phoebus plac'd,

Ordering through the bless'd abodes
All the splendid works of gods,
Sit the sisters in a ring,
Round the golden-shafted king:
And with reverential love
  Worshipping the Olympian throne,
The majestick brow of Jove
  With unfading honours crown.

Aglaia, graceful virgin, hear!
And thou, Euphrosyna, whose ear
Delighted listens to the warbled strain!
Bright daughters of Olympian Jove,
The best, the greatest pow'r above;
  With your illustrious presence deign
  To grace our choral song!
Whose notes to victory's glad sound
In wanton measures lightly bound.
  Thalia, come along!
Come, tuneful maid! For lo! My string
With meditated skill prepares
In softly soothing Lydian airs
  Asopichus to sing;
Asopichus, whose speed by thee sustain'd
The wreath for his Orchomenus obtain'd.
    Go then, sportive Echo, go
    To the sable dome below,
    Proserpine's black dome, repair,
    There to Cleodemus bear
    Tidings of immortal fame:
    Tell, how in the rapid game
O'er Pisa's vale his son victorious fled;
Tell, for thou saw'st him bear away
The winged honours of the day;
And deck with wreaths of fame his youthful head.[1]

THIS POEM WAS WRITTEN BY Pindar probably in 488 BCE, when he was about 30 years old, to celebrate the Olympic victory of a runner from the town of Orchomenus, not far from Pindar's native Thebes. While there is no 'typical' Pindaric ode, this poem exhibits many of his most notable qualities: the striking opening;[2] the prominence of the gods; the naming of the victor, his town and his family; the specification of the event in which Asopichus won; the musical setting (available to us only through allusions); the complex metre and the rich language full of imagery and metaphor. Only a mythical narrative is absent in this case. It is these qualities that made Pindar a classic in his own day, and which still inspire readers more than two thousand years later to delight in his poetry.

Gilbert West, who made this translation of Pindar's *Olympian* 14 in the 1740s or '50s, entitled it simply 'Address to the Graces'. The title accurately describes a large part of the poem but obscures the significance of the second part of his second stanza, where the poet turns to celebrate the victory in the *stadion* race at Olympia of Asopichus of Orchomenus. The poem seems easy to appreciate because of its sustained and beautiful evocation of the trio of goddesses called the Graces (*Charites*), whose task it is to shed beauty and delight on those who deserve it. 'Shining', 'gold', 'flowery', 'unfading': such are the colours of perfection that the gods enjoy constantly, but which are available to men only in fleeting moments of grace – 'a grace beyond the reach of art', as Pope called it, because it is a gift of the gods.

West's diction seems rococo: the picture evoked is like a painting by Poussin where shapely maidens in pastel colours dance sedately in mathematically determined motion, yet Pindar's own epithets are no less sensual: the 'fair' Orchomenus in Pindar is *lipara*, 'glistening'; the 'golden-shafted' Apollo is *chrysotoxon*, 'with golden arrows'; the 'tuneful maid' Thalia is *erasimolpe*, 'delighting in song'. The mathematical analogy is not misleading, either, since Pindar's verse holds to a rigid though complex metrical scheme, and the two stanzas respond precisely (a detail obscured by West's metrical scheme).

The poem paints a picture, and Pindar loves to evoke the world of the gods in vignettes like this one. In *Nemean* 5 it is the marriage of Peleus and Thetis:

> Then from heaven beholding
> The king of the high gods, cloud-gathering Zeus
>   With nodding brow forthwith ordained
> A sea-nymph of the golden-spindled Nereids
> His bride should be, and to accept this kinship,
> 'listed Poseidon's favour, who from Aigae
> Not seldom journeys to the far-famed Dorian isthmus. There
>   The flute's high note and joyful throngs,
>   With bold contests for strength of limb,
>   Receive him as their god.
> His inborn fate decrees each man's achievement.
> For you, Euthymenes, at Aegina
> The goddess victory opened her embrace.[3]

Here, too, gold and song are leitmotifs of the celebration of the god, in this case Poseidon, presiding deity of the Isthmian Games, where the young Euthymenes has won his victory. In both of these poems, the triumphant athlete's achievement has allowed him to enter for a moment into the glory of the gods. When Pindar enters the text of the poem to Asopichus, tuning his lyre to sing his victory, it is as a craftsman who speaks with the authority of a skill with which he was endowed by the gods. The poem thus presents two important strands of Pindar's poetry: contact with the gods and the poet's authority to praise. It also presents Pindar's intense sense of place (evident also in the *Nemean* 5 extract): if any Greek poet is a 'poet in a landscape' it is Pindar, whether he evokes the grassy plains of Nemea, 'pasture of the Lion'; the smoking, snow-capped peak of Mount Etna (in *Pythian* 1 – see Chapter 2); the baby Iamos – the future prophet – 'nourished with the blameless venom of bees... while his tender body was bathed by the golden and purple rays of violets';[4] or the creation of the island of Rhodes, when Zeus 'could see a land rising from the floor of the grey sea that would be bountiful for men and favourable for flocks'.[5] The places, too, are not just bits of landscape but gain further meaning because of their association with the gods. Even the olive that crowned the victor at Olympia was not just an olive; it was 'the grey-coloured adornment of olive, which once Amphitryon's son brought from the shady springs of Ister to be the fairest memorial of the contests at Olympia'.[6]

Finally, this poem, like all of Pindar's epinician odes, has a 'programme' to follow:[7] to include praise of the victor's homeland and his family as well as his own deeds. So the victor's father must be evoked, and it is no obstacle that he is (perhaps recently) dead, for another goddess is available to carry to the Underworld the tidings of Asopichus' fame. In West's translation his fame is 'immortal', but this is an over-translation of *klytan angelian*, 'message of renown'. However, the question of whether athletic victory confers actual immortality in making the victor a hero, with cult, has recently been raised,[8] and will need to be considered in its place. A neat example of praise that brings in all the elements of the programme in a short space is found in *Olympian* 8:

> Timosthenes,[9] destiny allotted your family
> to Zeus, its progenitor, who made you famous at Nemea,
> but by the hill of Kronos made Alkimedon
> an Olympic victor.
> He was beautiful to behold, in action he did not discredit
> his looks, and by winning in the wrestling match
> he proclaimed long-oared Aigina as his fatherland,
> where Themis, the saving goddess
> enthroned beside Zeus, respecter of strangers, is venerated
> most among men.[10]

Here, too, it is the presence of gods that gives the terms of praise a deeper meaning.

It was the quality of Pindar's poetry sketched here that drew the German poet Friedrich Hölderlin to his work. More about Hölderlin's response can be found in Chapter 7 of this volume, but in brief, the poetry seemed to him to offer glimpses into a world where gods had been present in the landscape and where gods and men could meet face to face, as they do in tragedy, but with happier consequences. To use a phrase that has been employed in another context, Pindar's world was a world full of gods.

But, important as the gods are, Pindar's work is for very human patrons. He is engaged, for a fee, to celebrate victors in the Panhellenic Games. The importance of the Games in Greek life, and in the definition of what it was to be a Greek, can hardly be exaggerated. To be Greek was to be permitted to compete in the Games; thus the kings of Macedon, who were descended from Greek gods, could participate, but other Macedonians could not. Competing in the Games was an expensive business, even if all that was required was systematic training in running, jumping or contact sports, while to field a team of horses for the chariot race was the mark of the wealthiest citizens only. Pindar's patrons are drawn from the wealthy aristocratic clans of the Greek cities, especially the Dorian cities. The majority of Pindar's odes, other than those for the tyrants of Sicily, are for aristocrats from Aegina or other Dorian cities including Pindar's own Thebes and nearby Orchomenus; the brilliant *Olympian* 7 is for Diagoras of Rhodes. This circumstance has seemed to some to make his work beneath contempt as hireling work for the rich. Moses Finley summed up the attitude in his essay 'Silver Tongue':

> The one choice Pindar did not have if he was to continue in his profession, was in his patrons. The tyrants of Sicily and of Cyrene in North Africa, the traditional aristocracies of Aegina, of his native Thebes, even of Athens – they and their protégés dominated the sporting events at the games, and it was their world and their values which Pindar celebrated, and obviously shared. His poetry therefore raises, within limits, the question which exercises critics of T.S. Eliot. Can one divorce a great poet from his deeply felt but odious beliefs? ... His athletes were still everyman's heroes, but their class and their class-values were being challenged. Even Aeschylus, who is regularly bracketed with Pindar in modern accounts, worried about the implications of the received myths. Hence the *Oresteia* is a serious, if ultimately unresolved, discussion of an ancient moral dilemma. There are no such discussions in Pindar; there are not even any dilemmas, only successes and failures.[11]

That Pindar did not worry about the meanings of the myths seems to me simply false. The charge of being a lackey of the ruling class is a harsh one: a poet is a craftsman, and it is no more shame for a craftsman to work for a rich man than a poor man; even the rich need shoemakers and plumbers. The further objection – that Pindar celebrates the repulsive ideology of an aristocratic class doomed to extinction – will be discussed further in the chapter here on patrons. Recently both Leslie Kurke and Laura Swift have argued forcefully that one of the functions of epinician is the reintegration of the hero into his *polis*: epinician poetry, which praises the city as well as the victor, is consciously civic in its purpose. That does not make it 'democratic', but it does mean that the odes are addressed to a public and not just to a self-regarding clan. David Fearn, however, has taken an opposing line, arguing that the Aeginetan odes at least are documents of the rivalry of different clans on that island as they jockey for supremacy.[12] Kurke further argues that only chariot racing is *really* elitist: athletes in other events simply become wealthy – so much so that they might turn to equestrian competition later.[13] Anne Burnett points out that chariotry is different from boxing, and kings are different from boys. Pindar varies his praise according to his subject.[14] This may in fact push the argument for social accessibility of the Games too far. Still, there can be no doubt that the festivals at which Pindar's odes were performed were public events, and events of religious life as well. Stesichorus called his own songs *damomata*, works for the people,[15] and Pindar's no doubt reached the same audience.

The corollary of the fact that Pindar is writing to commission is that he cannot be interpreted as a free-spirited genius pouring out words as the inspiration takes him. This Romantic view is part of what lies behind the disparagement of him as a lackey of the rich. It also lies behind Wilamowitz's bemusement as to what made him love Pindar when the poet seemed to represent everything he disapproved of. Ulrich von Wilamowitz-Moellendorff (1848–1931) virtually created modern classical scholarship in his work, which integrated history, literature, religion and the developing understanding of art and archaeology.[16] Every line he wrote breathed his passionate belief in the enduring value of the Greek experience for the modern world:

His world is quite strange to us; its customs, its thoughts and desires for us charmless, if not actually objectionable. He himself is no richly endowed spirit. He knows nothing of the power and greatness of fatherland, nothing of progress in any directions. Neither the exploration of the broad earth nor the solving of the thousand riddles that Nature arouses in and around us, attracts him at all. He has no conception of science; were it to come near him, he would reject it as godless foolishness. All the greatness that our souls depend on is Ionic-Attic; but he will know nothing of its nature; not only Odysseus, but even Homer are antipathetic to him. His art itself is alien to us, no less in what is unique to him than in his traditional style. But yet: he is Pindar, a complete man, and human, and prophet of the Muses. He compels us first to attend to him, and then to love him. The longer one lives with him, the faster one clings to him. I have experienced this; I hope that I have succeeded in showing him in some measure as he was, in making the path to him easier, so that others too may learn to understand him. Then we shall love him and win a loyal companion for our lives: πιστον το θειον [loyal are the gods].[17]

The American classicist Basil L. Gildersleeve (1831–1924) reflected on Wilamowitz's view:

The German attitude to Pindar is the attitude of Carducci towards Dante. Pindar's soul dwelt apart from the great cause of Greece against Persia, Hellene against Barbarian... His lofty praise of Athens has enhanced value coming from a Theban, but the liberation of Ionia left him cold... His dislike for the Ionians shows itself in his treatment of that incarnation of the Ionians, Odysseus... But it is our business to study Pindar night and day, as Carducci studied Dante, and Wilamowitz's essay is an effective incitement to the study, and needless to say illuminating.[18]

In fact, praise poetry is no very unusual thing in world culture, and romantic outpouring is far from being the norm by which all poetry operates or should be judged. One may, for example, compare the praise poetry of Tswana kings:

I shall keep on telling about you,
My voice is now used to you;
I now want to make you my friend,
Hail to you, son of a fine person![19]

J.A. Burrow has argued in his book *The Poetry of Praise* (2008) that praise is a much-neglected category in poetry. His main focus is on the Middle Ages, where he convincingly demonstrates an essentially didactic aim encoded in the celebration of the good and the shaming of the bad. He shows how this model was applied, for example, to Ovid's *Heroides,* 'a poem interpreted by medieval readers as concerned with the praise of virtue and the blame of vice'.[20] This may have been how medieval readers experienced the classics, but it is not one that we should regard as doing justice to, say, the *Iliad*, however important the veneration of its heroes may have been for contemporary listeners. However, in his discussion of classical origins Burrow usefully shows how far the Greek poets were concerned with *kleos*, fame – and *kleos* was also the mainspring of the actions of the aristocrats who commissioned Pindar's poems, as Kurke has clearly shown. The *kleos* of the house suffers entropy, and must be won again and again.[21]

In the 1960s a sea change took place in Pindaric interpretation with the publication of E.L. Bundy's *Studia Pindarica*, first published in 1962. Bundy's mantra was that everything in a Pindaric poem is designed to conduce to praise of the victor. We must remember that

> This is an oral, public, epideictic literature dedicated to the single purpose of eulogizing men and communities; that these eulogies are concentrated upon athletic achievement; that the environment thus created is hostile to an allusiveness that would strain the powers of a listening audience, hostile to personal, religious, political, philosophical and historical references that might interest the poet but do nothing to enhance the glory of a given patron, hostile to abruptness in transitions, to gross irrelevance, to lengthy sermonizing, to literary scandals and embarrassments, hostile in short to all the characteristics of style and temper that we ascribe to Pindar.[22]

All these things had indeed been attributed to Pindar by one critic or another, and Bundy's trenchant dismissal of them all opened the way to an understanding of the poems as, in essence, rhetorical compositions. The style of interpretation that Bundy rejected had begun in the third century BCE, with the ancient commentators. Wherever they could not understand a passage, they cast around for supposed historical allusions or private concerns of the poet to explain it. Later scholarship, up to the middle of the twentieth century, generally accepted the scholiasts' interpretations at face value. Wilamowitz set about his great book on Pindar by constructing a biography using the suspect allusions dreamt up by the scholiasts. For example, Pindar's allusion to the hero Alcmaeon in *Pythian* 8, 56ff., 'I am glad to pelt Alkmaion with wreaths and sprinkle him with song, because as my neighbour and guardian of my possessions, he met me on my way to the earth's famed navel and employed his inherited skills in prophecy', is explained by Wilamowitz straight-faced, following the scholiasts:

> So, Alkmaion appeared to Pindar when he was on his way to Delphi and prophesied something to him; what, we do not discover, but it is enough that he indicated that good fortune awaited him... Alkmaion is not a prophetic deity; it is exceptional that he adopts the art of his father [Apollo]. How did Pindar receive the revelation? One may suppose it was in a dream, and that is the only thing imaginable. And if Alkmaion was Pindar's neighbour and guarded his property, it is not wonderful that Pindar should dream of him. So one may presume that a sanctuary of Alkmaion stood near Pindar's house. But can one imagine that one of the Epigoni, the destroyers of Thebes, and in particular this much-reviled matricide, received cult in Thebes? Or was Pindar perhaps living abroad, in Argos for example, and thus had the occasion to store his property in a temple while he was travelling? That simply moves the problem on, since it is remarkable that there should be a Heroon of Alkmaion anywhere at all. So this passage will remain forever impossible to understand'.[23]

Wilamowitz's questions are not foolish ones, nor are his speculations unreasonable; the problem is that, even if we knew the answers to his questions, they would not actually help us to understand the passage in its context. The evocation of the god is reduced to a biographical puzzle.

C.M. Bowra, writing in 1964, relied heavily on this kind of cart-before-the-horse approach. He was reduced to despair by the attempt to explain such passages as the end of *Nemean* 7:

> In this poem Pindar sees that his two main themes cannot really be united, and this is why he keeps them apart but confronts them at three separate points. He shows that for him a poem need not be confined to a single theme and variations and can in fact carry two main themes different in both subject and in temper. His joy in the boy's victory and prowess is quite different from his feelings about himself, and though these are not out of control or even angry, they create a series of contrasting effects.[24]

Many readers must have felt themselves none the wiser as to why we would bother reading Pindar, if this is all that can be said to elucidate him. Truly, to interpret a poem as a kind of catch-all of private obsessions goes beyond Romanticism to a kind of anti-poetry. Bundy's revolution, though it shocked some scholars whose genius was for problem-solving,[25] in fact made it much easier to approach the poems as pieces of literature.

To carry out his analysis, Bundy invented a rather rebarbative set of technical terms, which one must perforce use since no one has come up with better ones: the person praised in the poem is the *laudandus* (I use victor or addressee when the context allows), and the means of praise are *crescendo*, *vaunt* (the actual matter of praise), *gnome* (moralising or otherwise sententious comment) and *foil*. The clear recognition of purpose has enabled a much richer understanding of the quality of Pindar's poetry. Few now would reject Bundy's insight, and the criticism of Pindar has been enabled to take giant strides into other, more fruitful fields in the succeeding forty years. Mary Lefkowitz and Hugh Lloyd-Jones were among the first to apply Bundy's insights to odes other than Bundy's own two specimens and to develop what often seemed a mechanical technique into a tool of humanist interpretation. David Young, A.P. Burnett, Christopher Carey,

Andrew Morrison and others have shown how different kinds of questions, about the individuality of Pindar's patrons, about performance scenarios and about the nature of the victor's glorification, can bring us much closer to an understanding of Pindar's poetry as a social as well as a literary phenomenon. David Fearn has extended the approach to Pindar's contemporary Bacchylides, the recovery of whose poems at the beginning of the twentieth century provided valuable comparative material for the understanding of Pindar's odes; but Bacchylides, despite the delicate ornamental quality of his poetry, has always suffered in critical comparison with Pindar. This more rounded approach should not go so far as to deny the relevance of biographical data, only to insist that inventing bits of biography is not a way to explain the poems. Where historical contexts can be divined they can be enormously helpful. W.S. Barrett demonstrated this in his articles[26] and Simon Hornblower has revealed some unsuspected connections by applying prosopographical techniques to Pindar.[27]

As noted above, the use of supposed external biographical data to explain problematic passages in the odes goes back to the ancient commentators; we possess an unusually large amount of these *scholia*, which are often useful but need to be employed with extreme caution.[28] Also from the pen of an ancient scholar comes the 'Life' of Pindar,[29] which gives a scrappy account that modern scholars have perforce to follow when other evidence does not show it impossible. To quote it in full will give both some salient details about Pindar and a view of the approach of ancient scholarship, though almost every statement requires critical inspection before it can be taken as fact.

[1] The poet Pindar was a Theban from Cynoscephalae, which is a village in the territory of Thebes. He was the son of Daiphantus, or according to other authorities, of Pagondas. Still others trace his genealogy to Scopelinus. Some say that Scopelinus was his uncle and that, since he played the *aulos*, he taught his skill to Pindar. His mother was Cleodice. Other authorities spell it Cledice. [2] When Pindar was a boy, according to Chamaeleon and Ister, he went hunting near Mt Helicon and fell asleep from exhaustion. As he slept a bee landed on his mouth and built a honeycomb there. Others say that he had

a dream in which his mouth was full of honey and wax, and that he then decided to write poetry. [3] Some authorities say that at Athens his teacher was Agathocles, others say Apollodorus. Apollodorus also, when he was in charge of the dithyrambic choruses and had to be out of town, entrusted their direction to Pindar even though he was still a boy. Pindar directed them so well that he became famous. [4] When he said that Athens was the bulwark of Hellas [fr. 76] he was fined one thousand drachmas by the Thebans, and the Athenians paid the fine on his behalf. [5] He was not only a beautiful poet, but he was a man dear to the gods. For example, the god Pan was seen between Cithaeron and Helicon singing a paean of Pindar. Accordingly Pindar wrote a song to the god in which he offers his gratitude for the honour, the poem that begins 'O Pan, Pan protector of Arcadia and guardian of sacred shrines' [fr. 95]. And Demeter also appeared in a dream and blamed him, because for her alone of all the gods he had written no hymn. So he wrote her the poem that begins 'Queen, lawgiver [?] with golden headband' [fr. 37]. And he also built an altar to the gods outside his house. [6] When Pausanias the king of the Lacedaemonians was razing Thebes, someone wrote on Pindar's house: 'Don't set fire to the home of the poet Pindar.' As a result his was the only house that remained unburned, and it is now the magistrate's hall in Thebes. [7] At Delphi when the priest is getting ready to close the temple he announces each day: 'let Pindar the poet come to join the god at dinner.' For the poet was born during the Pythian festival, as he himself says 'the quadrennial festival with its procession of oxen, in which I was first put to bed in swaddling clothes' [fr. 193]. [8] There is a story that pilgrims went to the temple of Ammon to ask for Pindar what was best for men, and the poet died on that very day. [9] He lived at the time of Simonides, though he was younger, Simonides older. In fact both of them celebrated the same events. Simonides wrote about the naval battle at Salamis [fr. 536] and Pindar celebrated the kingdom of Cadmus [fr. 272]. Both of them were together at the court of Hieron the tyrant of Syracuse. [10] He married Megacleia the daughter of Lysitheus and Calline and had a son Daiphantus, for whom he wrote a song for the Daphnephoria. He had two daughters, Protomache and Eumetis. [11] He wrote seventeen books: hymns, paeans, dithyrambs (2), prosodia (2), partheneia (2), hyporchemes (2), encomia, lamentations, victory odes (4). [12] There exists an epigram with the following conclusion: 'How Protomache and Eumetis weep for you in shrill voices, your wise daughters, when they came from Argos bringing home in an urn your remains which had been gathered from a foreign funeral pyre.'[30]

A variant version in hexameter verse is included in the *prooemium*, or introduction, to Pindar by the twelfth-century bishop and scholar Eustathius: I translate it into English here for the first time.

High-speaking Pindar was born in the land of Cadmeian Thebes
To Cleidice, the bride of Daiphantus, steadfast in war,
Who lived near the place called Cynoscephalae.
Not he alone, but his brother was Eritimos, skilled in hunting,
And skilled too in boxing and wrestling that brings pain.
Once when his mother laid him on the ground to sleep, still a baby
A bee settled on his childish lips to store its honey as if in a hive.
Then the divine Corinna, as his teacher, filled him with shrill-voiced verses and
melodies
And first gave him the foundations of his stories.
After her he listened to the voice of Agathocles,
Who explained to him the paths and measures of song.
When the Macedonians came to destroy the city of the Cadmeans
Because of the anger of Alexander the son of Philip,
The god-kindled fire did not touch the house of Pindar.
But that was later. While the poet was still alive
Lord Phoebus decreed that gifts and sweet wine should be brought
Forever from Pytho, rich in gold, to him at Thebes.
They also say that Pan of the fine horns was accustomed to sing
A melody of Pindar's on the mountains, and never tired of singing.
But when the doughty Persians stood at Marathon
And Salamis with Datis of the wild cry,

That was when he lived, at the same time as Aeschylus in Athens.
His wife was the noble Timoxeine,
Who gave birth to great-hearted Eumetis and Daiphantus,
And also Protomache. He sang the successes of the four great games,
Weaving paeans of praise to the blessed ones,
As well as songs for dancing, hymns to the gods
And melodious chants of honey-voiced maidens.
Thus he was, and that is what he did and experienced,
And he died when he had accomplished eighty years.

Some fragments of a life of Pindar survive on an Oxyrhynchus papyrus:[31] this contains an argument about the date of Pindar's death, referring to Psaumis' victory in *Olympiad* 82 and asking 'how could he have written an epinician for him if he was dead?' This was a sharp scholar indeed. A writer called Aristodemus also wrote a work 'On Pindar', which does not survive.[32]

These 'Lives' represent what the ancients thought they knew about Pindar, and moderns cannot do much better, though careful criticism has elicited a chronology for at least a large proportion of his poems. The leitmotifs of these brief accounts are divine favour (from bees, Apollo and Pan), training in music, and a list of the types of his poetry, which is fuller in the prose Life. This list originates from the cataloguing activity of the scholars in the library at Alexandria and, like any cataloguing system, is designed more to organise than to reflect the actual occasions of the poems. Thus some poems are clearly misattributed even in the books we have, while other genres, such as *partheneia*, are probably not the names of any kind of poem that Pindar knew: these were just songs sung by choruses of girls, which could be varied in purpose.[33] Of the 17 books of the Alexandrian classification, four have survived – the victory odes; in the early twentieth century the sands of Egypt yielded a papyrus of a large part of the book of paeans. Of the rest we have a few, mostly small, fragments. So our judgment of Pindar as a poet is based on a very small sampling of his poetry; furthermore, the difference in style between the paeans and the much more complex epinicians, or victory odes, suggests that what we know best – the poems for human addressees – may not be typical of his output as a whole.

We are able to extend the basis of comparison a little because we have some of the poems of his younger contemporary Bacchylides, who also wrote victory odes, which were likewise recovered from the sands of Egypt in the early twentieth century. We also have a few fragments of Bacchylides' uncle Simonides, but these are mostly from his elegiac poems and not from his lyric poems. As practitioners in the same line of business as Pindar, Bacchylides and Simonides provide helpful background.

Pindar was the first and greatest of the nine lyric poets canonised by Alexandrian scholars, and his reputation has outlasted the centuries. Consideration of his poetry needs to have regard to his predecessors in both monody (Sappho, Alcaeus, Anacreon) and choral poetry (Stesichorus, Simonides). If we had more of all of them we should be the richer, but our valuation of Pindar would not be diminished. Among the things that make him special are the qualities of his language; his metaphors, which recall the Metaphysical poets; his narratives of the myths of the heroes and gods; and his intense religious sensibility. This book will try to demonstrate all of these things.

PINDAR'S CAREER

Pindar's Thebes

THE WORLD INTO WHICH PINDAR was born, probably in 518 BCE, had a very different atmosphere from that of the Athens with which we are familiar from the pages of history. In 518 BCE the reforms of Cleisthenes had set the Athenian *demos* free and started the city on its road to the radical democracy of the mid fifth century. Other *poleis*, including nearby Corinth and Argos, had weathered tyrannies – the emergence of powerful leaders – and relapsed into aristocratic rule. The islands, too, had seen civil strife and the rise of tyrants in the sixth century BCE, which threatened the way of life of the aristocrats for whom Alcaeus of Mytilene wrote his poetry. But Thebes had, apparently, remained undisturbed by social upheaval and continued to be run by *aristoi*, 'the best people'. It was protected to some extent from civic discord by prosperity; the fertile lands of Boeotia provided sufficient grain, and there was also plenty of wild game to add meat to the diet. Horses could also be bred in the plains, as they were further north in Thessaly. Athenian writers wrote enviously of the game birds of Boeotia.[1] Aristotle tells us that the legendary legislator of Thebes, Philolaus, created laws about procreation and adoption that 'were intended to preserve the number of the lots of land'.[2] (Philolaus perhaps foresaw the difficulty of a system like the Spartan, or the

French, which split up holdings into smaller and smaller pieces with each successive death.) If landholding remained stable, there was little sinking from prosperity to debt, such as the Athenian legislator, statesman and poet Solon seems to have had to deal with in Athens in the sixth century. The large landowners made the decisions, and the populace remained tribal, as was common in many other parts of Greece, though Cleisthenes' reforms had begun to turn Athens' structure from a tribal to a predominantly civic one.

In short, Pindar's Boeotia was a land in which nothing seemed to have changed for centuries. It was largely rural, with only small urban centres, and the rhythms of life were pegged to the revolving agricultural seasons that Pindar describes:

> Now Alkimidas makes it clear to see that his inherited
> nature is like crop-bearing fields, which alternate
> and at one time give men abundant sustenance
>   from the plains,
> but at another rest to gather strength.[3]

The generations of men may be like leaves, for Homer,[4] but here they are part of a cycle: a generation fallow of athletic success is followed by a bumper crop.

Besides agriculture, the year was punctuated by the festivals of the gods. Though we can name only a few of the festivals of Boeotia, the countryside aspect is dominant in the cult of Pan, to whom Pindar made a dedication, and in that of Apollo Galaxios ('Milky'), of which we know from a *daphnephorikon* by Pindar:

> For, like the finest water from springs,
> milk gushed forth from the teats
> of all the flocks; the people rushed to fill the jars,
> and not a single wineskin or amphora remained in their homes,
> for all the wooden buckets and jars were filled.[5]

The *Daphnephoria* – a celebration that involved bringing a branch of bay to Apollo – seems to have been the main festival of Thebes, and was probably performed annually, like the *Panathenaea* at Athens. Pausanias described the events of his own times, the second century CE:

> They take a strong, good-looking boy from a distinguished house and make him priest of Ismenian Apollo for a year with the title of the bay-boy [*daphnephoros*], as the boys wear wreaths of sweet-bay leaves [...] The richer boys dedicate tripods. One tripod really distinguished for its antiquity and its famous donor is the one Amphitryon dedicated when Herakles was the bay-boy.[6]

A later author, Proclus, adds the detail that the nearest kinsman of the 'bay-boy' or *daphnephoros* carried a staff of olive wood, called a *kopo*, which was wreathed in laurels and flowers and topped with a bronze globe from which dangled smaller balls, to signify the sun and stars. The bay-boy wore a bright robe and special shoes, and was followed by a chorus of pubertal girls who sang as the procession advanced to the god's temple. Pindar composed several *daphnephorika*, which were classified by Alexandrian scholars among the *partheneia* or maiden-songs, of which they are a species.

Quickly tying up my robe
and carrying in my gentle[7] hands a splendid branch
of laurel, I shall hymn
        the all-glorious house of Aioladas
and of his son Pagondas,
my maidenly head flourishing
with garlands,
        and I shall imitate in my songs,
to the accompaniment of lotus pipes,
        that siren's loud song
which silences the swift blasts
of Zephyr, and whenever with the strength of winter
    chilling Boreas rages
        swiftly over the sea.[8]

We do not learn what flowers were worn, but the mention of dispelling winter's blasts makes it sound like a spring festival celebrating the return of life to the land.

Besides Apollo Ismenios, the chief deity associated with Thebes was Heracles, the 'hero-god' who achieved divinity after much toil and suffering. He was celebrated in an annual two-day festival with games, but if Pindar wrote any songs for his festival, we do not have them. Heracles is important for Pindar as an emblem of the successful athlete who touches divinity through his achievement; more on that topic can be found in chapter four of this volume. Though he comes up repeatedly in the odes, the only Theban victor in whose song Heracles appears is Melissus of Thebes, who won the wrestling at the Isthmian Games in, possibly, 477 BCE.[9] He was a small man for a wrestler,[10] so Pindar makes Heracles a shortie too, in combat with the giant Antaios:

> Long ago a man came to Antaios' home
> in wheat-bearing Libya from Kadmeian Thebes
> short of stature, but of unbending spirit,
> to wrestle with him and stop him from roofing
> Poseidon's temple with the skulls of strangers.
> He was Alkmene's son, who went to Olympos,
>   after exploring all the lands...
> In his honour, above the Elektran Gates
> we citizens prepare a feast.[11]

Cadmus, the founder of Thebes, is taken for granted by Pindar, but his story is never told at length. Pindar also has little to say about the other great myth of Thebes, that of Oedipus and his family, which dominates our knowledge of Attic tragedy.

Pindar was probably of aristocratic birth himself,[12] otherwise he would have had no opportunity to learn the arts of music and song. Other archaic poets are similarly of aristocratic extraction: witness Alcaeus' scorn for populist tyrants who emerge from the rabble,[13] and Theognis' contempt for the lower orders.[14] We can recover nothing of his training except that the Ambrosian Life tells us his teacher was his uncle, Scopelinus. We might draw an analogy with the education described in even more rural Arcadia by Polybius in the second century BCE:

> The Arcadians are the only people among whom boys are by the laws trained from infancy to sing hymns and paeans, in which they celebrate in traditional fashion the heroes and gods of their particular towns. They next learn the airs of Philoxenus and Timotheus, and dance with great spirit to the pipers at the yearly Dionysia in the theatres, the boys at the boys' festival, and the young men at what is called the men's festival. Similarly it is their universal custom, at all festal gatherings and banquets, not to have strangers to make the music, but to produce it themselves, calling on each other in turn for a song. They do not look upon it as a disgrace to disclaim the possession of any other accomplishment: but no one can disclaim the knowledge of how to sing, because all are forced to learn... Their young men again practise a military step to the music of the pipe and in regular order of battle, producing elaborate dances, which they display to their fellow-citizens every year in the theatres, at public charge and expense.[15]

What Polybius describes in the second century BCE as unique to the old-fashioned Arcadians was surely generalised among most of the cities of archaic Greece.

Plato thought that dance was the origin of education:

> Whereas animals have no sense of order and disorder in movement ('rhythm' and 'harmony', as we call it), we human beings have been made sensitive to both and can enjoy them. This is the gift of the same gods who we said were given to us as companions in dancing [...] So [...] Can we assume that education comes originally from Apollo and the Muses, or not?[16]

Pindar composed his first dateable poem, and probably his first epinician ode, *Pythian* 10, in 498 BCE for the Thessalian boy-racer Hippocleas. In 497/6 he composed a dithyramb for Athens, which does not survive. Within a very few years he was receiving commissions from distant patrons: two Pythian victors from Acragas in Sicily in 490 prompted *Pythian* 6 and *Pythian* 12. The proximity of Thebes to Delphi gave Pindar the opportunity to show his skill and seek commissions at the Pythian Games held there every four years. Should we imagine the poets and sculptors setting up stalls at the Games to display their wares and offer their services to the wealthy victors?

Paean 2.96–101 evokes the songs of the mountain: 'songs are calling through fragrant [...], and among the lofty rocks of Parnassos often do the maidens of Delphi with shining headbands join in swift-footed dance and sing a sweet strain with ringing voice'. The lacuna is perhaps to be filled by Mount Pindos, or more probably the plain of Kirrha, though Race in the Loeb edition makes the reference to the island of Delos; a characteristic passage of Gildersleeve interweaves humour, poetic sensibility and scholarly acumen in discussing the problem:

> The woods of Pindos may be fragrant. The woods of other Greek mountains are fragrant, but Pindos is so remote and [Κίρρα]ν is so near. Kirrha was the seat of the hippodrome, and so we should have both ends of Delphi represented... It is no valid objection against calling Kirrha εὔοδμος (sweet-scented) that there was a decree against planting trees in the plain. That decree – if such decree there was – could hardly have held its sway over the whole stretch from Itea to Kastri, and when one rides through the olive groves, marvellous today for their vigour, one becomes incredulous as to the whole thing... Was there no ἄλσος [grove] by the hippodrome, no laurel grove for the wreaths, no beds of flowers which the Greeks prized for the 'nosegays' they yielded, no θυοεις βωμός?[17]

Pindar's contemporaries, the older Simonides and the younger Bacchylides, both among the nine canonical lyric poets, also wrote epinician odes, though Simonides' fragments are hard to make much of. Another Boeotian poet, Corinna of Tanagra, was regarded by later authors as a contemporary of Pindar: she was said to have defeated him in a contest, and in an egregious instance of pseudo-biographical interpretation, his phrase 'Boeotian sow' was turned into a jibe at his rival. On present evidence, though, it is more likely that Corinna lived in the third century BCE.[18] Most of her very damaged fragments are scraps of mythical tales, several on Boeotian themes; at least some are for girls' choruses, for instance 655: 'Terpsichore summons me to sing fine tales for the white-robed women of Tanagra.'[19]

At all events, Pindar's fame spread rapidly, and in the 480s he composed a series of songs for Olympic and Pythian victors from Orchomenus,[20] Athens,[21] and Thebes.[22] Theban victors were never absent from his work, though *Isthmian* 1 *and Isthmian* 7, both for Theban victors, can be dated only conjecturally to his late period, 458 and 454 respectively. Also in the 480s he first established the connection with the island of Aegina, for whose boy athletes he composed a large number of songs. In 476 his fame took him back to Sicily with a commission from Hieron of Syracuse, who also commissioned the younger Bacchylides to celebrate his same victory in the chariot race. The Sicilian connection lasted for some years, even after the fall of the tyrants. While Pindar's best-known epinician odes cluster in the 470s (the Sicilian years) and 460s, we may imagine him constantly busy with other commissions, for the epinician odes filled only four books of the 17 into which Alexandrian scholars classified his works. If the year 474 is his *annus mirabilis*, with six epinician odes completed, each year of his 50-year career may have been equally filled with commissions of other kinds.

Patronage and Praise

Pindar's job in the epinicians was to praise victors in the Games, and many of the other types of poetry he wrote, including laments and love poems, were also in praise of individuals. When he was not praising humans he was praising gods. If praise has always been seen as one of the functions of poetry, praise of individuals has often been seen as toadying.[23] We should consider exactly what is involved in the relation between the praising poet and his patron – and on the technique of praise, see Chapter 5.

The most fruitful and subtle way of theorising the function of Pindar's poems for mortals is that developed by Leslie Kurke in 1991, in which she viewed the poems in the light of their function in the *polis*. Epinician is a way of reintegrating the victor, with his more-than-mortal achievement, into the society of the *polis*.[24] In 2011 David Fearn offered some modification of this view, forwarding the notion that the poems bolster the status of one clan against another rather than their position in the *polis* as a whole.[25] Bruno Currie sees an interesting blend of public festival with private performance.[26] Sponsoring part of the show was a way of drawing attention to the family's merits. Pindar always celebrates his addressee as a member of his *oikos*, his family or household, and these families by their conspicuous wealth have made themselves pre-eminent in their societies; but their *kleos*, their fame, needs to be maintained by new achievements and displays. This entails various features of the relationship of poet and patron.

Pindar's very first patron, Hippocleas, the victor of *Pythian* 10, was a member of the Aleuad clan of Thessaly, whose name had been a byword of extravagance and luxury since at least the time of Alcman;[27] the horse-breeders of Thessaly were prominent members of the international aristocracy and went in for bull-riding rodeos as well as more conventional sports.[28] Simonides and Bacchylides had also written odes for them. The international network spread the fame of good poets and meant that a poet who was to make a career from praise had to be a 'wanderer'. The case is far from unique: think of the troubadours, or of Minnesang (the model for Wilamowitz's understanding of Pindar). Just as Richard Wagner was a wanderer from city to city until he entered the good graces of Ludwig II of Bavaria, who gave him the security he needed to compose what he wanted, so ancient Greek poets moved from city to city in pursuit of new patrons.[29]

As Geoffrey Lloyd has demonstrated in the case of philosophers and intellectuals, Greek thinkers and poets were essentially freelancers (unlike in ancient China, where a bureaucratic structure provided the setting for intellectual activity).[30] As a result, they relied on the institution of *xenia*, guest-friendship. Pindar frequently describes himself as the *xenos* of the victor, and this is crucial to the matter of remuneration.

The traditional relationship between *xenoi* was that of gift-giving. The gift that is the poem of praise requires a reciprocal gift from the one praised. To take an example from a completely different milieu, the fourteenth-century Persian poet Hafez of Shiraz writes:

> Possessor of the world, Nusratu'd-Din, the perfect Khusrau
> Yahya ibn Muzaffar, just ruler of the world,
> O your Islam-sheltering Court has opened
> On the face of the earth a window for the soul and a door for the heart.
> Honouring you is incumbent on the soul and sense, and obligatory.
> Your largesse to beings and places is abundant and universal.[31]

The poet expects support from the person he praises. As Greek society moved from the world of aristocratic *xenia* to that of the democratic *polis*, this kind of reciprocity came to be re-conceptualised in monetary terms.[32] The issue comes to the fore in *Isthmian 2*:

> The men of long ago, O Thrasyboulos,
>   who used to mount
> the chariot of the golden-wreathed Muses,
>   taking with them the glorious lyre,
> freely shot their honey-sounding hymns of love
> at any boy who was beautiful and had the sweetest bloom
> of late summer that woos fair-throned Aphrodite.
> For at that time the Muse was not yet
>   greedy for gain nor up for hire
> nor were sweet, soft-voiced songs
>   with their faces silvered over being sold
> from the hand of honey-voiced Terpsichore.
> But now she bids us heed the Argive's adage,
> which comes [...] closest to the truth:
> 'Money, money makes the man.'

For Leonard Woodbury these lines signalled a 'change in the condition of poetry' from the spontaneous compositions of earlier poets to lyrics composed to commission.[33] The change was often associated with Pindar's older contemporary Simonides, though an old Attic song attributed to Homer makes the most blatant claim:

> If you will pay me for my song, o potters,
> Come then Athena and hold your hand over their kiln.[34]

An ancient scholar wrote, 'Simonides seems to have been the first to introduce money-grabbing into his songs and to write a song for pay. This is what Pindar says in riddling fashion in his *Isthmians* [quoted above] [...] Xenophanes calls him a skinflint.'[35] Aristotle tells a story that Hieron's wife asked him whether it was better to be wealthy or wise, and he answered, 'Wealthy; for I see the wise spending their days at the doors of the wealthy.'[36] So Mary Renault in her well-imagined novel about Simonides, *The Praise Singer*, has Simonides say:

> Like every poet, I have sold my praises, in the sense that I've been paid
> for them; but, like Lyra with her lovers, I want freedom to pick and
> choose. Praising excellence, one serves the god within it; and false
> praise insults him, it has always seemed to me. The only worse thing is
> detraction of the good.[37]

Another anecdote about Simonides depends on the idea that the patron is paying for a good job.[38] Here, the patron complains that he wants praise of himself, not all this stuff about Castor and Pollux. But the last laugh is on Simonides when two elegant young men enter the dining hall and call Simonides outside; moments later the hall collapses, killing everyone inside. (The main point of the story as told by Cicero is that Simonides, by virtue of his art of memory, was able to identify every corpse in the rubble because he remembered where they had been sitting.)

Poets no doubt had sought patronage from the earliest times. The point of Pindar's lines in *Isthmian* 2,[39] as Leslie Kurke analyses them, is not that payment has supplanted the freedom of the inspired poet who knows no master (an inappropriately Romantic conception), but that Pindar moves from the negative point of view of the older poets who disapproved of money[40] to 'a view that appropriates the money economy and validates expenditure in the service of the epinikian ideal'.[41] *Isthmian* 1, 68–70 makes clear this duty of conspicuous consumption and conspicuous expenditure: 'If a man keeps wealth hidden inside, and attacks others with laughter, he does not consider that he is paying up his soul to Hades devoid of fame.' You must spend money to win immortal glory, and spending it on a poet is one of the best ways to achieve that. In an age, Kurke suggests, when democratic ideas and sumptuary legislation are beginning to bite, even in traditional aristocracies, epinician provides 'a new outlet for prestige displays'.[42] The need of aristocrats to draw the attention of fellow citizens to themselves is managed by the poet in such a way that the victor brings glory not just to himself and his *oikos*, his family or household, but also to his *polis*.

The ways in which Pindar fits himself to his patron vary according to his milieu, and as we shall see he has to develop an even more sophisticated portrayal of the relationship between poet and *laudandus* in the poems for the absolute rulers of Sicily. But we can trace this kind of patron/poet relationship in all of the poems for aristocratic victors: in Thebes, in Aegina and even in Athens, a city to which Pindar is often supposed to have been antipathetic because of its democracy. In fact he wrote poems for Athenian clients throughout his career. Anne Pippin Burnett has also detected a difference of tone in the poems written for boy athletes of Aegina: here it has to be the family, not just the individual, who is the object of praise.

By the Banks of the Asopos...[43]

By the banks of a spring in the island town of Aegina, in 487 BCE, a group of young men, no more than teenagers, assembles for a celebration. The spring itself is holy, even though it is an artificial creation, made by channelling water from Mount Panhellenios underground to the centre of the town.[44] This spring commemorates the gift of rain by Zeus in response to the prayers of the hero Aeacus, who is himself commemorated in the Aiakeion, a sanctuary in the town, perhaps right by the spring.[45]

The youths are preparing to perform not one but two odes in celebration of the Nemean victory of a boy between seven and fourteen years old, Pytheas of Aegina, in the *pankration*. With the wounds and bruises of the contest now healed, the lad sits in the place of honour while the youths, dressed in their finest robes, process, maybe with the victor's prize of a crown of wild parsley, and then assemble into position for a stately dance and song.

It requires an effort of imagination to picture the scene. Nowadays, not even the spring survives: Aegina is a waterless island, dependent on rainfall. Much greater is the effort required to picture the statue of Aeacus before the temple, the harbour full of merchant ships and the quay with stalls busy with the chinking silver drachms stamped with the island's signature turtle, the audience whose eyes are on the chorus as their leader strikes up the *kithara* and they begin to sing:

> I am not a sculptor, so as to fashion stationary
> > Statues that stand on their same base.
> Rather, on board every ship
> > And in every boat, sweet song,
> Go forth from Aigina and spread the news that
> Lampon's mighty son Pytheas
> Has won the crown for the pancratium in Nemea's games.[46]

Pindar evokes the scene around them in his opening lines. Perhaps besides the cult statue of Aeacus there were statues of other athletic champions, for this form of honour had begun as early as the sixth century.[47] The Aeginetan school of sculpture was particularly celebrated in antiquity, as Pliny tells us,[48] and the new pediments of the Temple of Aphaia on Aegina were being erected at exactly the time this ode was performed.[49] Sculptors in their time were as famous as poets, and the impressive fee recorded for one of Pindar's odes, 3,000 drachmas, would have been cheap for a statue;[50] but their works, melted down for their metal or smashed by Christians, have lasted less well than the products of the poets: Pindar's older contemporary Simonides summed it up in some famous lines:

What man who can trust his wits would commend Cleobulus, dweller in Lindus, who against ever-flowing rivers, spring flowers, the flame of the sun or the golden moon or the eddies of the sea set the might of a statue? All things are less than the gods. Stone is broken even by mortal hands. That was the judgment of a fool.[51]

No doubt Simonides, like Pindar, went on to assert the superior staying power of words remembered and recited.

Was Pindar's short poem of 54 lines the overture, as it were, to the much more extensive poem by Bacchylides that told the story of half the Trojan War and the central part that the heroes of Aegina played in Troy's fall?[52] Just the theme, in fact, that was depicted on the pediments of the Aphaia temple: Peleus on the east pediment in the first Greek assault on Troy, Ajax and Achilles on the west, in the campaign famous from Homer. The old pediments of the temple were replaced at the beginning of the fifth century, the west pediments in the 490s and the east in the 480s, according to the most reliable dating.[53] One might imagine that it was for the rededication of these pediments that Pindar composed his *prosodion* (processional) 'For the Aeginetans to Aphaia', of which nothing remains but the title. A dedication on such a scale must be the act of a state, not just of a family, however prominent, as Watson argues. If Pindar came to the attention of the Aeginetans through a state commission, the family of Lampon would have known who to call on when an epinician was needed a year or two later.

You, son of Lampon, have won all this at Nemea, and, your hair crowned with garlands of luxuriant flowers, you [have come bringing distinction to] the city with its lofty streets, [so that] your native island [is rich in] soft-voiced revels that give joy to men, thanks to your display of overpowering might in the *pancration* fighting. Daughter of the eddying river, gentle-hearted Aigina, truly [the son of Kronos] has given you a great honour, displaying among all the Greeks [a new victory] like a beacon; and some high-vaunting girl sings in praise of your [power], often springing lightly on [white?] feet [over your sacred soil], as a carefree fawn towards the flowery [hills], with her illustrious near-dwelling [companions]; and garlanded with the local adornment of crimson flowers and reeds those maidens sing, queen of a hospitable land, of your [child] and of rose-armed Endais, who bore godlike Peleus and Telamon after her union with Aeacus.[54]

The ode contains, as it were, a virtual second ode,[55] a chorus of girls with poppies, perhaps, or summer's roses in their hair, joining the youths to celebrate the glamorous young bruiser.

Pytheas' father, Lampon, had the wealth to commission two of Greece's leading poets to celebrate his son. Pindar's shorter ode might have been the pricier, line by line. Or was there some other reason that Lampon gave more space to the fluid and decorative poetry of Bacchylides than to the sinewy and occasionally foreboding language of Pindar? Where Bacchylides knows only the glories of the Aeacids, Pindar hints at their criminal tendencies in murdering their half-seal brother, before going on to evoke one of the clan's closest approaches to godhead: the marriage of Aegina's son Peleus to the goddess Thetis. Nothing is said of a marriage in the poem, but was one of the poppy-haired girls already in the eyes of Lampon and his son?

All that Pindar says in conclusion is:

> Proclaim that as a boxer and in the pancratium
> he won at Epidaurus a double
> victory; and to the portals of Aeacus' temple
> bring the leafy crowns of flowers
> in the company of fair-haired Graces.[56]

Like the girls, Pytheas too has flowers in his hair.

The scene evoked encapsulates many of the features of a victory ode. It associates the victor with local heroes and gods, it introduces proud family members and the cohorts of his peers, it places him in a context of divine and heroic achievement and gives him, by association, a portion of that divine radiance. The status of the maiden chorus celebrating a god is brought into play in the song of the youths celebrating a boy.[57]

Pindar was to write another 11 odes (that survive; maybe there were more) for victors from Aegina, all of them youths who triumphed in athletic events, and many of them related. (Pytheas did not win again, but his uncle Euthymenes was victorious at the Isthmian Games a year later and again in 484, and Pytheas' younger brother Phylacidas won three victories over the next five years or so.) Bacchylides, by contrast, has only one other surviving epinician ode for an Aeginetan victor (Bacchylides 12, for Teisias, a wrestler at Nemea), which is undateable. Clearly Pindar developed a warm rapport with the leading families of the island, whose landscape and economic background were so different from his own.

Unlike the plains of Boeotia, the rocky island of Aegina supported few horses and was unsuitable for chariots, so no chariot victors came from Aegina. Both were Dorian states, but their mythologies were very different, though linked by the companionship of Boeotian Heracles and Aeginetan Telamon in the first assault on Troy. A.P. Burnett convincingly shows how a mythical first ancestor of the Aeginetans, Aeacus, was gradually inserted into the myths of wider Greece.[58] The companions Zeus created for Aeacus – ants who became the island's first human inhabitants – became identified with the troops of the Homeric hero Achilles, the Myrmidons, because of the similarity of the word for ants, *myrmekes*; with Achilles came his father, Peleus, and his mermaid-goddess bride, Thetis. Peleus killed his half-brother, Phokos – the Seal Prince, as Burnett calls him – and the Salaminian hero Telamon was made into a third son of Aeacus (Aiakos), since Telamon's son had the similar name of Ajax (Aias). The deeds of this family provide most of the mythological background that Pindar uses to illumine his island champions.

Thebes and Aegina also differed in their economic bases. Where Boeotia was rural and agricultural, the rocky island supported few crops. Its people, like those of Attica, claimed to be autochthonous, and the myth of the Myrmidons (ant-men) recalls their deep digging of the soil to bring more fertile layers to the surface.[59] Since it had gained independence from the city of Epidaurus, perhaps at the end of the seventh century, a class of leading families had emerged in Aegina whose wealth was so great that the society became polarised – to such an extent that the *demos* rose up against the 'fatties' (*hoi pachees*), probably in the 490s.[60] Where did the wealth come from? Certainly from maritime activity, for Pindar's odes for Aegina are infused with the breath and imagery of the sea, as in the ode under discussion. Myth suggested that Aeginetans had been trading to Arcadia already in the seventh century or earlier,[61] while an interesting anecdote in Polyaenus suggests that they were known as pirates in the 560s. A man called Thrasymedes fell in love with the daughter of the tyrant of Athens, Pisistratus; he and his friends,

> Forcing their way through the crowd with drawn swords, carried her on board a ship, and set sail for Aegina. Hippias, her eldest brother, was at that time scouring the seas of pirates: and supposing the vessel from the expedition with which it sailed, to be of that description, bore down upon it, and took it.[62]

The story ends happily when Pisistratus agrees to give his daughter to Thrasymedes, but the point that interests us is that Hippias naturally assumes an Aeginetan ship to be a pirate one. The involvement of Aegina in slaving would be consonant with the report in Aristotle's *Athenaion Politeia* (*Constitution of the Athenians*) that the small island had a population of 70,000 (or, by a variant reading, 470,000) slaves in the fifth century. But if slaves were part of the merchandise, they were not everything, for the word for small trading items in antiquity was 'Aeginetica'. Aeginetans transported small-scale merchandise of all kinds throughout the Greek world. Herodotus tells us that they were trading in the Black Sea in his time,[63] and there are remains of their settlements there. (Though they never established colonies, like other land-poor Greek *poleis*.)

Thomas Figueira, who has analysed the economic base of Aegina in exhaustive detail, concludes that aristocrats sought treasure above all for *kleos*.[64] He concurs with the view, first put forward by C.O. Mueller in 1817,[65] that Aegina had a trading aristocracy.

This has sometimes been thought impossible in economic theory, since aristocrats essentially base their claims on landholding. Nothing in the odes tells us where the wealth of these families came from,[66] and one scholar stridently insisted that this picture of commercial success was anachronistic, and that if Aegina had been so commercially active one would have expected it, like other Greek trading states, to have sent out colonies, which it did not.[67] But even if the ships in the harbour at the beginning of *Nemean* 5 were not all Aeginetan,[68] it seems inescapable that trade was the foundation of the island's prosperity.[69] Trading aristocracies are not unknown to history. The merchants of medieval Italy and Flanders were of just such a kind, and in antiquity one may perhaps compare the case of Palmyra in the first centuries C E, which was analysed by Michael Rostovtzeff as being home to merchant aristocrats (though they used the ships of the desert, not the sea).[70] Aegina thus became antipathetic to its neighbour, Athens, not just for its rivalry for mastery of the sea, but for its antithetical political system. The Athenians had abetted the revolt of the *demos* in the 490s, and in 431, nine years after Pindar's death, they took control of Aegina, expelled the entire population, and replaced them with Athenian settlers.

Pindar, from landlocked Boeotia, found charm in the company of these cosmopolitan islanders who welcomed visitors from, or sent out ships to, not just the Black Sea, but Rhodes, Naucratis and Etruria. He celebrates them for their justice to strangers,[71] which could be interpreted in economic terms as reasonable trading tariffs. A man named Xenarches (ruler of the foreigners) even appears in *Pythian* 8.

A man called Sostratus of Aegina was mentioned by Herodotus as the richest trader ever,[72] and he had traded with the Etruscans. Another Sostratos was the father of the Syracusan Hagesias, celebrated in *Olympian* 6. Is it possible that there is a family connection: that a descendant of the great trader settled in the west, and that his Aeginetan cousins mentioned to him the admirable poetry of their favourite poet Pindar, so that his fame reached Sicily? For within ten years of his first commissions in Aegina, Pindar was in demand in Sicily. The ode for Hagesias dates from 468, and is almost the last of his surviving Sicilian odes, while two odes for champions from Acragas – *Pythian* 6 and *Pythian* 12 – predate any of the Aeginetan songs; but family networking would be entirely characteristic of everything we know about Greeks both ancient and modern.

Sicily, or Once upon a Time in the West

Sometime in 476 BCE, Pindar saw his first volcano. The sight impressed him greatly, and he describes

> Snowy Aetna, nurse of biting snow all year round.
> From whose depths belch forth holiest springs
> Of unapproachable fire; during the days rivers of lava
>> Pour forth a blazing stream
> Of smoke, but in times of darkness
> A rolling red flame carries rocks into the deep
>> Expanse of the sea with a crash.[73]

This awesome natural phenomenon is explained by Pindar – as it was by Greeks generally – as the complaining of the hundred-headed monster Typhos, enemy of the gods, whose vast body Zeus had imprisoned beneath the flaming fields of Cyme as well as the 'dark and leafy peaks' of Etna; 'and a jagged bed goads the entire length of his back that lies against it'.[74]

In Pindar's poem, the monster Typho (otherwise called Typhon or Typhoeus) becomes an emblem of discord in the universe that throws into sharp relief the power both of Zeus and of music: 'those creatures for whom Zeus has no love are terrified when they hear the song of the Pierians [Muses]'.[75] The ode begins as an invocation of the lyre, the source of music itself, and its great power: 'you quench even the warring thunderbolt of ever flowing fire; and the eagle sleeps on the sceptre of Zeus'.[76] All this is in order to bring praise to Hieron, one of the most powerful men in the Greek world, following his victory in the chariot race at Olympia in 470 BCE. At the same time it celebrates his foundation of the new city of Aetna (founded *c*.480 BCE), which, we may presume, is to be as inimical to civil discord as the rule of Zeus is to cosmic discord: the factionalism of the cities whose populations were moved to create Aetna is to be no more. The eagle was a favourite symbol of Hieron's: it appears on the coins of Aetna and surely represents the bird that adorned the cult statue of Zeus in the temple, of which Hieron was priest.[77]

But to begin at the beginning. Sicily had become part of the Greek world as a result of colonisation from the second half of the eighth century BCE onwards. Successive Greek colonies were established at Naxos, Syracuse (founded from Corinth) and then Leontini and Catana (founded from Naxos), Megara Hyblaea and Gela (founded by a Rhodian and a Cretan), Acragas (founded from Gela), Zancle (from Cumae) and Himera (from Zancle). Thucydides describes the process,[78] which involved the displacement of the native Sicans, Sicels and Elymi, as well as rivalry with the Phoenician settlers, who were allied with their fellow Semites in Carthage. At the beginning of the fifth century, a number of 'tyrants' became rulers of the major Greek cities, beginning with Hippocrates of Gela (from 498), who failed in an attempt to capture Syracuse in 492. A revolution followed in which the democrats expelled the *gamoroi* (landholders), and in the aftermath Gelon became tyrant of Syracuse, with its excellent harbours and fertile hinterland, and entered into an alliance with Theron of Acragas.

Acragas had been founded about 580 by the people of Gela and was notorious as the erstwhile home of the vicious tyrant Phalaris (*c.*570–549), who had been overthrown by Theron's great-great-grandfather. Theron became tyrant in 489 and, after the major battle fought against the Carthaginians at Himera in 480 (legend said on the same day as the mainland Greeks defeated the Persians at the Battle of Salamis),[79] set about the rebuilding of his city. Chained Carthaginian prisoners carried out the work. Beside these public slaves, Diodorus tells us that the captives were so numerous that some private citizens took possession of as many as 500 personally.[80] The chain gangs quarried the stone for the three great temples with which Theron adorned Acragas; they dug underground water conduits and even created a fish pond. As a result, Polybius (writing in the second century BCE) tells us:

> Acragas is superior to all cities in beauty and elaborate ornamenta-
> tion [...] Its wall is placed on a rock, steep and precipitous, on one
> side naturally, on the other made so artificially. And it is enclosed by
> rivers. The citadel overlooks the city exactly at the south-east, girt on
> the outside by an impassable ravine, and on the inside with only one
> approach from the town. On the top is a temple of Athene and of Zeus

Atabyrius [...] The city is sumptuously adorned in other respects also
with temples and colonnades. The temple of Zeus Olympius is still
unfinished, but in its plan and dimensions it seems to be inferior to
no temple whatever in all Greece.[81]

The phenomenon of tyranny – the emergence of a populist ruler who
displaced and eroded the privileges of the ruling aristocrats – had been a
phenomenon of mainland Greece and the islands in the sixth century BCE.
The poet Alcaeus had been a vocal opponent of the tyrant of Lesbos, Pittacus
(who was in fact something like an elected dictator).[82] Besides calling him a
lot of rude names referring to his flat feet and fat belly,[83] he wrote numerous
poems inspiring aristocratic solidarity against the tyrant and his associate
Myrsilus (the name is Lydian):

> Come, with gracious spirit hear our prayer, and rescue us from these
> hardships and from grievous exile; and let their avenger pursue the
> son of Hyrrhas [Pittacus], since once we swore, cutting [...], never
> [to abandon] any of our comrades... But Pot-belly did not talk to
> their hearts; he recklessly trampled the oaths underfoot and devours
> our city.[84]

But by the fifth century the Greek world had moved on from tyranny to
a more civic conception of the *polis* (unless, like Boeotia, it had remained
aristocratic and had never seen this kind of upheaval). Sicily, by contrast,
for reasons we can hardly fathom, came later to this form of government.
Wealth came no doubt mainly from the rich cornlands of the island, from
which the Sicans and Sicels had been displaced, and perhaps also from the
trading activities of the Phoenicians at their settlement of Motya.

Gelon was tyrant of Syracuse from 485 until 478, while his brother
Hieron was appointed regent of Gelon's former stronghold of Gela in the
same years. After the battle of Himera in 480 the island was divided into
a Punic west, the two despotates based on Syracuse and Acragas, and the
eastern part, which fell under the sway of Anaxilas of Rhegium (modern
Reggio). Gelon died in 478, and his modest and beneficent rule (according to

Diodorus 11.38) concluded with exequies, which adhered to the provisions of the law prohibiting costly funerals – a law that echoed the ban by Solon on funerals as occasions for aristocratic display in Athens. Hieron now became tyrant in his own right and reigned in Syracuse until 466, while his younger brother Polyzalus became governor of Gela. Hieron subjugated several of the other Sicilian cities, and at some time, perhaps as early as 476, he refounded the city of Catana under the new name of Aetna. This involved expelling all the existing inhabitants, along with those of Naxos, and deporting them to Leontini. Aetna was repopulated with 5,000 settlers from Syracuse and a similar number from the Peloponnese.[85] The foundation of the new city was celebrated by the Athenian dramatist Aeschylus in his *Women of Aetna,* commissioned for the occasion.

Positioned on the slopes of Mount Etna, the site was notably fertile on account of the rich volcanic soil:

> Although the ash is an affliction at the time, it benefits the country in later times, for it renders it fertile and suited to the vine, the rest of the country not being equally productive of good wine; further, the roots produced by the fields that have been covered with ash-dust make the sheep so fat, it is said, that they choke.[86]

Hieron's third wife was a niece of Theron, who had become tyrant of Acragas in 489 and reigned until 473, and whose daughter Demarate was married to Gelon. In 483 Theron seized Himera and made his son Thrasydaeus its governor. Though the brothers fought alongside one another in the decisive battle against the Carthaginians at Himera in 480, they came close to war in 476 when the oppressed Himeraeans called in Hieron's aid, but were reconciled, we are told by a scholiast on *Olympian* 6, by the intervention of the poet Simonides. In the same year, Hieron celebrated his victory over Anaxilas at Cumae and marked the occasion with dedications at Olympia, a victory referred to in muted terms by Pindar in *Pythian* 1.72–3: 'I beseech you, son of Kronos, grant that the war cry of the Phoenicians and Etruscans may remain quietly at home, now that they have seen their aggression bring woe to their fleet before Kyme [Latin Cumae].'

PINDAR

The tyrants, with their sudden new-found wealth, sought recognition as equals of the aristocracy of old Greece: one might think of them as Henry-Jamesian wealthy Americans eager to reach a position of equality with the aristocrats of Europe (though hardly as bemused as James' Americans often are by the subtleties of European culture). One way of expressing their status was through architecture, the great temples of Syracuse, Acragas and Selinus; another was through competition in the Games, and the commissioning of adequate celebrations from the greatest poets of the age.

Hieron gets a poor press from history. Diodorus[87] says he 'did not rule over his subjects in the same manner [as Gelon]; for he was avaricious and violent and, speaking generally, an utter stranger to sincerity and nobility of character. His network of spies, including women who were trained to trick his enemies into betraying themselves, was much feared'.[88] Plutarch, however, regarded his reign as an example of *eunomia*, good government. The other side of the coin was his extensive patronage of the arts.

> Hieron of Syracuse, they say, was a philhellene with a great enthusiasm for culture. And they say he was very quick to perform generous acts, being more anxious to confer favours than petitioners were to take them. [...] Simonides and Pindar, they say, lived with him; and Simonides, weighed down by his years, did not hesitate to join him. The man from Ceos was by nature keen to make money, but it is reported that Hieron's love of generosity was even greater.[89]

Xenophon composed a fictional dialogue between Hieron and Simonides that remarks on the tyrant's 'unrivalled power to confer benefits on friends',[90] but for the most part the dialogue is given over to Hieron's assertions that the tyrant has a much worse life than the private citizen. The protestation is hardly convincing, but in the conclusion 'Simonides' urges him to be as generous as possible:

> Thus you will be not only the loved, but the adored of mankind [...] Enrich your friends, and so you will enrich yourself. Exalt the state, for so you will deck yourself with power [...] And if you do

all these things, rest assured that you will be possessed of the fairest and most blessed possession in the world; for none will be jealous of your happiness.[91]

Hieron started his career as 'an ordinary citizen of no culture, and in his boorishness did not differ in the least from his brother Gelon'.[92] But all that changed when he became ill, apparently with chronic gallstones that plagued him all his life. He devoted the leisure enforced by illness to cultural pursuits, and created a salon of poets in Aetna.

Poets had visited Sicily from the east before this. Some lines attributed to the sixth-century poet Theognis (though West thinks they might be by another Megarian poet, Philiadas, *c.*480) describe how

I've been a gangrel bodie, I've been to Sicilie,
And owre til Euboia wi the vines upon its howe,
Bonnie Sparta on Eurotas whaur the rashes grow
And aa the fowk in ilka place were guid to me.
But I'd nae rowth o pleisure for aa that I micht see.
Och, I'd suner be at hame in my ain countrie.[93]

Ibycus, who was born in Rhegium but spent most of his life at the court of Polycrates on Samos, may have revisited the west, since a fragmentary poem celebrates a victory by an athlete from Leontini.[94]

But the flow of poets increased markedly during Hieron's reign. Xenophanes, exiled from his native Colophon, made his home at Hieron's court. Aeschylus not only composed *Women of Aetna* for the tyrant, but produced a performance of *The Persians* there in 471, and may have spent a longer time there;[95] he died in Gela. Some lines of *Prometheus Bound* (363–72) have been thought to reflect his observation of an eruption of Etna: the play may not be by Aeschylus, but whoever did write it can thus be added to the catalogue of poets who went to Aetna. Simonides' role in reconciling the brother tyrants has already been mentioned; he wrote odes for Theron's brother Xenocrates and for Anaxilas; he too died in Sicily. Bacchylides, Pindar's younger contemporary, wrote poems for Hieron and may have visited the island. The rhetorician Corax is also said (dubiously) to have been based at Hieron's court.

But undoubtedly the greatest of the poets who wrote for Hieron was Pindar. Pindar's first Sicilian commissions were for Theron's brother Xenocrates,[96] and for the flute-player Midas of Acragas in the same year, 490 B C E.[97] The latter opens with a beautiful evocation of the site of Acragas, 'lover of splendour, loveliest of mortals' cities, abode of Persephone, you who dwell upon the well-built height above the banks of the Acragas, where sheep graze'. Xenocrates' son Thrasybulus, who acted as his charioteer, received the burden of praise in this ode, and again in *Isthmian* 2 (which was probably written in 470). Pindar's *annus mirabilis* for Sicilian odes was 476: in that year he composed *Olympian* 1 for Hieron, which was also celebrated in Bacchylides 5, and two odes for Theron, *Olympians* 2 and 3, as well as, probably, *Nemean* 1 for Chromius, a general in Hieron's army, which opens with another celebration of a natural beauty of the victor's city: the spring of Arethusa on the island of Ortygia, where, according to legend, the nymph Arethusa re-emerged from the ground after fleeing beneath the sea to escape the clutches of the god of the river Alpheus in the Peloponnese.[98]

Pindar's *Pythian* 1, the last of his odes for the tyrants, composed in 470, is one of the greatest of his poems, though it is often overshadowed by *Olympian* 1, which had the good fortune to come first in the Alexandrian edition. It can stand as an almost perfect example of praise poetry. It is not just an epinician but a panegyric of Hieron in the guise of ideal ruler. Its structure is pellucid and the focus on praise of Hieron is steadily maintained. From the brilliant opening – 'when a work is begun, it is necessary to make its front shine from afar'[99] (the metaphor is architectural) – describing the repose of the eagle of Zeus (perhaps the performance took place in front of the cult statue: see above), it moves through three myths that all cast glory on the figure of Hieron. Typhon's bestial nature is suppressed and there follows a prayer to Apollo that he will 'make this a land of brave men: for from the gods come all the means for human achievements'.[100] A second myth alludes to Philoctetes, the hero whose aid, despite his sickness, was indispensable to the conquest of Troy: Hieron's sickness is undoubtedly in view here, as it is throughout the magnificent *Pythian* 3. A third myth associates the people of Aetna with the Dorian sons of Herakles and leads to a prayer, this time to Zeus, who is perhaps watching over the proceedings from his throne in the temple: 'Zeus Accomplisher, determine such good fortune as this always for the citizens and their kings.'[101] Pindar now alludes to Hieron's victories over the Carthaginians and prays that their defeat will be final. In the last triad, Pindar addresses himself: 'If you should speak to the point by combining the strands of many things in brief, less criticism follows from men, for cloying excess dulls eager expectations, and townsmen are grieved in their secret hearts especially when they hear of others' successes.'[102] The lines encapsulate epinician etiquette (on which more in Chapter 5 of the present volume): the poet must hit the mark, get praise just right, and not overdo it. If he goes too far, people will be enraged, not with the poet, but with the *laudandus* whose fame is being trumpeted to excess. Pindar's next words are addressed both to himself and to Hieron: 'But nevertheless, since envy is better than pity, do not pass over any noble things. Guide your people with a rudder of justice; on an anvil of truth forge your tongue.'[103] And then Pindar sets himself up as not just a *xenos*, an honoured guest, but a *philos*, an intimate, of the king:

> Do not be deceived,
>> O my friend, by shameful gains,
>> for the posthumous acclaim of fame
>> alone reveals the life of men who are dead and gone
>> to both chroniclers and poets. The kindly
>> excellence of Croesus does not perish,
>> but universal execration overwhelms Phalaris, that man
>> of pitiless spirit who burned men in his bronze bull,
>> and no lyres in the banquet halls welcome him
>> in gentle fellowship with boys' voices.[104]

Pindar evokes the legendary cruelty of the tyrant of Acragas, who ruled less than a century before Hieron; his advice not to follow his example is tantamount to an assertion that Hieron does not do so, that he is a wise and just king. In these lines Pindar speaks as an equal who may expect to be listened to by the king: his praise is thus made adequate and the ode comes to a fitting conclusion.

As was noted earlier, to praise an absolute ruler is a different thing from praising a fellow aristocrat. The ploy that Pindar here carries off seemingly effortlessly was developed with more complexity and some awkwardness in the earlier *Pythian* 2. That poem ends with 25 lines of meditation on the nature of praise, starting from the admonition to Hieron, 'Become what you are': it is a virtual textbook on the modalities of praise, and will be discussed as such in Chapter 5. In contrast to the odes for aristocrats, the theme of 'generosity' hardly occurs in the tyrant odes. 'The bounty of tyrants is an easy virtue,' remarks Freeman,[105] and Pindar steered clear of any suggestions that his work was that of a hireling: he was a king's counsellor.

A third great poem for Hieron, *Pythian* 3, will be discussed in Chapter 6 as an example of Pindar's narrative art. This was probably composed in 474 and was thus Pindar's last ode for Hieron. Despite his illness, Hieron went on to win further chariot victories at Delphi (474) and Olympia (468), but these were celebrated in poems by Bacchylides, not Pindar. One would love to know what caused Hieron to change his poetic allegiance. He died in 467. His successor Thrasybulus was a murderous tyrant; he was overthrown and democracy established in Syracuse until the ascent of Dionysius.[106]

Persephone's Island

In the year that Pindar celebrated Hieron's Olympic victory in *Olympian* 1, he also celebrated the Nemean victory of a citizen of Aetna, Chromius (*Nemean* 1), and also offered two odes to Hieron's wife's uncle, Theron of Acragas. A notable feature of *Olympian* 2 is that it contains no myth as such, but a description of the life of the Blessed, who have been initiated in the Mysteries, in the Underworld. There are close resemblances between this passage and two fragments of Pindar's laments,[107] both addressed to Theron. The usual explanation for this unusual feature is that Theron was himself a devotee of a mystery religion, as befitted the inhabitant of an island whose chief goddess was the underworld deity Persephone. The appearance of the

theme in the ode, however, is a variation on the idea of 'reward for pains':
after the opening praises of Olympia, Pindar goes on: 'Under the force of
noble joys the pain dies and its malignancy is suppressed, whenever divine
Fate sends happiness towering upwards.'[108] He goes on to illustrate the point
with allusions to several mythological characters who suffered but were
rewarded with heavenly life: Semele and Ino, and even Oedipus. The praise
of Theron himself at 53ff. is expressed in the following terms:

> Truly, wealth embellished with virtues
> Provides fit occasion for various achievements
> By supporting a profound and questing ambition;
> It is a conspicuous lodestar, the truest
> Light for a man. If one has it and knows the future,
> That the helpless spirits
> Of those who have died on earth immediately
> Pay the penalty – and upon sins committed here
> In Zeus' realm, a judge beneath the earth
> Pronounces sentence with hateful necessity;
> But forever having sunshine in equal nights
> And in equal days, good men receive a life of less toil...
> [68] But those with courage to have lived
> Three times in either realm, while keeping their souls
> Free from all unjust deeds, travel the road of Zeus
> To the tower of Kronos, where ocean breezes
> Blow round
> The Isle of the Blessed, and flowers of gold are ablaze...
> [78] Peleus and Kadmos are numbered among them,
> And Achilles too...

The august expectation of a blessed afterlife is a symbol of the glory that
has fallen on Theron as a result of his victory. Just as aristocratic victors are
illuminated with a flash of heroic glory, so the greater status of the tyrant
demands a higher level of religious reward; and whereas the god-given gleam
is normally shed on an athlete in his lifetime, Theron can look forward to

it also after his death. The same *topoi* about the afterlife occur in two fragments – 133 and 137 – of Pindar's laments, which may come from a poem
on the death of Theron.[109] After Theron's son, Thrasydaeus, fell from power
in 471, democracy was established, and all the Sicilian tyrannies had fallen
by 462; the exiled populations returned to their own cities.

Cyrene

Pindar's next commissions took him to another distant Greek corner of
the Mediterranean: the Libyan city of Cyrene. Cyrene had been founded
in 630 BCE by colonists from Thera; further waves of colonists followed
until the settlers were able to inflict a defeat on the native Libyans in about
570 BCE. Cyrene became a large *polis* surrounded by villages; the Libyan
people provided labour in the cities. Conquest by Persia in 525 was followed by renewed independence. The attraction of Cyrene was, as usual, its
agricultural promise: the land was productive of cereals, vines and olives as
well as grazing for flocks and herds; in addition, the plant silphium was a
precious export. This now extinct plant was probably a relative of *Scorodosma
foetidum*, from which asafoetida is derived; its leaves and stems were eaten
as a vegetable while its root and sap were valued for their wide-ranging
medicinal properties. A famous black-figure vase painting shows the king
of Cyrene overseeing the harvest of the silphium.

The founder, Battus, had a hero's tomb in the agora of Cyrene, and the
rulers of Cyrene, who took the title of 'king', were regarded as his descendants.
The dynasty was overthrown in 440. The king of Cyrene, Arcesilas, commissioned two poems from Pindar, but Pindar's first poem for a Cyrenean
was *Pythian* 9 for Telesicrates, winner of the race in armour at the Pythia of
474. Most of the ode is dominated by the myth of the nymph Cyrene, the
happy victim of an amorous pursuit by the god Apollo. The girl loved hunting
and was spotted one day by the god as she wrestled with a lion. Impetuous
Apollo immediately called out to the wise centaur Chiron (whose home
was on Mount Pelion, rather far from Libya) to ask him for information
about the girl, and to enquire, 'Is it right to lay my famous hand on her?'[110]

2.1   King Arcesilas overseeing the silphium harvest in Cyrene.
Spartan black figure kylix, c.550 BCE. Bibliothèque Nationale de France.

One does not often discover jokes in Pindar, but there is definitely
humour in Chiron's reply to Apollo:

> Do you ask from where
> the girl's lineage comes, O lord? And yet you know
> the appointed end of all things and all the ways to them,
> and how many leaves the earth puts forth in spring,
> and how many grains of sand in the sea and the rivers
> are beaten by the waves and blasts of wind,
> and what will happen and whence
> it will come.[111]

The erotic theme of the myth, taken with later allusions to the marriage of the daughters of Danaus[112] and that of the daughter of the Libyan king Antaeus to Alexidamus – he won her as a prize in a race – has suggested to many commentators that Telesicrates himself was about to be married. The interpretation is attractive, but the motif might be woven into the poem into a more subtle way than that. One form of the brightness that adorns the victor may be the glow of youthful attraction; Woodbury suggested that the girls of Cyrene are all gazing on Telesicrates as Apollo does on Cyrene.[113] Kurke however, following Carson,[114] suggests that in this poem glory itself is the victor's bride: 'Kyrene will welcome him gladly to his country of beautiful women, having brought delightful fame [*doxan himertan* – better, 'desirous glory' or, as Conway has it, 'the fame all men desire'] from Delphi'.[115]

A dozen years passed before Pindar was back in Cyrene – possibly in person, since *Pythian* 4 begins, 'Today, Muse, you must stand beside a man who is a friend, the king of Kyrene.' Pindar composed two odes for the same chariot victory of King Arcesilas at Pytho, *Pythians* 4 and 5. Both are devoted to the founding myth of Cyrene, the story of Battus, whose stutter (that is the meaning of his name) was cured by an encounter with a Libyan lion. *Pythian* 5 is a straightforward encomium of Arcesilas with extensive praise also of his charioteer, Carrhotus, the king's brother-in-law: it was performed at the festival of Carneian Apollo,[116] possibly very soon after the victory, since the festival took place in July/August while the Carneia of the ancestral city Sparta took place in the same period (though it is possible that the Cyrenian Carneia took place at a different season).

Pythian 4 is the longest ode that Pindar wrote, by far: it is 299 lines long and its linear narrative style is indebted to the approach of the early sixth-century poet Stesichorus.[117] Most of it is devoted to the story of the Argonauts, one of the participants in whose expedition was Battus' ancestor Euphemus, and to prophecies of the future glory of Cyrene. Towards the end Pindar inserts himself into the setting by referring to his *xenia*, 'guest friendship', with one Damophilus when the latter was at Thebes. It has been suggested that Damophilus commissioned this extraordinary ode as a way of regaining the favour of the king who had banished him.

Certainly the plea for forgiveness is explicit: 'But almighty Zeus set free the Titans'[118] – not that any other source says he did. More generally, the link with Damophilus is used to create the necessary link of poet and patron as *xenoi*, which is indispensable to the epinician 'fiction' that the two are involved in an exchange of gifts.

Last Years: Dancers in the Dark

Besides these commissions from across the sea, Pindar's work as far as we know it was carried out for cities of mainland Greece.[119] There are several poems for Athens as well as for Argos and Corinth. For a poet who was supposed to favour the cause of Aegina against its hated rival, Pindar wrote quite frequently of Athens,[120] suggesting that political considerations were not the only thing that determined where Pindar accepted his commissions. Poems for Athenian individuals are rare, but *Paean* 5 (undated) as well as the early *Pythian* 7 (486) are for Athenian occasions, and three dithyrambs were also written for Athens, *Dithyramb* 1, Fragment 75 and Fragment 76 (post-Artemisium). Most of the other poems and fragments cannot be dated, though *Paean* 9 for the Thebans is most probably anchored to 463 by its reference to an eclipse of the Sun: 'Beam of the Sun, what have you contrived, far-seeing one, O mother of eyesight, supreme star, by being hidden in daytime?' The only total eclipse of the sun in Pindar's lifetime took place in 463; there was an annular eclipse in 478. Rutherford notes that the poem need not have been performed on the actual occasion of the eclipse, but perhaps at Apollo's New Year festival; however, it loses point if it did not coincide with the actual phenomenon, and scientists were perfectly capable of predicting the eclipse in time for Pindar to get his poem ready. *Paean* 4, for Ceos, was probably not composed until after the death of the Ceans' own poet, Bacchylides, in 458. *Paeans* 5, 7 and 12 are for Delos, 1 for Thebes and 2 for Abdera.[121]

Dithyramb 2, unusually in Pindar, is for a festival of Dionysus, and evokes how

The whirling of the drums begins
beside the holy Great Mother,
and the castanets clatter
while the feast is lit by bright pine-torches.
The loud shrieking of the Naiads is roused,
their wailing and whooping as their necks arch back
in the wild clamour.[122]

The chorus is of maidens, and they are dancers in the dark.

Two poems, one possibly late, the other certainly so, may bring to a conclusion the trajectory of Pindar's composing life. *Nemean* 11 is not an epinician but was included among the epinicians by the Alexandrian scholars because of its references to athletic prowess. It is in fact an encomium for Aristagoras of the island of Tenedos on his installation as a councillor. The congruence of its themes and method of praise demonstrate how far epinician is merely a subspecies of encomium: it opens with an address to a goddess (Hestia, protector of city halls) and evokes the sound of music that accompanies the festival. It praises his father Arcesilas, and Aristagoras' sixteen victories in lesser games. Its very short myth describes the colonisation of Tenedos from Sparta, and the closing lines have struck many as notably melancholic: 'The talents of ancient time produce their strength in alternating generations of men... we embark on ambitious projects and yearn for many accomplishments, for our bodies are enthralled to shameless hope, and the streams of foreknowledge lie far off.'[123] In this poem the dark foil to praise follows rather than precedes it and gives a very downbeat ending to the poem.

A shaky argument has proposed that the poem might date from very late in Pindar's career, around 446;[124] if this were so, its mood would chime with that of what is known to be his last poem, *Pythian* 8, which is, fittingly, for a victor from his beloved Aegina, for which he had first composed a poem over 40 years before in 487. It is for a boy-victor, Aristomenes of Aegina, and the scholiast tells us that it was written for a victory in 446. Here, too, sombre tones outweigh the celebratory character of the ode, and explanations have been sought in possible civil strife in Aegina at the time. The evocation of the defeated contestants slinking home by the back roads is an unusual way of celebrating achievement. The final lines, however, read like the words of an old man saying farewell to life and a city he loves:

> Creatures of a day! What is someone? What is no one?
> A dream of a shadow
> Is man. But whenever Zeus-given brightness comes,
> A shining light rests upon men, and a gentle life.
> Dear mother Aigina, on its voyage of freedom
> Safeguard this city, together with Zeus and king Aiakos,
> Peleus and noble Telamon, and with Achilles.[125]

III

THE RANGE OF
PINDAR'S POETRY

PINDAR'S LIFETIME OUTPUT OF POETRY amounted to 4,000 poems.
So we are told by Eustathius, the twelfth-century bishop of Salonica who
wrote an introduction to Pindar that contains many still-pertinent insights.[1]
Whether Eustathius had access to all these poems we do not know:[2] the
number is in any case suspiciously round, and Eustathius' range of reference
does not seem to be greater than the odes we have, while his information
about Pindar replicates what was current already in antiquity. What is
without question is that we only have a tiny amount of what Pindar wrote,
and we cannot be sure that the epinician odes are particularly typical of
his poetry as a whole. Eustathius says, 'The epinicians are the most widely
diffused because they are more human and concise and do not present
obscurities, at least in comparison with the others.'[3] The judgement that
they are concise and lack obscurity might be opposed by some students of
Pindar, but it is almost certainly the human focus of these odes that ensured
their preservation in antiquity.

The Survival of Pindar's Poetry

Pindar himself never made a collection or published a book of his poetry. His poems were written for specific occasions, and no doubt those who commissioned them kept copies of them: one of the best-known examples is the report in the scholia to *Olympian* 7 that this poem was inscribed in letters of gold in the temple of Athena at Lindos. Pausanias tells us that his Hymn to Ammon, 'which he sent to the Ammonians in Libya, in my time still survived on a triangular stone tablet beside the altar'.[4] But Greek lyric poetry is full of remarks to the effect that poetry is more lasting than sculpture. The word is always privileged in Greek thinking, from the Homeric idea of *kleos* onwards, and in a poem for an unknown occasion Simonides had asserted that statues do not last.[5] The poem surely went on to announce that poetry was a more reliable source of eternal fame, as does Pindar in *Nemean* 5: 'I am not a sculptor, so as to fashion stationary statues that stand on their same base. Rather, on board every ship and in every boat, sweet song, go forth from Aegina and spread the news...'[6] The sailors of Aegina swung their oars whistling an ode of Pindar. Sometimes a well-remembered song could save your life, as the Athenian prisoners taken in Syracuse in 414 discovered after being spared execution because their jailers were charmed by their ability to sing the latest choruses of Euripides.[7]

Pindar's odes were among the popular hits of their day, though by the late fifth century they had come to seem old-fashioned, at least according to the Athenian poet Eupolis,[8] who died some time after 415 and was thus some 20-odd years younger than Pindar. His poems were widely known; our evidence comes inevitably from Athens, but we may presume they were sung elsewhere too: Aristophanes several times quotes from Pindar, usually for purposes of parody, which implies familiarity,[9] and Bacchylides has been thought to refer to the famous opening of *Olympian* 1 in his *Ode* 3, 85–7: 'I utter words which the wise man may understand: the deep heavens are unsoiled, and the water of the sea does not decay, and gold is a joy...' Then as now, people would remember 'lollipops', and one thing that made a passage memorable was a quotable moral: hence the survival of many passages from Simonides, who seems to have been amenable to this kind of excerpting. Plato preserves one of our longest fragments of Simonides in his *Protagoras*, where Socrates constructs a lecture on the text: 'It is difficult for a man to be truly good, four-square in hands, in feet and in mind, fashioned without flaw';[10] the fragment continues for a further 30 lines.[11] Plato also refers to Tynichus of Chalcis, who 'never composed any poem worth remembering with the exception of the paean which everyone sings, almost the most beautiful of all lyric poems and truly, as he himself puts it, "a discovery of the Muses"'.[12]

Simonides, like Pindar, could be seen as old-fashioned by the avant-garde, as Aristophanes' character Strepsiades found when he started to sing one of Simonides' poems and his son 'at once told him it was old-fashioned to play the lyre and sing while drinking, like a woman grinding barley'.[13] Nonetheless, in the middle years of the fifth century it was undoubtedly customary to sing such things at symposia. Party poetry was not limited to monodic lyric like that of Alcaeus in the sixth century, but comprised solo renderings of what had originally been choral poetry, with appropriately reduced accompaniment. (The singer played his own lyre.)

These highly wrought poems, with their involved metres and complex grammatical structures, were particularly suitable for solo performance, and it has sometimes been assumed that they must have been written for such performance. Scholars have had difficulty in envisaging a chorus of twelve or more persons dancing (or even processing) in step and singing audibly and intelligibly at the same time. Anyone who has seen a modern performance of a Greek tragedy that attempts this knows how difficult it is, and one is tempted to imagine a separation of roles, with two groups, singers and dancers, performing simultaneously, as in Carl Orff's *Carmina Burana*, or in extreme cases a solo singer (the poet himself?) performing in front of a troupe of dancers. The image belies what we know of the ritual nature of Greek choral performances, though particular difficulty has arisen with a very long poem like *Pythian* 4: could this really have been sung and danced for the half hour or more it would take to get through? The question arises also with the sixth-century lyric poet Stesichorus. It has generally

53

been assumed that his epic-lyric narrative compositions were choral (partly because his name happens to mean 'establisher of the chorus'), but West has argued that they were in fact performed solo.[14]

The susceptibility of the odes to solo re-performance should not blind us to the fact that in many cases choral performance is implied by the text. The *locus classicus* is *Olympian* 6, 87–92: 'Now, Aineas, urge your companions first to celebrate Hera the Maiden... for you are a true messenger, a message stick of the fair-haired Muses, a sweet mixing-bowl of loudly ringing songs.' The scholiast explains that Aineas was the trainer of the chorus: in referring to him as a message stick Pindar names the *skytala*, a Spartan stick of set diameter around which parchment or other material was wound in a strip: the message written hereon could only be read when the material was wound again around an identically sized stick. So Aineas reproduces at a distance the exact instructions (music, dance steps) of the chorus, from a written text (though hardly a coded one in reality).

But this passage alerts us to another feature that would have made some poems more suitable for re-performance than others: the presence of specific allusions to the occasion of performance. These are very numerous in Pindar's epinicians: 'in this land of Zeus',[15] 'this city',[16] 'this island',[17] 'this people',[18] 'this man'[19] are just a few examples. The adjectives undoubtedly refer to the occasion of performance, though Sean Harrigan[20] has called attention to similar deictic expressions in tragic prologues – 'These are the streams of the Nile'[21] – which would make a reference to 'this island' easier to pull off in central Athens. But considerations like these must have favoured the frequent performance abroad of poems with less specifically local reference – a Euripides chorus, for example, would be suitable anywhere.

However, the local references draw attention to another context for re-performance, namely in the city for which the original performance was commissioned.[22] In *Pythian* 1, 95–8 Pindar refers to the tyrant Phalaris, dead now a hundred years, who because of his bad reputation does not get celebrated in repeated songs: 'no lyres in banquet halls welcome him in gentle fellowship with boys' voices.' Pindar makes the possibility explicit in *Nemean* 4, 13–17:

And if your father Timokritos

were still warmed by the blazing sun, often would he have

played an elaborate tune on the lyre, and, relying on

this song,[23] would have celebrated his triumphant son

for bringing a wreath of crowns from Kleonai's games...

Later in the same poem Pindar envisages the victor's grandfather, Euphanes, singing a song (a solo) for the boy's uncle, who is dead.[24] In this poem, which like *Nemean* 6 is about the durance of glory through generations, repeated performance of old epinicia is one of the means of preserving the memory of past achievements.

Similar consideration may help to explain another problematic question: are *Isthmians* 4 and 3 one ode or two? Though composed for different victories, they are both in the same metre, and Bruno Currie follows G. Aurelio Privitera in suggesting that this was done to enable a chorus to learn the second one without additional training, and to perform the two together on the occasion of the second victory; thus the earlier is being re-performed on this occasion.

Currie also wonders whether an ode like *Nemean* 4 might be performed regularly at a specific festival in Aegina, such as the new moon festival held when games took place. *Pythian* 2.15–7 tells us that 'the Cyprians often celebrate Kinyras, whom golden-haired Apollo heartily befriended'. The same could have been done to keep the aristocrats of Aegina in the public eye at city festivals: see, for example, *Isthmian* 8.8, 'let us sing for the citizens a sweet song'. The poems might have been inscribed locally to keep them available for re-performance, though more portable copies would have been more useful in rehearsals. Just as the poems of Homer were performed regularly at the Panathenaea, so the poems of Pindar might have been performed regularly at Aeginetan festivals. In Euripides' *Alcestis*, in the ode for Alcestis, who is about to sacrifice her life for her husband, the chorus sing:

Servants of the Muses

will sing many hymns for you, on the seven-stringed lyre

and unaccompanied,

when the hour comes to pass in the Carneian

month in Sparta, at the all-night

festival of the risen moon,

and in the blessed city of shining Athens.[25]

(The importance of the moon as a festival occasion is apparent here, as is the quotation from Pindar in the reference to 'shining Athens'.)[26] A more historical parallel is provided by a fragment of the historian Sosibius[27] that refers to paeans[28] being composed to celebrate those who died at the battle of Thyrea in c. 545 BCE, and being regularly performed at the annual festival of the *gymnopaedia* in Sparta.

Once the poems had been composed, how were copies kept? Pindar probably made multiple copies of his own poems and circulated them among his acquaintances as well as his patrons. (A manuscript copy would be a gift of guest-friendship, like the performance itself.) The first edition will in many cases have been on stone, as in the case of the later paeans that have survived at Delphi.[29] The famous case of *Olympian* 7, inscribed in letters of gold on the wall of the Temple of Athena at Lindos on Rhodes, might not be unique. Beyond Pindar's lifetime, many people might have kept collections of at least some of his books, though we do not know of any editions like those that were made of the Attic tragedians in Athens. A famous story tells how Ptolemy II, in collecting texts for the library in Alexandria, paid an enormous deposit to Athens for the loan of these texts for copying; he then kept the originals, returned the copies and forfeited the deposit. Furthermore, every traveller visiting Alexandria was compelled to surrender any books he had with him, and was then given replacement copies while the originals were added to the library collection. No doubt the librarians went to similar lengths to collect complete sets of the other poets designated as classics, though where they acquired their Pindars we do not know. It has been suggested by Thomas Hubbard[30] that Pindar's house in Thebes, which Alexander spared when he destroyed the city, may have functioned as an archive. Scholarship on the history of the Games began in the fourth century with Philochorus, and Aristotle wrote books on the history of the Games that revised Hippias' victor lists; so this would provide another context for the collection of material relating to the Games, including Pindar's poems.

Genres

Our knowledge of Pindar's poetry, as of most Greek literature, is the result of the work of the scholars of Alexandria in the third and second centuries BCE. It was they who catalogued the classical authors and in part they who determined which works would become classics by their regular inclusion in school syllabuses. Callimachus (320–240 BCE), the librarian of Alexandria and also a distinguished poet, established the categories into which Pindar's surviving poems were divided. (Of course some might already have been lost before Callimachus began work.) Then Aristophanes of Byzantium (265–190 BCE) refined his cataloguing method into an edition, in which he was followed by Aristarchus (215–144) and Didymus (in the first century BCE), who wrote numerous detailed notes, or scholia, on the epinicians.

The Alexandrians divided Pindar's poems into 17 books. The list given in the Ambrosian *Life*, which Eustathius follows, runs thus: hymns; paeans; dithyrambs (two books); prosodia or 'processional songs' (two books); *partheneia* (two books); 'separate *partheneia*' – whatever that means; hyporchemes (two books); encomia; laments; epinicians (four books).[31] The list given by the Ambrosian *Life* conveniently mirrors the classification of lyric genres devised by Proclus in the third century CE into poems for gods, poems for humans, poems for both and poems for particular occasions. The genres in this list begin with poems for gods, while the last three categories are 'for humans'. It is notable that there are no epithalamia, such as are so prominent among the remains of Sappho's poems.

The schema is neat, but it is unlikely that it reflects the practice or understanding of Pindar and his contemporaries. It seems to derive at least in part from Plato's over-tidy comments on the regulation of genres in some unspecified 'old days':

In those days Athenian music comprised various categories and forms. One type of song consisted of prayers to the gods, which were termed 'hymns'; and there was another quite different type, which you might well have called 'laments'. 'Paeans' made up a third category, and there was also a fourth, called a 'dithyramb' (whose theme was, I think, the birth of Dionysus). There existed another kind of song, too, which they thought of as a separate class, and the name they gave it was this very word which is so often on our lips: '*nomos*' ('for the lyre', as they always added). Once these categories and a number of others had been fixed, no one was allowed to pervert them by using one sort of tune in a composition belonging to another category.[32]

However, Ian Rutherford argues convincingly that the 'normative' application of genre names is a product of the Hellenistic period:[33] though Pindar and his contemporaries used genre names, they reflected a functional understanding of the occasions of the poems – that is, the name of the kind of poem is determined by its purpose and not by any formal features such as metre, instrumentation, gender of performers or type of content. So, for example, a paean in Hellenistic terminology designates a poem addressed to Apollo, with a refrain and a mythical narrative on an Apolline theme; and that is what our fragmentary book of Pindar's paeans contains, though some of the odes are primarily addressed to relevant heroes instead.[34] Pindar seems to support the classification in Fragment 128c: 'On the one hand there are paeanic songs in season belonging to the children of Leto of the golden distaff; on the other there are also [songs] ... from crowns of blooming ivy belonging to Dionysus.' Indeed, the genre is one of the easier ones to identify through its function. Paeans go back to the earliest stages of Greek poetry and are mentioned in, for example, the *Iliad* 1.472–4 and the Homeric hymn to Apollo, 516–9. Originally they seem to have had an apotropaic function, to ward off sickness or the dangers of battle, and to have been addressed to an actual deity called Paieon, who already occurs in Bronze Age Linear B texts under the name Paiawon; these, though, might have been simple short invocations and not developed poetic compositions at all. They were probably accompanied by pipes, not stringed instruments. So Pindar's compositions represent a relatively advanced stage in the development of the genre, and Rutherford ventures a definition of the fifth-century paean: 'A song addressed to "Paian", who is an old Greek god, connected with war and usually identified with Apollo. *Paianes* tended to be performed by groups of males, often *epheboi*, who have a special interest in the area of life represented by Paian and Apollo';[35] he goes on to conceive the 'paean' as really a loose federation of subgenres including the purposes of averting disaster, pre-battle, and celebration. Known poems that the ancients call *paian* but which are difficult to fit into this definition are mostly not by Pindar. A problem is created by his address to the Sun, *Paean 9*, which being addressed to the Sun God should be thought of as Apolline, but the critic Dionysius of Halicarnassus identifies it as a dithyramb or hyporcheme. The dilemma seems to show mainly that the definitions cannot be clear-cut, and for Pindar it was probably not a problem: this was a poetic invocation of the Sun, and he may have classified it no more precisely than to use the all-embracing term 'hymn'. Paeans were performed so frequently in ancient Greece that the term must have become pretty inclusive: in Rhegion, for example, there was a spring festival that lasted 60 days, and on every day 12 paeans were sung by choruses to Artemis Phakelitis.[36]

The problem is just as apparent with the other main surviving body of Pindar's work, the epinician odes (odes for victors). As Nick Lowe trenchantly expresses it, 'By the time the epinikian genre was invented it had been dead for two centuries.'[37] Paeans were still being sung in the third century, but nobody composed victory odes any more. Euripides' epinician for Alcibiades was probably the last, though Diodorus refers to an exceptionally elaborate epinician festival in Acragas in 412, when the *stadion* victor Exaenetus entered the city with a procession of three hundred chariots.[38] The term Pindar uses to refer to his epinician odes is *enkomion*, which literally means 'a song performed in a revel-procession';[39] but he once also calls it an *enkomios hymnos*, a hymn sung in a revel,[40] thus instantly blurring Proclus' neat distinction of gods and men. When he (twice) uses the word *epinik(i)os*, it is as a descriptive adjective 'for a victory', and has no technical sense. It was the Alexandrians who devised the term as a generic name, in order to separate these from other kinds of praise poems, which is what *enkomion* meant by this time. Laments, which, like epinician, share most of the programmatic traits of encomium, were likewise given a separate book. Some poems that we would regard as love poems fall under the bracket of encomia as poems of 'erotic praise', so to speak.

The classification of the epinicians was further subdivided according to contest, probably by Callimachus, who used a different principle for the epinicia of Simonides – classifying them by event – while the poems of Bacchylides were given titles according to their subject matter. The order of the four books of the epinicians is contested; ours was probably devised by Aristophanes of Byzantium to reflect the hierarchy of importance attached to the four Panhellenic Games.

The problems become greater when we turn to the other genres to which Pindar's poems are ascribed, particularly since what we have is small fragments; not a single complete poem except Fragment 123, the erotic encomium to Theoxenus of Tenedos. After the paeans, the dithyrambs are best represented. As the paean is for Apollo, so the dithyramb is a choral song for Dionysus,[41] and 'dithyrambos' might originally have been a title of the god. According to the scholiast Pindar at *Olympian* 13.19 it was invented in Corinth by Arion of Lesbos (c.625–585 BCE) and introduced to Athens by Lasus in the age of the tyrants. Herodotus[42] says that Arion first established a definite routine movement for the chorus and provided words to sing, on a subject from which it took its title. It was often accompanied by pipes rather than lyres, and the music was in the Phrygian mode.

In Pindar's day the dithyramb (like the tragic drama) was a piece with a title, consisting predominantly of a mythical narrative, and at Athens it was the subject of a competition like those for tragedy and comedy. Simonides, in the generation before Pindar, is said to have won 56 dithyrambic victories, but no certain fragment of his dithyrambs survives. Bacchylides' dithyrambs[43] are better represented, with reasonably substantial portions of six plus smaller fragments of a number of others surviving; they offer narratives on subjects varying from 'The Recovery of Helen' to two complete poems about the exploits of Theseus and shorter ones on the Argive heroine Io and on the Spartan hero Idas. There is nothing obviously Dionysiac about these themes, and Rutherford suggests that Bacchylides 17 may in fact be a paean.[44] But Pindar's dithyrambs, as far as we can tell, locate themselves within the worship of Dionysus:

> ...how the sons of Uranus
> celebrate the rites of Bromius [Dionysus]
> in the halls by the sceptre of Zeus...
> The loud shrieking of the Naiads is roused,
> their wailing and whooping as their necks arch back
> in the wild clamour...
> Artemis the shepherdess strides swiftly through,
> yoking the tribe of lions in Bacchic frenzy...[45]

In the century after Pindar's death, the dithyramb became a virtuoso set-piece performance, in the hands of poets such as Melanippides, Philoxenus, Timotheus, probably Pratinas (see below on hyporcheme), and others.

The Alexandrian list also includes three books of *partheneia,* or maiden-songs. We have small extracts of two of these poems. The classification is of a different kind from the preceding genres, since it refers to the gender of the performers, not to the subject or occasion of the odes. As Claude Calame has shown,[46] there were an enormous number of occasions on which girls ripe for marriage might perform songs in religious rituals, and this usually constituted some sort of rite of passage.

A number of surviving poems are designated *partheneia*, most famously those of the seventh-century BCE Spartan poet Alcman, of which the first is performed by a chorus of girls who constantly refer to each other in the course of the poem; this *partheneion*, for all its loveliness, remains enigmatic, but there is no doubt that the maidens are celebrating the sacred ritual, whatever it is.[47] Corinna Fragment 655, which is possibly the opening of her book, begins, 'Terpsichore summons me to sing fine tales for the white-robed women of Tanagra... having adorned stories from our fathers' time I begin them for the girls.' But a *partheneion* could be for any deity worshipped by young women; it is not defined by its god as paeans seem to be and as dithyrambs might at some stage have been. Nor, as far as we know, are the style of dancing, music or metre prescribed.

The non-exclusive nature of the term *partheneion* is shown by the fact that Pindar's *Partheneion* 2 is actually called a *daphnephorikon* (laurel-bearing procession), which elsewhere appears as a genre name. It might be supposed to be a poem for Apollo, as bay is sacred to him, or to his sister Artemis. The main subject of this poem is undiscoverable, but it is also a celebration of a family, as epinicia are, and therefore the category is presumably suitable for both gods and men:

> Dressed in my robe swiftly
> And bearing in my tender hands
> The bright branches of laurel,
> I will sing the dwelling of Aioladas
> And of his son Pagondas,
> Adorning my maidenly head with garlands.[48]

The singer goes on to speak of a younger member of the family, Agasicles, and his chariot victories, so the overlap of theme with epinician is palpable, though it is noticeable that the words are clearly placed in the mouth of the maiden singer, not that of the poet, as is common in the epinicians.

The general style is recognisably similar to the earliest *partheneia* we have, those of Alcman, in which the personal utterances of the chorus members combine with mythical narrative and gnomic statements, as in the lapidary lines of Alcman Fragment 1: 'There is such a thing as the vengeance of the gods: that man is blessed who devoutly weaves to the end the web of his day unweeping.'

The fact that the Alexandrians added to the two books of Pindar's *partheneia* a third book of 'separate *partheneia*' suggests that they were uncertain what held the poems in these three books together, and were at a loss to know how to classify some of them, so lumped them all into this puzzling third book. One formal feature of the *partheneion* seems to be that the 'I' who speaks is the chorus (leader), not the poet in person as in the epinicians. The same seems true of some of the paeans, for example *Paean* 4, but in *Paean* 6 it has been supposed that the speaker who calls himself 'I' is the poet, not the choral entity.[49] The question has been much debated, and may come closer to being a true generic marker than anything the Alexandrians devised. Or is the distinction between poems for gods and for humans? Or perhaps the practice varies?

Of the other genres in the Alexandrian list, we have too little remaining to say much. Hymn seems to be a straightforward category, though it may be supposed to encompass all hymns for gods. Pindar may have called all his divine poems hymns, but he also sometimes uses the term 'hymn' as in *epinikios hymnos*, to refer to a poem for a human. So separating out paeans and dithyrambs may give a false impression of diversity of style or mode.

Prosodion, 'processional', would seem to be another kind of poem directed at a shrine of the gods, here distinguished only by manner of performance: it is sung in a procession rather than in a (usually) circular dance. It ought logically to encompass other such designations as *daphnephorikon* (laurel-bearing) and *oschophorikon* (branch-bearing: an *oschos* is a branch with clusters of grapes attached). According to Monica Negri,[50] *Isthmian* 8 was actually an *oschophorikon*. In Athens at least, the boys who carried the branches were dressed as girls,[51] which may portend a further blurring of categories. One of the *partheneia* is also called a *daphnephorikon*: the maidens process with their laurel bough rather than dancing. Because of the Apolline connection, such a *daphnephorikon* could easily overlap with paean.[52] One's head begins to spin.

The last three Nemeans may not be epinicia, but they were composed for particular momentous occasions: *Nemean* 11 is for the inauguration of Aristagoras as a *prytanis*, a chief magistrate of Tenedos. *Nemean* 10, though it mentions athletic victories, is not designed to celebrate a particular one; it was performed at the festival of Hera at the Argive Heraion and its specific purpose is hard to define. For *Nemean* 9 we have no clues as to the occasion.

Some erotic poems could also be classified as *skolia*, drinking songs: for instance, Fragment 122, part of a poem for Xenophon of Corinth, who sacrificed to Aphrodite at Corinth with the assistance of the temple prostitutes:

Lady of Cyprus,
it is to your sanctuary
that Xenophon has come

shining with glory
and accompanied by a herd of a hundred young ladies.

The complete poem of 15 lines for Theoxenus of Tenedos, Fragment 123, which extols his beauty, is clearly erotic but was classified as an encomion. It could very readily be performed as a party piece, and no doubt was in later years, as was the surviving portion of the poem for Xenophon:

Anyone who sees the shafts of light flashing from
Theoxenus' eyes
and does not swell up with desire,
has a dark heart, forged of steel or adamant
in a cold fire.

Another genre of which we have no significant fragments is the hyporcheme. Fragments 105–11 are attributed to this book, but it is impossible to see many common features in them. Fragment 106, a priamel, looks like the beginning of praise: 'The Laconian hound of Taygetus is the fastest creature for the hunt; goats of Syros are best for milking. Armour from Argos, war-chariots from Thebes – but for a well-made racing chariot look in Sicily of the glistening fruit.' Fragment 107 is also about hunting dogs, but Fragment 108 is a gnome: 'When a god shows the beginning in any matter, the path is straight to seize achievement: and the conclusion is glorious'; and Fragment 109 is a prayer: 'Let someone bring the community of the citizens into clear day by seeking out the bright light of noble-hearted Tranquillity...'

The word 'hyporchema', which Proclus classifies among the songs for gods, means a song accompanied by dance; while this description fits all of choral lyric, the particular feature of this genre seems to be that the dancing played a primary role, and often took the form of mimesis: hyporchemes could include imitations of animals and might often have been very wild, like the *kordax* of comedy. According to Lucian in *On Dance*,[53] the dancers enacted a narrative, and Athenaeus tells us that the dancers and the singers were separate.[54] Pratinas' 'hyporcheme', quoted by Athenaeus,[55] is certainly a metrically wild piece, and may be irrelevant here. Richard Seaford suggests, surely rightly, that the definition of hyporcheme is a creation of musical theory, and that this poem of Pratinas is actually a dithyramb that appeared in one of numerous satyric dramas as part of an agonistic choral conflict.[56]

An interesting problem is raised by some lines of *Pythian* 2, which, if it is an epinician at all, was composed not for a Pythian victory but for some Syracusan event. In lines 67–72 Pindar, addressing Hieron, writes:

> Like to Phoenician merchandise
> this song is sent across the foaming seas;
> but for the song of Castor in Aeolian strains,
> pray you, in honour of the seven-stringed lyre
> greet it with favour.
> Become what you are.

The scholiast tells us that Pindar is here referring to his hyporcheme addressed to Hieron, Fragment 105: 'Hear what I say, eponymous father of sacred rites, founder of Aetna. He who does not have a house on a wagon is a wanderer among the peoples of the Scythians and is without honour.' The point of the lines, taken out of context, is highly obscure.

According to antique generic theory, hyporchemes were a type of armed dance,[57] like the *pyrriche*, and had been invented by the Couretes of Crete, legendary warriors who protected the infant Zeus from harm by clashing their shields. Here Pindar seems to be following an alternative Spartan genealogy, according to which it was invented by Castor, and he follows his predilection for referring to poems by archaic generic terms, just as he uses *kallinikos* to refer to an epinician, or *linos* to imply more generally lament.[58] Some scholars have supposed that Pindar is using this expression – *kastoreion* in the Greek – to describe *Pythian* 2 itself,[59] but this seems unlikely as there is no particular difference between the first part of the poem and the second. If he is referring to a separate poem, it becomes one of the best pieces of evidence we have of a kind of generic awareness, perhaps based on musical categories, in Pindar himself. But what he actually meant by *kastoreion* is imponderable. And what was in the two books of hyporchemes, we have no way of characterising.

Hymns for Humans: A Short History of Epinician

The epinician odes constitute the bulk of what we have of Pindar's output, and it is worth examining the model to see how it developed in the century or so preceding Pindar. We shall look in more detail in the next chapter at the importance of athletics in archaic Greece; here I would like to trace briefly the way in which the poet's task of celebration, of giving *kleos*, developed into the complex form that we call epinician or victory ode. It is important to remember that the term, as a generic name, was not known to Pindar: he normally refers to his poems for victors as *enkomion*, a song sung 'in a *komos*' or celebratory rout.[60] At the beginning of *Olympian* 9, for the wrestler Epharmostos, Pindar writes, 'The song of Archilochos resounding at Olympia, that triumphal refrain swelling with three refrains, sufficed for Epharmostos to lead the way to Kronos' hill as he celebrated with his close companions.'[61] The poet evokes the celebration that followed immediately on the victory, when the young man and his friends raced across the sanctuary singing an old refrain, '*tenella kallinike*', which means much the same as 'hip-hip-hooray'. He contrasts this with the elaborate production of the Muses that he is now going to provide to celebrate the same victory. The epinician ode elaborates the basic ritual act in much the same way as the literary paeans develop from the ritual cry to the god, or as the lament developed from the *Linos*-song.[62] The merry *komos* may not look much like a ritual act, in comparison to the solemn cries to a god of healing or battle, but the essential relation between the original act and its literary development is similar.

Poetry specifically for athletic victors arose with the growth of aristocratic display in the sixth century BCE. Simonides was traditionally regarded as the earliest epinician poet, but some papyrus finds of poems by Ibycus suggest that he had a predecessor:[63] Ibycus' Fragment 282B (i), which is actually part of a Hellenistic commentary on the poet, refers to athletic contests, the winner's success, and someone's boasts; the scattered words of Fragment 282A seem to be part of a mythical narrative about 'Castor the horse-tamer and Polydeuces, excellent boxer', while later on there are allusions to chariot victories by Heracles' charioteer Iolaus and his brother-in-law Euphemus, as well as to the killing of Geryon by Heracles, the pre-eminent 'athletic' hero. As Barron says, 'It is in the last degree improbable that archaic victors were content merely with the ritual cry of τήνελλα'[64] – 'tenella'. Pindar himself regards 'epikomios hymnos' as being of the hoariest antiquity.[65]

The fragments of Simonides' epinicians give disappointingly few clues as to what these poems may have been like in their entirety, as most of them have been preserved because they contain admirable moral sentiments. Like the verses of Ibycus just mentioned, Simonides Fragment 509 refers to the athlete–heroes Polydeuces and Heracles,[66] and a famous story[67] told how a patron, Scopas, tried to pay Simonides only half his fee because half of his poem had been not about Scopas but about Castor and Polydeuces.

But Simonides also composed epigrams, to be inscribed on stone, for victors in the Games, and we may imagine that these were not altogether different in content from the odes, though of course they were shorter and in different metre. Take, for example, Epigram xxx, preserved in the *Planudean Anthology*:[68]

> Know that you are looking at Theognetos the Olympic victor,
>   A boy, skilful charioteer of the wrestling match,
> Most beautiful to look upon, and in competition no worse than his appearance,
>   Who has crowned with garlands the city of his virtuous fathers.

This poem contains all the elements of the epinician 'programme' except a myth: it names the victor, the event, his city and his family; it praises him as an individual, notably evoking his physical beauty as well as his skill. Mere naming can be enough to confer immortality, as Carey comments.[69]

Even briefer is Epigram xxxi:

> Give your name, father's name, native city and victory.
> Casmylus, Euagoras, Rhodes, Pythian boxing.[70]

The inscriptional evidence could easily be extended with poems preserved on stone, usefully collected in Joachim Ebert's book. A poem as late as 49 BCE gives much the same details about Ariston, who brought 'immortal garlands' to his city of Ephesus, while another, dateable to later than 396 BCE, describes as unique a Spartan woman who had won a chariot victory.

Another epigram attributed to Simonides[71] breaks the bounds of the format: it is 12 lines long, and it adds extra information and a full catalogue of Games at which Nicolaidas won, but does not name the event;[72] it is composed in a metre that combines hexameters with lyric cola:

> Nicolaidas of Corinth dedicated this statue after his victory in Delphi,
> and carried off five crowns at the Panathenaea, and sixty amphorae [?]
> of oil, and at the glorious Isthmus [a line and a half corrupt], and won
> three times at Nemea and four more times at Pellana, and twice at the
> Lycaion, and at [Nemea] and Aigina and mighty Epidaurus and Thebes
> and the city of Megara; by winning the stadion race five times at Phlius
> he brought delight to great Corinth.

Some celebrations were evidently less poetic than others.

This was the tradition that Bacchylides and Pindar developed to a peak of artistry in the fifth century. In fact, the epinician became such a successful genre among aristocratic patrons that it began to absorb generic elements form other types of praise poetry as well. Anne Burnett has argued persuasively that *topoi* of the erotic epigram are frequently employed to add depth to the victory ode; we have seen this already in the epigram for Theoxenus, and it is particularly evident in the songs for boy victors from Aegina, in which physical beauty is regularly part of the praise. *Isthmian* 2 and *Pythian* 6 are good examples, and again there are precedents in Ibycus,[73] who was remembered for his poems to boys. Pederasty was a significant element of aristocratic culture. In Sparta erotic bonds between young adult men and teenage boys were fostered as a rite of passage as well as a military cement; many cities held male beauty contests, and the erotic attractions of boys at the dance (as well as competing naked in the Games) are evoked in the inscriptions relating to the Gymnopaedia ('Games of naked boys') on the island of Thera.[74] Aristophanes represents the old man Philocleon as enjoying looking at boys' genitals, an aspect of his old-fashionedness with which his son Bdelycleon, with his 'democratic' spirit, is not in sympathy.[75]

The tension between 'old' aristocratic ways and 'new' democratic principles can also be found in another genre that made its contribution to the apparatus of praise, namely the lament, '*threnos*'. If praise of the victor assimilates him in some sense to the dead hero at whose festival the Games were celebrated, the celebration of dead family members may be equally important. Ancestor cult in some form is crucial to the maintenance of aristocratic family consciousness. Fustel de Coulanges argued that the worship of the dead functioned as a justification of private property: unless you have your own house or tomb, worship of the dead is impossible.[76] Funeral games are not primarily contests but occasions for display and the confirmation of the social order. Lament can take the most primitive form: Lucian *On Grief* 12 refers to wailing, floods of women's tears, breast-beating, tearing of hair, bloodied cheeks, torn clothes, heads strewn with dust, so that 'the living become more wretched than the dead'. But in archaic Greece, lavish burials were accompanied by elaborate processions accompanied by song: Solon referred to such rituals as *threnein ta pepoiemena*, performance of especially composed laments. Not many examples survive, but one of the best known is Simonides' poem for the dead of Thermopylae,[77] which is not, except incidentally, a poem for aristocrats. The war-dead seem to have received divine honours in Sparta, though not in Athens.[78] He also wrote a poem for the dead of Marathon, though this was not a choral lyric but a long elegiac poem, intended for inscription but also no doubt for performance.[79] This was composed as an entry for a competition for the best such elegy, and Simonides was the winner.[80] It may perhaps have been frequently reperformed as a commemorative act,[81] as indeed might any epinician.

The fragments of Pindar's laments are exiguous and have mainly been preserved because they contain allusions to unusual mystery cults. Such cults were certainly widespread in Sicily, which is why Pindar's odes for Theron refers to the life of the blessed dead, but they were probably numerous in mainland Greece also, as Plato implies when he quotes Fragment 127 and refers to 'priests and priestesses' who make it their business to promote such cults.[82] Plutarch famously compares the experience of the soul at death to initiation.[83] The discovery of the Derveni papyrus has shown that there were people who went to their graves accompanied by detailed instructions on how to negotiate the Underworld.

However, we can observe elements of the lament occurring in Pindar's epinicia, notably *Olympian* 14. Here it is Echo who carries news of the victory to the dead, but often the newly dead are conceived as greeting those who have been in Hades for some time with updates from the world of the living.[84] The *topoi* of praise do not vary. What is notable is that the dead are regarded as heroes, and may as such have received cult honours. Bruno Currie has argued that the living victor in the Games – whether or not he is standing in for the dead hero – is in effect heroised, perhaps to the extent of receiving cult honours. Certainly a few athletes historically did become heroes (see Chapter 4), and this would represent a convergence of the worlds of lament and epinician.

Composed laments were generally regarded as characteristic of aristocratic milieux, which is why Solon forbade them in his rules for a more democratic society:[85] this was part of his legal assault on luxury and ostentation. Their role in democratic Athens came to be played by the *epitaphioi logoi*, the annual speeches honouring the war dead that began soon after the Persian Wars.[86] They were often delivered by the polemarch.[87] The earliest that we have is Pericles' of 439 BCE,[88] but they became annual events, as is indicated by Plato,[89] and could be accompanied by athletic and other competitions, including, from the second century BCE, torch races. It is reasonable to infer that the structure and content of these speeches resembled that of the earlier laments; rhetorical practice, as elsewhere, was to adopt the arrangement of material that had been created by the 'pre-rhetorical' praise genres.

Metre

One notable feature of the epinician odes that we have is their metre. With very few exceptions, they are composed in metrical triads: two stanzas that responded to one another metrically plus a third of different metre, the triad repeated a variable number of times. These divisions – strophe, antistrophe and epode – were Englished by Ben Jonson as 'turn', 'counter-turn' and 'stand': it is to be supposed that the chorus executed two similar movements, the one perhaps a mirror image of the other, and then sang the epode in a more stationary position, before starting the movement again. Though this metre was used in other contexts, notably Stesichorus' long narrative poem *Geryoneis*, it is especially notable in epinician odes, and was thereafter adopted in Attic tragedy.

The Music and Dance:
Heard Melodies Are Sweet, but Unheard Sweeter

Pindar's poems were multimedia performances, involving words, music and dance – and maybe special costumes as well, since we know that the leader of the procession in the *Daphnephoria* was a good-looking youth wearing a special garland of bay leaves,[90] and that the girls who danced by the Aeginetan river, the Asopos, wore flowers in their hair (see Chapter 2). Youths in the Athenian *Oschophoria* wore female clothes, and no doubt there were many other special costumes, even outside the drama. Of the varied spectacle that performances of Pindar presented, only the words survive to us. Much work has been done on the material side of dramatic performances in Athens, but much less on that of epinicia. The music and dance are beyond reconstruction, though a few things can be said.

The few examples of musical notation that we have from ancient Greece are all from later centuries and will not help us to imagine Pindar's unheard melodies, except in a general way. Ancient Greek music was based on a series of modes, somewhat resembling Indian ragas in lying between a scale and a melodic form. The music followed the metrical pattern of the lines, producing complicated rhythms that rarely corresponded to 4/4 time, except in the simplest cases, such as marching anapaests or the epic hexameter. The melody normally rose where the pitch accent rose, though strophic response often conflicted with this practice.

Instrumentation was on a small scale. There were various percussive instruments – mainly clappers and castanets rather than drums, which are not mentioned before the fifth century B C E, and then would have been small, like tablas – but besides these the music was produced by stringed and wind instruments. The stringed instruments were invariably plucked, not bowed. Pindar refers both to *phorminx* and *kithara*: the latter is large, with a square base and wooden sound-box, cradled in one arm and plucked with the other. The *phorminx* is similar but with a round base. The lyre (*lyra*) was a slighter instrument, traditionally constructed using a tortoise shell as the sound-box, and the *barbitos* was similar but with much longer arms and hence longer strings. The smaller lyres were more suited to solo performance, while the larger box lyres were better for choral and concert performance, and are what Pindar usually seems to use in the epinicia. Lute-like instruments existed in ancient Mesopotamia, and are depicted on Greek vases, but seem to have been mainly for solo use and hardly feature in accounts of choral poetry.

The Homeric *Hymn to Apollo* describes the dance of the gods accompanied by Apollo:

> The fine-haired Graces and the kindly Seasons,
> with Harmonia and Hebe, and Zeus' daughter Aphrodite,
> dance together holding each other by the wrists;
> Along with them there dances, divinely tall and fair,
> Artemis who delights in the bow, the sister of Apollo;
> in the midst Ares and the sharp-aimed Killer of Argus [Hermes]
> perform their turn. Meantime Phoebus Apollo plays the lyre,
> stepping high and fine, while radiance clothes
> his twinkling feet and his well-spun tunic.[91]

The scene must be modelled on a human dance, though we need not imagine Pindar, a mere mortal, managing to skip and prance as Apollo does while he plays his lyre for the singers and dancers. Lucian describes simply how the *aulete* sits in the centre of the dancers and taps his foot to keep the rhythm.[92]

The main wind instrument was the *aulos*, often misleadingly translated 'flute'. The *aulos* was a double-reed pipe, like an oboe, and is perhaps best compared to the medieval shawm, or the modern Greek *clarino* with its piercing wail. The player's cheeks had to be bound with straps to maintain the embouchure, making it an instrument scorned by those who wished to look elegant.[93] *Auloi* accompanied religious ceremonies, including paeans,[94] and were played when marching into battle; but Pindar makes uses of them as well, sometimes in a small band: 'Let us rouse up, then, the resounding *phorminx* and rouse the pipe for the very apex of contests for horses.'[95]

Music could range from wild to sedate, from the dithyramb to the stately marching hymn, and the modes too were perceived as having different moral characters. Dare we imagine Pindar leading something like a Cretan village band of the twentieth century, their reed pipes not dissimilar to the piercing reed instruments used on that island today, but with the quieter plucking and twanging of lyres to replace the strident bouzouki, and of course no bowed instrument like the modern Greek *lyra* or fiddle to add its distinctive texture? We can only imagine.

And while the music played, the dancers danced and sang. These two functions, which are invariably separate in modern musical performance, were regularly combined in ancient Greek music. Dance was inseparable from Pindar's poetry, though you would hardly know it from the two incidental references to Pindar in what remains the standard book on Greek dance, by Lillian B. Lawler.[96] Song-dance is *molpe*, from which the Muse Melpomene derives her name, and from earliest times it was an integral part of Greek life. Homer describes the archetypal dance, the wedding dance, as depicted on the Shield of Achilles:

> The one [city] did nuptials celebrate,
> Observing at them solemn feasts, the brides from forth their bow'rs
> With torches usher'd through the street, a world of paramours
> Excited by them; youths and maids in lovely circles danc'd,
> To whom the merry pipe and harp their spritely sounds advanc'd,
> The matrons standing in their doors admiring.[97]

Every religious celebration – that is, every important moment in public life – was marked by song-dance, as it was by sacrifice. Communal dance took two main forms: the circular dance and the *Reigentanz*, dancing in line. A famous line-dance was the *geranos*-dance, supposedly invented by Theseus.[98]

The only treatises on ancient dance that we have come from the second century CE: Lucian's *On Dance* and Plutarch's *On Music*, along with a section in Plutarch's *Table Talk* about dance.[99] In the same century Athenaeus collected a number of passages relating to dance in his *Deipnosophists*.[100] Though they wrote seven hundred years after Pindar's career, both Plutarch and Lucian interpret the dance as having a cosmic significance: it is an imitation of the godlike, eternal movements of the heavenly bodies. Lucian (7) writes:

> Those who speak most accurately about the genealogy of dance would say that dance came into being at the same time as the origin of all things, appearing at the same time as the cosmic Eros. Indeed, the dance of the stars and its interweaving with the wanderings of the planets are indications of this, as are their rhythmic community and the well-ordered harmony of the primal dance.[101]

That such ideas were not alien in the fifth century BCE is suggested by Pindar's lines at *Olympian* 4.1–3: 'Driver most high of thunder with untiring feet, Zeus: on you I call because your Horai [Seasons] in their circling round have sent me, accompanied by song with the lyre's varied tones, as a witness of the loftiest games.' Plato interpreted the movement of the heavens as a dance:

> Vain would be the attempt to tell all the figures of them circling as in dance, and their juxtapositions, and the return of them in their revolutions upon themselves, and their approximations, and to say which of these deities in their conjunctions meet, and which of them are in opposition...[102]

Gloria Ferrari has argued powerfully that the chorus in Alcman's *Partheneion* are a chorus representing stars, performing to mark a key point of the agricultural year: the setting of the Pleiades and Hyades.[103] She links the interpretation to an Attic red-figure vessel in the form of an *astragalos*, 'knuckle-bone', which depicts dancers who from an early date have been interpreted as the Pleiades, and also to a Lucanian volute-krater of 420–400 BCE depicting dancers wearing various strange headdresses that can be interpreted as stars and suns.

Not every dance is a cosmic ritual, but in dance humans can replicate the 'perfect' circular motion that is appropriate to gods, and which the gods themselves carry out in the passage of the Homeric *Hymn to Apollo* quoted above.

Lucian and Athenaeus both divide patterns of dance into three: movement, pose and gesture. That is, each dancer carries out a movement, and at the end of it is described holding a particular pose; that pose also incorporates a gesture, such as shading the eyes, stretching the hands down, grasping and so on.[104] The movements thus require to be interpreted as carrying some kind of meaning, and this is in concord with what we are told by earlier authors about the mimetic qualities of dance. It is not just costumed dancers like the satyrs of the dithyramb or the grotesque figures of Old Comedy that imitate something else: the problematic concept of the *hyporcheme* is defined through its mimetic quality, as well as through the subordination (contrary to the linguistic implications of the word) of music and song to dance.

To begin to catalogue and classify the many named types of dance is to court confusion. Athenaeus speaks of sedate dances,[105] though he includes among them, along with many names that mean little to us, the *kordax* and *sikinnis*, both of which other sources regard as wild dances. There was also a kind of dance in use among private individuals called the *anthema*, and they used to dance this while repeating the following words with a sort of mimicking gesture:

Where are my roses, and where are my violets?
Where is my beautiful parsley?
Are these then my roses, are these then my violets?
And is this my beautiful parsley?

He moves on to Satyric dance, and then to 'lyric dance', which he divides into pyrrhic (rapid and warlike), *gymnopaedic* (grave and solemn) and *hyporchematic* (resembling the comic *kordax*). The classification will hardly hold, but what he goes on to say of *gymnopaedic* dance is of interest: 'All the boys dance naked, performing some kind of movement in regular time, and with gestures of the hand like those used by wrestlers: so that the dancers exhibit a spectacle akin to the palaestra and the *pankration*, moving their feet in regular time.'[106] He then states that the *oschophorikon* is one form of the *gymnopaedia*.

All this has to be taken with a pinch of salt, as well as allowance for the changed conditions of performance in the second century CE, especially the prevalence of pantomimic styles and the usual complaint that dance was coming to occupy a more important place than the music – which was already being expressed by Pratinas in the fifth century BCE! But it is suggestive of the range of meanings that could be attached to dance. Lucian, while offering a roughly similar though less detailed account of types of dance,[107] goes on to emphasise the moral aspect of dance and the need for a dancer to be trained in knowledge of the myths: the singers sing the tales and the dancers 'show' them.[108] He offers a kind of definition of dance: 'Speaking with the hands'.[109] So dance – sometimes a solo dance – can be expressive, like sign language, and can convey passions and character, love and anger. The twists and twirls, leaps and steps of the dancer[110] are a kind of physical training, better than wrestling,[111] so dance 'sharpens the soul, exercises the body, delights the onlookers and teaches all kinds of things'.[112]

Some of the typical moves of the ancient Greek dance have been determined. They include knee bends, pirouetting and dancing on tiptoe, holding hands (in a file or in a circle), raising the hands above the head, shading the eyes, throwing the head back and sticking the buttocks out, as well as steps and kicks, jumps, turns, bends, swinging and shaking parts of the body. The movement could consist of a series of poses, or one continuous movement leading to a final, held pose.[113]

If Pindar's dancers conveyed even a fraction of what these later writers imagined that dance could represent, we are missing an incalculably large part of the meaning of his work. William Mullen has tried to divine some of the specifics of Pindaric dance, such as death being always mentioned in the epodes when the chorus is stationary with their hands pointing down to earth, but such inferences can be no more than speculation, though his peroration is eloquent:

Whether as a place for narrative of divine favour, for precepts on the limits of mortality, or for confrontation with the dead themselves, the epode reminds us that we are earthly beings whose destiny is, at best, to be briefly irradiated by the light from above before passing forever into the soil below. The dancers acknowledge as much when they come to a stand on the patch of earth that has been cleared for their dancing floor. It is by such a stand, if at all, that an axis through our transience can be established.[114]

But for the most part, we as interpreters are dancers in the dark. We wish we could follow the invitation in *Paean* 2.96–100:

> The dances summon you to sacred Delos
> And the shining-armed Delphian maidens
> Who regularly dance their soft measures
> Around the high Parnassian rocks
> Sing their melody with sweet voice.

IV

ATHLETES AND HEROES

Athletics in Greek Culture

The central importance of athletic contests in Greek culture requires some explanation. At one level it arises from the intense competitiveness of the ancient Greeks, which Jakob Burckhardt identified in the nineteenth century as a driving force of Greek civilisation. But there are also historical and anthropological reasons for their importance. First of all, the four-yearly cycle of the great Games provided the one Panhellenic armature on which to hang a chronology of the ancient world, and this was in use at least from the fourth century BCE. The earliest secure date in Greek history was the foundation of the Olympic Games in 776 BCE. They were celebrated every four years thereafter until their abolition, along with all other forms of pagan observance, by the Christian emperor Theodosius I in 393 CE. As the occasion when the oft-warring Greek states set aside their differences and met as Hellenes to celebrate Zeus and the other gods and heroes with contests, sacrifices and other rituals, the Olympic Games had an enormous symbolic significance for all Greeks. The other Panhellenic Games – the four-yearly Pythian, founded in 586 or 582, dedicated to Apollo and held in the third year of every Olympiad; the two-yearly Isthmian, founded in 582 for Poseidon; and the two-yearly Nemean, in 573 for Zeus – had a significance almost as great. Numerous local festivals also involved games. Pindar mentions more than twenty such, with lists of individual local victories at *Olympian* 13.107ff. and *Nemean* 10.43ff.; see also Bacchylides 10.305. One major festival was the Argive Heraea, mentioned in *Nemean* 10. Athens, for example, had 18 annual festivals – that we know of – that involved athletic competitions, scattered throughout the year: the greatest of these was the Panathenaea, reorganised in 566. In fact, it was unusual for any Greek festival to take place without involving some form of contest, including music competitions, beauty contests, races and other things as well as athletics. Though the four Panhellenic Games were *stephanitic* games, where the prize consisted of a wreath (olive at Olympia; bay at Pytho; parsley [or celery] at Nemea; and pine, later celery [or parsley], at the Isthmus), other Games involved high-value prizes. At the Heraea the prizes were objects of valuable bronze, either tripods or shields, while at the Panathenaea in the fourth century the total value of prizes awarded was one talent, or six thousand drachmas – equal to nearly twenty years' salary for a skilled worker.[1] Victors in Athens were also awarded free meals in the *prytaneion* (council house),[2] but statues of athletes were never erected in the agora at Athens, in contrast to other cities.

But why should athletic contests be central to the worship of the gods? An anthropological perspective might help to shed light on this phenomenon.[3] The first athletic contests described in Greek literature were those held by Achilles at the pyre of his dead comrade Patroclus. Such contests are an essential part of funeral rites or honours to a dead hero. They may be understood as a way of placating the dead by performing a mock sacrifice in the form of an endurance test, in which the victor becomes the sacrificial victim and is, in a sense, offered for the life of the dead man. The fundamental insight into the centrality of sacrifice to Greek culture was developed by Walter Burkert in his book *Homo Necans*, and its results were applied to the particular case of sport by David Sansone and to that of epinician poetry by Gregory Nagy.[4] All the major Panhellenic festivals, besides their dedication to a particular god, had a foundation legend that involved their institution as the funeral celebrations for the death of a hero, and took place around the tomb of that hero: Pelops at Olympia, Neoptolemus at Delphi, Archemorus/Opheltes at Nemea, Melicertes/Palaemon at the Isthmus. Thus Games may be a 'reaffirmation of life in the face of death'; an alternative view, deriving from the Homeric description and the informality of the arrangements, may regard them simply as an 'expression of life'. No doubt there was always some tension between the religious perspective, which is the one Pindar emphasises, and the humanist approach that seems to be characteristic of Homer, with his limited concentration on religious observance.[5]

In historic times such ritual origins of the Games may have been as little understood as are, say, the origins of Orthodox church ritual in Byzantine court procedures among present-day churchgoers, or the origins of the Christmas tree in pagan Germanic practice; but, like these things, their origins gave an atavistic dimension to the celebrations and imbued the festivals with solemnity and depth. So athletic activity was a part of the worship of the gods and heroes. A beautiful passage of the Homeric *Hymn to Apollo* suggests that participants in the glorious festival on Delos achieve a kind of immortality:

> To fill thy fane
> there flocks so many an Ionian,
> with ample gowns that flow down to their feet,
> with all their children, and the reverend sweet
> of all their pious wives. And these are they
> that (mindful of thee) even thy Deity
> render more spritely with their champion fights,
> dances, and songs. Perform'd to glorious sight,
> once having publish'd, and proclaim'd their strife.
> And these are acted with such exquisite life
> that one would say, 'Now, the Ionian strains [i.e. families]
> are turn'd Immortals, nor know what age means.'[6]

Athletics, as remarked, also captured the famous competitive spirit of the Greeks. An anecdote about Pythagoras illustrates this well: the ruler of

Phlius once asked him what the new-fangled word 'philosopher' – which Pythagoras used to apply to himself – implied. Pythagoras' answer was:

> The life of man is like a fair, the one considered to be celebrated with the greatest ostentation by the whole of the Greek world [i.e. the Olympic Games]. Some people go there to seek the glory and nobility of victory in the athletic exertion of their bodies; some go to buy and sell in the hope of gain and profit; but there is a certain class of person, the noblest, who neither seek applause nor gain, but come only to watch and view intently what and how things happen. Likewise we are present, as it were, at a thronging fair, come from some city; changing thus from one life and form to another some come to serve glory, others money, but there are a chosen few who study the universe, considering everything else of no importance. These people call themselves lovers of wisdom, in other words, philosophers.[7]

For those who were not philosophers, winning became important for its own sake. The ascetic hero Hippolytus in Euripides' play, rejecting the life of the autocrat, says that his highest ambition would be to win in the Panhellenic Games, and second to that to live happily in his city with his fellows: athletic success is even more glorious than royal state.[8] In another revealing passage, Thucydides describes the welcome of the victorious Spartan general Brasidas in Scione: 'He was publicly crowned with a gold crown as the liberator of Hellas, and private individuals used to come up to him and deck him with garlands, as though he were a famous athlete.'[9] The status of athlete is seen as higher than that of general. Athletes were often pelted with leaves (like with confetti), and an intriguing comment by a scholiast on Euripides' *Hecuba* 573, where Polyxena is pelted with leaves before she goes to be sacrificed to the shade of Achilles, remarks that she is being treated 'as if victorious in a contest' – another hint of a conceptual connection between athletic victor and sacrificial victim.

The events varied from one festival to another but there was a standard core at all the Panhellenic festivals. From its foundation in 776 until 724 there was only one event at the Olympic Games, namely the *stadion*, a foot-race down a single length of the stadium, about 200 metres. By the time of the foundation of the Pythian Games, the *stadion* had been joined by the *diaulos* (two lengths), the *dolichos* (20 or 24 lengths, or about 4,000 metres), and in 520 at Olympia, followed by Delphi in 498, the *hoplitodromos* (two lengths in full armour). There were several forms of combat sport:

(1) Wrestling. Tactics included controlling the opponent by seizing his wrists; head-lock and neck lock; the 'underhook' (holding under the shoulder); the waist lock, the leg trip, and the shoulder throw. The aim was to ground the opponent, but fighting might continue after the fall.

(2) Boxing, carried out with the hands bound with leather thongs, which protected the wrists but could also cut an opponent badly. Boxing with extended thumbs meant there was a possibility of eye-gouging. Death was not unknown in both boxing and wrestling.[10]

(3) The *pankration*, a form of no-holds-barred wrestling. The only things forbidden were biting and gouging. Finger-breaking, choking and limb-wrenching were commonly employed. The contest could take place on the ground as well as in the standing position of normal wrestling. The bout ended when a competitor signalled his submission.

The pentathlon was rewarded by a single prize for victory in five combined events: discus, long jump, javelin, running and wrestling. The method of victory is not certain, but it is likely that if any contestant won the first three contests, he would be declared overall winner and the running and wrestling cancelled. The boys' pentathlon was introduced at Olympia in 628 but discontinued; it continued to take place at other venues. (*Nemean* 7 is for a boy pentathlete.) The weight of the discus seems to have varied considerably, and victory in this event, as with the javelin, was won by distance, but we know that the javelin also had to land within defined limits[11] and that the thrower had not to overstep a mark in throwing.[12] The long jump was a standing jump, and the jumper carried weights known as *halteres*, by swinging which he increased his momentum. The Greeks never practised the high jump.

It should be noted that all these events are for individual athletes. No team events were involved in the Games or in any other area of Greek life as far as is known: the spirit of individual competition ruled supreme. All athletes competed naked; they oiled their bodies and then sprinkled them with dust, of which special supplies were kept at most sites.[13] There were two age classes – boys and men – though a third category, of *ageneioi*, 'beardless (youths)', existed at some festivals.[14] Pindar almost always makes clear in his words if it is a boy that is being celebrated, though *Olympian* 11 is an exception, and Bacchylides 6 does not state that it is for a boy victor, though we know from the inscribed victor lists that it is so. It has been suggested that the mention of a trainer in an ode implies that the victor is a boy, but this is not certain. At Athens the *choregoi* of boys' choruses had to be men over 40 to reduce the likelihood of their interfering with the choirboys; young athletes (who could also be choristers) could equally be celebrated for their beauty and sexual attractiveness. On Samos, for example, in the second century BCE there were some unusual additional events, including *philoponia*, 'stone-throwing' (literally love of labour, perhaps weight-lifting), and *euexia* and *eutaxia*, probably respectively a beauty contest and a competition in good deportment.[15] Other common events included a torch race (six in Athens' annual calendar of festivals) and musical contests of all kinds, at Athens eventually including those that introduced dithyramb, tragedy and comedy to the public. Musical contests were important at the Panhellenic Games – *Pythian* 12 is for a victor in the *aulos* competition at Delphi – as were Olympic events for trumpeters and heralds.

As important as the athletic events were the equestrian events. These were not displays of the contestant's skill (though the charioteers could become famous) but of their wealth. The most conspicuous was the four-horse chariot race, the *tethrippon*, consisting of 12 laps around the hippodrome, but the length of the latter is unknown. Pindar's best-known odes are for victors in the *tethrippon*; in 416 BCE the Athenian politician Alcibiades entered no fewer than seven *tethrippa* for the Olympic Games; his victory was celebrated by Euripides with an epinician ode whose few remaining fragments suggest something less magnificent than Pindar's. In 648 a horseback race, or *keles,* was added to the Olympic programme, and in 408 a two-horse chariot race, *synoris.* There were also races for two-year-old foals. In 500 a mule-cart race was added, but it did not last long, being discontinued in 444. Apparently it was regarded as undignified.[16] Pindar's *Olympian* 4 and 5 are for a victor in this event; when Simonides (515) had to write an ode for a mule-cart victory by Anaxilas of Rhegium, he addressed them as 'daughters of storm-footed steeds'.[17] Horses themselves could become celebrities – as did Hieron's Pherenikos, 'Bringer of Victory', celebrated by both Pindar and Bacchylides – and a nameless charioteer was immortalised in a statue at Delphi.

Beginning as a communal ritual, the Games soon became the occasion for a growing professionalism among performers and trainers. The concept of amateurism never existed in ancient Greece, despite some idealistic modern misconceptions.[18] This is one reason that the criticism of Pindar by Moses Finley is not well taken: Greek athletics was not an elitist pursuit, it was not even an elite one, though given the nature of early fifth century society most participants in the Games were no doubt not drawn from the class of those at subsistence level; some degree of leisure was required. Chariot-racing, to be sure, is a form of ostentation by members of the elite, as was made very clear by Alcibiades when he entered seven chariots for the race at Olympia in 416 (see above, p. 84). But chariot-racing was a special case, requiring large stables and expensive equipment. The paradigm competitor in Greek games was a boxer or wrestler, and few young men could avoid taking part in races in some festival or other, just as few young people if any would escape being a member of a chorus at some time in their lives. These physical contests celebrated excellence of body, not wealth. One may reflect on the importance attached to sport in former communist countries of Eastern Europe, where physical excellence is of as much service to the state as intellectual; even a successor state like Uzbekistan has to have its national sport. (The president chose tennis.)

If you did not need wealth to become a boxer, there is no doubt that a successful boxer could acquire great riches. As early as the end of the sixth century the poet and philosopher Xenophanes of Colophon was attacking the excessive honours and rewards lavished on athletes (in his view, his own thoughts were of much greater social value, and perhaps Pythagoras would have taken a similar view):

> But if a man wins a victory by speed of foot,
> Or in the pentathlon, in the close of Zeus
> By Pisa's stream at Olympia, or in the wrestling,
> Or by enduring the pains of the boxing match,
> Or the fearful trial which they call the pankration
> He is honoured in the eyes of his fellow-townsmen
> With a seat of honour at the Games and festivals
> And maintenance at the public cost
> And a gift of treasure form the city.
> Even for a horse victory he gets all that,
> Though he is not as deserving as I, for my wisdom
> Is better than the strength of men and horses.
> From none of these...
> Will the city be better governed.[19]

Another fierce attack on athletes was delivered by an unidentified character in Euripides' *Autolycus* :

> In youth they walk about in fine attire,
> And think themselves a credit to the city;
> But when old age, in all its bitterness
> O'ertakes their steps, they roam about the streets,
> Like ragged cloaks whose nap is all worn off.
> And much I blame the present fashions, too,
> Which now in Greece prevail; where many a feast
> Is made to pay great honour to such men,
> And to show false respect to vain amusements.
> For though a man may wrestle well, or run,
> Or throw a quoit, or strike a heavy blow,
> Still where's the good his country can expect
> From all his victories and crowns and prizes?[20]

Though he is an aristocrat, Xenophanes' concern is with his city as a whole, and the speaker in Euripides starts from the same standpoint.[21] Athletic achievement was seen by some politicians as benefiting only the clan to which the victor belonged. Certainly Pindar's odes are celebrations of family as well as of the individual, but they do very evidently shed radiance on the city too. In democratically minded Athens, the lawgiver Solon thought little of athletes. Diogenes Laertius tells us that

> he curtailed the honours of athletes who took part in the games, fixing the allowance for an Olympic victor at 500 drachmae, for an Isthmian victor at 100 drachmae, and proportionately in all other cases. It was in bad taste, he argued, to increase the rewards of these victors, and to ignore the exclusive claims of those who had fallen in battle, whose sons, moreover, ought to be maintained and educated by the State... Athletes [unlike soldiers] incur heavy costs in training, do harm when successful, and are crowned for a victory over their country rather than over their rivals.[22]

Solon similarly attempted to limit the ostentation of the aristocracy, by forbidding the performance of pre-composed laments at funerals (for more on this topic, see Chapter 3). Two centuries later, the Athenian thinker Isocrates could describe the Games as a contest of, above all, wealth: they were an occasion not for civic pride but for lavish and conspicuous expenditure.[23]

Diagoras – A Fighter by His Trade

Pausanias devoted two books of his guide to Greece, written in the second century CE, to the region of Eleia, where Olympia was situated. The second of these two books, Book VI, is almost wholly devoted to the monuments standing at Olympia. To visit one of these great shrines, like Delphi or the Athenian Acropolis, must have felt like wandering in a forest of bronze statues. Almost all of them have been melted down for their metal by subsequent conquerors. At Olympia Pausanias describes dozens of statues, many for political figures but by far the majority (80 or so, erected between 544 and 400 BCE and covering 35 Olympiads) for victors in the Panhellenic Games.[24] Among these was a group of statues of Diagoras, a great athlete from Rhodes, and his family.

Originally from Messene, Diagoras had come to Rhodes probably in the 470s. He won a famous victory in the boxing in 464. His sons Akousilaos and Damagetos won the boxing and *pankration* respectively, while the sons of Diagoras' daughters were also boxing champions. See Pausanias 6.7.3:

> They say Diagoras came to Olympia with his sons Akousilaos and Damagetos, and when the young lads had won they carried their father through the festival crowd, while all Greece pelted him with flowers and called him happy in his sons.

Another son, Dorieus, won eight victories at the Isthmus and seven at Nemea, but an Olympic victory eluded him. Nonetheless he became a prominent citizen of Rhodes and supplied and commanded his own ships on the Spartan side in the Peloponnesian War. He was captured by the Athenians in 407, and

> The Athenians were threatening and furious with him, but when they met in their assembly and saw a man so big and tall and so extremely famous presented as a prisoner they changed their minds about him and let him go without doing him the least ungracious action, though they could have done many, and with justice.[25]

This little story effectively illustrates the immense prestige attached to athletic success.

The base, but alas only the base, of Diagoras' statue at Olympia has been found,[26] but Diagoras did not rely on bronze alone to preserve his memory. He also commissioned an ode from Pindar for his victory of 464; it splendidly evokes the atmosphere of the celebratory banquet back home in Rhodes:

As when a man takes from his rich hand a bowl
foaming inside with dew of the vine
and presents it
to his young son-in-law with a toast from one home
    to another – an all-golden bowl, crown of possessions –
as he honors the joy of the symposium
    and his own alliance, and thereby with his friends
present makes him envied for his harmonious marriage,
so I too, by sending the poured nectar, gift of the Muses
and sweet fruit of the mind, to men who win prizes
gain the favour
of victors at Olympia and Pytho.
    Fortunate is the man who is held in good repute.[27]

Pindar goes on to evoke Charis – Grace – who turns her favours now to one man, now to another. The allusion, which can be regarded as normal 'foil' to praise, is part of an unusually insistent pattern in this ode, which also narrates three wonderful myths about the legendary past of Rhodes. The three myths are told in reverse chronological order, each leading to an earlier event which deepens the perspective on the island's present glory. ('Three' seems to be a leitmotif of the ode, as 'bronze' is in *Nemean* 10.) The three myths also share a common feature, namely that each tells how wrong-doing or mischance led ultimately to a happy outcome. Tlepolemus' murder of Licymnius led to the colonisation of Rhodes; the negligence of the sons of Helios in founding a sanctuary 'without holy fire' was nonetheless rewarded by Zeus' gift of craftsmanship; and Helios' unfortunate absence from the original distribution of the parts of the world among the gods led to the creation of an island especially for him – Rhodes:

He said that he himself could see a land
    rising from the floor of the gray sea
that would be bountiful for men and favourable for flocks...
        the island grew
from the watery sea and belongs to the father

who engenders the piercing sunbeams,
the master of the fire-breathing horses.[28]

The common theme of these stories must have been part of Pindar's conscious design, but it is not now possible to discern what external cause may have prompted him to write the ode in this way. The downbeat ending, too, with its typically Greek warning of mutability of fortune, may also recall this theme of uncertainty and chance. Carol Dougherty, in a powerful analysis of this ode, proposes that the trials and purification of the founder–hero are a potent analogy for the sacred value to the city of the much-enduring athlete: 'By comparing Diagoras with Tlepolemus, Pindar suggests that a victorious athlete has similar powers to confer on his city, and he thus deserves the reward of fame in return for the toils of victory in the boxing competition.'[29]

Whatever the trials of the heroes of the ode, nothing seems to have disturbed the high social position of Diagoras and his sons for some 60 years. The scholiast on the poem tells us that Diagoras had the entire poem inscribed in letters of gold in the temple of Athena at Lindos on Rhodes. This is one of the earliest known 'publications' of an ode of Pindar. The letters of gold are gone, of course, but we still have the words.

Not many of Pindar's victors can be matched to known dedications at Olympia or elsewhere: Ergoteles of Himera, winner in the long foot-race, is one who can.[30] The poem is brief but focuses on Ergoteles' past misfortune and present success: exiled from his native Knossos, he has become a citizen of Himera in Sicily:

Truly would the honor of your feet,
Like a local fighting cock by its native hearth
Have dropped its leaves ingloriously,
Had not hostile faction deprived you of your homeland, Knossos.
But now... you exalt the Nymphs' warm baths, living
By lands that are your own.[31]

Perhaps one may imagine a similar back-story for Diagoras, originally from unhappy Messenia.

Athletes Who Become Heroes

Pausanias' book about the dedications at Olympia contains many vivid stories about the athletes, and shows how men of great prowess attracted legend and, eventually, cult, even if their actions off the games field seem less than admirable.[32] (The stories that arose in the Christian period about saints, those 'athletes of faith' are similar.) Two famous examples are Cleomedes of Astypalaea and Theagenes of Thasos.[33]

Cleomedes killed a man in a boxing match, was condemned by the judges and went out of his mind with grief:

> He went home to Astypalaea and attacked a school there where there were 60 boys: he overturned the pillar that held up the roof, and the roof fell in on them: the people stoned him and he took refuge in Athena's sanctuary, where he climbed inside a chest that was kept there and pulled down the lid. The Astypalaeans laboured uselessly to open it; in the end they broke open its wooden walls, but they found no trace of Cleomedes, alive or dead. So they sent to Delphi to ask what had happened to Cleomedes and they say the Pythian priestess gave them this oracle:
>
> > Astypalaean Cleomedes is the last hero:
> > Worship him: he is no longer mortal.[34]

Here is a remarkable instance of bad turning to good in a story of an athlete. Despite his violence and his murders, Cleomedes becomes divine and an object of worship. Greek gods and heroes do not need to be good, but one of their defining characteristics is that they are powerful, even violent. In this way every athletic victor elevates himself above his fellow men by his powers and is touched by divinity.

An example of the power of the athlete, even dead, is given by Theagenes of Thasos, who in his lifetime won 1,400 wreaths in boxing. A statue of him was erected in his town, but every night one of his enemies came to flog the statue as if he were beating up Theagenes himself. The statue fell on the man and killed him. The Thasians then put the statue on trial, condemned it and drowned it in the sea. Pretty soon the crops and fruit on Thasos ceased to grow; the Delphic oracle commanded them to take back the exiles. It took them a while to work out that Theagenes was meant, but eventually they dredged the statue out of the sea and commenced to offer sacrifices to it as to a god. Prosperity returned.

An athlete from Italian Locri called Euthymos won three victories at Olympia in 484, 476 and 472. Though his father was a man named Astycles, he was remembered as a son of the local river, the Caecinus,[35] and the base of his statue at Olympia was altered to remove the name of his father; it reads instead 'Euthymos... set up this figure to be admired by mortals,'[36] implying that Euthymos had passed beyond the mortal state.

Bruno Currie develops a vigorous argument that Pindar's victors are at the least candidates for heroisation: 'The heroizing theme... might hover in the background of epinician poetry, and might be brought into the foreground to a greater or lesser extent according to the exigencies of the commission'.[37] By this argument, the victor's immortality is not simply given through song, but is on a par with the heroes of old and, it seems, the war dead of some cities, including Sparta but not Athens.[38] The argument has particular force for the analysis of the odes for kings and tyrants, such as Arcesilaus in *Pythian* 5 and Hieron in *Pythian* 2 and 3. Currie states forcefully:

> In the songs of the Locrian maidens the heroic, still-living Hieron was celebrated, not a hero of myth like Kinyras. The encomiastic function of the comparison in *Pythian* 2 is clear: it serves to elevate Hieron to a heroic status. The 'obvious differences' which have struck scholars are in fact the essence of the comparison.[39]

He goes on to mention the paeans offered to Lysander at the end of the fifth century, and the 'ithyphallic songs' for Demetrius Poliorcetes at Athens in the fourth. The argument is worth pursuing, though it may be doubted whether it really gets beyond the level of metaphor; we know of no actual religious dedications to any of Pindar's victors, even Hieron. But of course something might always turn up. Currie's perspective can fruitfully be borne in mind when reading the odes. Currie also extends the theory to an illuminating analysis of the problematic ode *Nemean* 7, on which more in Chapter 6.

Heroes in Pindar: Heracles and the Dioscuri

Pindar tells the stories of many heroes in his epinicians, but the one who recurs perhaps most often is Heracles. His story is alluded to, often in detail and at length, in no fewer than fourteen of the odes.[40] Because of his strength and his victory in a series of contests, *athloi*, Heracles was regarded as the prototype of the athletic hero. He shared this reputation with the Dioscuri (or Dioskouroi) – the twin sons of Zeus and Leda, Castor and Polydeuces (Pollux, in Latin). Simonides had already named them in the same breath in what seems to have been an encomium for the Olympic victor Glaucus:[41] 'Not even mighty Polydeuces would raise his hands to fight him, nor Alcmena's iron son.'[42] A passage in Pindar's *Isthmian* 1, in praise of a Theban chariot victor named Herodotus, brings them all together, referring to his

> Fatherland, in which
> Alkmene too bore her dauntless
> son, before whom Geryon's fierce dogs once cowered.
> But for my part, in rendering honour to Herodotos
>   for his four-horse chariot, whose reins
> he guided with no other hands than his own, I wish
> to include him in a hymn to Kastor or Iolaos,
> for they were the mightiest charioteers of the heroes,
> one born in Lakedaimon, the other in Thebes,
> and in athletic games they took part in the most contests,
> adorning their houses with tripods,
> cauldrons and bowls of gold,
> whenever they savoured the crowns of victory.[43]

(Iolaus, or here Iolaos, is the son of Heracles' brother Iphicles, and acted as the hero's driver and assistant.)

Heracles' unique status in Greek religion is that he started life as a hero but became a god: in *Isthmian* 4 he is 'Alkmene's son, who went to Olympos after exploring all the lands and the cliff-walled hollows of the grey sea,'[44] and in the unique phrase of *Nemean* 1, *heros theos*, 'the hero-god'.[45] He is thus a model for the successful athlete who perhaps transcends human status by becoming a hero. This change of status is also the theme of the beautiful myth of Castor and Polydeuces told in *Nemean* 10. Polydeuces was the immortal twin, but when Castor was fatally wounded in a fight, Polydeuces could not bear immortality without him and surrendered his own immortality so that he could share with Castor an alternating life on Olympus and in Hades. Zeus spoke to him:

> 'If you prefer to escape death and hateful old age
>   and come by yourself to live on Olympos with me and
>   with Athena and Ares of the darkened spear,
>   that destiny is yours. But if you strive on behalf of your
> brother, and intend to share everything equally with him,
> then you may live half the time beneath the earth
> and half in the golden homes of heaven.'
> When he had spoken thus, Polydeukes set no twofold plan in his judgement
> but freed the eye and then the voice
> of bronze-armored Kastor.[46]

There is no such ambiguity in Heracles' case, as the prophecy uttered by Tiresias when the hero is still in his cradle makes clear. In a phrase that echoes the reward-after-pains *topos* of athletic victory, he announces that Heracles

> In continual peace for all time
>   will be allotted tranquillity as the choicest
>   recompense for his great labours
>   in a blissful home, and, after receiving

> flourishing Hebe as his wife
> and celebrating his wedding feast with Kronos' son Zeus,
> will praise his hallowed rule.[47]

As well as being the prototype athlete, Heracles is important in epinician ideology as the legendary founder of the Olympic Games. Pindar tells portions of this story in several odes, notably *Olympians* 3 and 10. *Olympian* 3 tells how he brought the olive, used to garland Olympic victors, from the happy people of the far north, the Hyperboreans, and made the bare space of the Altis into a shady grove with its foliage. *Olympian* 10 tells of Heracles' defeat of the villainous King Augeas of Elis, after which 'he made the surrounding plain a resting place for banqueting, and honoured the stream of Alpheos along with the twelve ruling gods'.[48]

Pindar rarely has a bad word to say of the great Theban hero, but in *Olympian* 10 he pulls himself up short when Heracles finds himself in conflict with the immortal gods:

> Men become brave and wise as divinity
> determines: for how else
> could Herakles have brandished
> his club in his hands against the trident,
> when Poseidon stood before Pylos and pressed him hard
> and Phoebus pressed him while battling with his
> silver bow, nor did Hades keep still his staff, with which
> he leads down to his hollow abode the mortal bodies
> of those who die? But cast that story
> away from me, my mouth!
> For reviling the gods
> is a hateful skill, and boasting inappropriately
> sounds a note of madness.
> Stop babbling of such things now![49]

The passage is a good example of the 'break-off formula', which allows the poet to name a touchstone of excellence before moving on to a different subject; yet the move is not merely formal, but motivated religiously, by the need to speak only well of the gods. Did Heracles perhaps go too far on this occasion in his demonstration of prowess?

The hero's all-conquering strength and accomplishment might have raised a moral doubt in the minds of listeners to Stesichorus' *Song of Geryon*, too. The poem is very fragmentary, but the three-headed monster Geryon, from whom Heracles steals his cattle, is given very sympathetic treatment before he meets his end at the hero's hands: there is a long and pathetic speech in which Geryon's parents try to dissuade him from fighting Heracles, and when Heracles' arrow pierces his third and last head, 'it stained with gushing blood his breastplate and gory limbs; and Geryon drooped his neck to one side, like a poppy which spoiling its tender beauty suddenly sheds its petals and...'[50] The episode is the subject of a fragment from one of Pindar's poems that has long been known from the discussion of it in Plato's *Gorgias*. It begins:

> Law, the king of all, of mortals and immortals, guides them as it justifies
> the utmost violence with a sovereign hand. I bring as witness the deeds
> of Herakles, for he drove Geryon's cattle to the Cyclopean portal of
> Eurystheus without punishment or payment.[51]

In Plato's dialogue, Callicles uses Heracles' behaviour to justify his doctrine that 'might is right': the stronger have the right to rule the weaker. It has long been agreed that Plato (or Callicles) is misrepresenting Pindar, who, whatever he meant in these lines, cannot have meant this. Many discussions have been devoted to the problems, well summarised in a classic article by Hugh Lloyd-Jones.[52] The most satisfactory approach seems to be to take the first word, *nomos*, which in classical Greek means 'law', or more generally 'custom', as meaning 'whatever is accepted as the order of things, as a norm', and that the participle *dikaion* means 'making just' in the sense that whatever attitude one might normally take to an act, acceptance of it as a norm can make it right. That is, Heracles is a great hero and a touchstone of excellence; so whatever he does, even if it looks like criminal behaviour, must be accepted as just in the order of the universe. Clearly the character of

Heracles was far from unproblematic for Greek thinkers, including Pindar, despite his reverence for the hero.

The purely heroic Heracles has his tragic side as well. Euripides' *Heracles*, which incorporates both a long choral ode describing his twelve labours and a further ode that takes the form of an epinician, focuses not on Heracles' glory but on the wretched fate that can entrap a man even in the moment of his pride. Fresh from his labours, and from rescuing his wife and children from the usurping tyrant Lycus, Heracles is struck down by the vengeance of his inveterate enemy Hera, who sends the goddess Lyssa to drive him mad and, in his madness, to kill the children he has just rescued. The hero here is a broken man, and the prospect of eventual immortal glory is hidden from view.[53]

A similar ambiguity seems to characterise the account Bacchylides gives of Heracles in his Ode 5, where he describes Heracles' descent to the Underworld. Strangely, he concentrates on the hero's melancholy encounter with the dead Meleager, which seems chosen to illustrate the preceding gnome that no man is happy in all things. The encounter ends when Meleager proposes his own daughter to Heracles as a wife on his return to the world. She is unnamed, but we know that she is Deianeira, who in due course will unwittingly kill Heracles by her gift of a magic robe that she thinks contains a love philtre; in fact it contains a poison that causes Heracles' flesh to burn until he dies. Bacchylides, perhaps because of his Ionic background, tells a far darker story of the great hero than the Dorian Pindar will admit. But it can be seen as prefiguring, however remotely, Heracles' deification. The difference in treatment encapsulates something of the difference between the two poets: Bacchylides weaves a far looser train of thought than Pindar.

The Dioscuri offer a rather different kind of link between the worlds of gods and men. They were the gods most commonly entertained at rituals known as *theoxenia*, 'god-entertaining'.[54] In *Nemean* 10 we learn that an ancestor of the victor Theaeus once received these gods into his home:

> But given that Kastor and his brother Polydeukes came
> for hospitality to the home of Pamphaes, it is no wonder
> that they have inborn ability to be good athletes, because

those stewards of spacious Sparta, along with Hermes and Herakles,
administer their flourishing allotment of the games
and are very solicitous for men who are just. Yes, truly
the race of the gods is faithful.[55]

Friedrich Deneken surmised that such festivals often commemorated the origin of a *genos*, so that Pamphaes here would be the clan ancestor.[56] (At Sparta a series of priests of the Dioscuri were all members of a single family.) However, the ode was performed at the Argive state festival, the Heraea, not at a *theoxenia*, so the clan's interests are subsumed in the city's.

It was the Dioscuri who saved Simonides from a banquet at Scopas' house (by arriving and calling him outside just before the house collapsed in an earthquake), and they could be malevolent if not properly received, as a story in Pausanias shows: they knocked at the door of one Phormion of Sparta and asked to be put up for the night in their favourite room; when he refused, on the grounds that that room was now occupied by his virgin daughter, they punished him by stealing his daughter and leaving behind a little bunch of silphium on the table. If they gave Pamphaes' descendants athletic skills, they were gods to be approached with awe and placated with meals, as much as any god.

Other Heroes

Other heroes are more rarely brought into play as paradigms of athletic achievement, though the nymph Cyrene takes on this role in *Pythian* 9, and Simonides once (to our knowledge) describes a prize (presumably) as 'deservedly given by Hermes, lord of contests' (which acts as a transition to a myth about Atlas, father of the seven Pleiades, of whom one was Hermes' mother).[57]

The picture is rather different when we turn to Pindar's poems that are not for athletic victors. Those we know best are the Paeans, all connected with the worship of Apollo. In *Paean* 5, for the Athenians to Delos, whatever myth there was has been lost, though *Paean* 7b, for an unidentified *polis* to

Delos, tells the story of the origin of the island of Delos, which floated at random across the Aegean sea until Leto arrived there to give birth to Apollo and Artemis. (See also *Paean* 12, for the Naxians to Delos, for a repetition of the theme of the birth of the twin gods.) *Paean* 4, for the Ceans to Delos, is unusual in its patrons, since Ceans in other cases commissioned their native sons, Simonides (who was perhaps dead by this point) or Bacchylides. The best-preserved passage begins with the words, 'Truly I dwell on a rock, am renowned for achievements among Hellenes in games, and also known for providing poetry in abundance.'[58] Note how the poet here speaks in the person of the Cean chorus, not in his own persona, as in the epinicians. After these compliments to his two contemporary poets, Pindar goes on to retail some fairly obscure local myths of Ceos. In the preserved portion it is not possible to see any particular connection with Apollo.

Choruses to Delos were an important of the quadrennial cycle of Apollo worship, and in Athens these choruses were, like those at home, the responsibility of a *leitourgos*, a rich man who took on the burden or liturgy (which means 'work for the people') of funding and organising it. Games took place and the contestants were transported in a special oared ship. When Nicias, perhaps in the 420s, was in charge of the choruses, he found that

> The dancers and singers which the cities of Greece sent there to sing rimes and verses in the honour of Apollo, were wont before to arrive disorderly: and the cause was, for the numbers of people that ranne to see them, who made them singe straight without any order, and landing in haste out of their ships, they left their apparel, and put on such vestments as they should weare in procession, and their garlands of flowers on their heads, all at one present time. But Nicias... landed first on the ile of Renea, hard adjoining to the ile of Delos, with his singers, his beasts for sacrifice, and with al the rest of his traine, carrying a bridge with him, which he had caused to be made at Athens, upon measure taken of the channel, betwixt the one and the other ile, set out with pictures and tables, with gilding, with nosegays and garlands of triumph, and with excellent wrought tapestrie, which in the night he set up upon the channel, being not very broade, and the next morning

by break of day caused his singers to pass over upon it, singing all the way as they went in his procession so nobly set forth, even unto the very temple of Apollo.[59]

Similar processions were also sent to Delphi, and again the emphasis seems to have been on local myths. In *Paean* 2, for example, for the men of Abdera, the beginning invokes the local hero Abderus, but the 'myth' is scarcely a myth at all; it is, rather, a piece of history about how the people of Abdera drove out a local people, the 'spear-bearing Paiones' in order to establish their city. The involved story elicits from Pindar (speaking in the person of the Abderitan chorus) the remarkable statement, 'I am a young city: yet I bore my mother's mother, shattered by the fire of war.'[60] The paradoxical statement recalls the riddling style of Old English poetry, for example Riddle 3 from the Exeter Book: 'My mother is my daughter.' Here, the speaker is an iceberg. In Pindar's case, the point is that the city was originally settled by Greeks from Clazomenae in 654 or 652; they were driven out, and later the Teans, driven from their home by the Persian general Harpagus, resettled the site.[61] At a later date some of the Tean settlers in Abdera returned to Teos and refounded that city.[62] Abdera came under Persian rule by 514 and was freed after the defeat of the Persians at Eion in 475. Only a local could reasonably be expected to understand what this chorus was singing about.

Delos had a strong connection to Crete, since the ritual of the crane-dance there was supposed to have been established by Theseus when he returned from Crete leading the Athenian youths and maidens he had rescued from the labyrinth: this dance was 'an imitation of the winding twists and turns in the Labyrinth, contrived in a certain rhythm which had complicated turns. This type of dance is called *geranos*... and he danced it around the horned altar.'[63] Pindar never speaks of the great Athenian hero Theseus, whose career was partly modelled on that of the Dorian Heracles, but he features frequently in the surviving poems of Bacchylides. Bacchylides 1, an epinician for a Cean boy boxer, told how 'warlike Minos came with a throng of Cretans on fifty glittering-sterned ships, and by the favour of Zeus, god of glory, he bedded the slim-waisted maiden Dexithea; and... sailed away to the lovely city of Knossos.'[64] The connection with the victor is unknown, but

4.1 Theseus, protected by Athena, visits the under-sea kingdom of Amphitrite. Attic red-figure cup by Onesimus, from Cerveteri.

perhaps Ceos felt an affinity with nearby Delos and its Cretan connection, as the Cretan theme recurs in Pindar's *Paean* 4. Bacchylides 17, 'The Young Athenians, or, Theseus; for the Ceans to perform in Delos', is classified by the ancient editors as a dithyramb, but is surely a paean. It tells the story of how Theseus, on his way to Crete, was ordered by Zeus to leap into the sea, and all his companions thought his end had come.

> But sea-dwelling dolphins were swiftly carrying great Theseus to the house of his father, god of horses, and he reached the hall of the gods. There he was awe-struck at the glorious daughters of blessed Nereus, for from their splendid limbs shone a gleam as of fire, and round their hair were twirled gold-braided ribbons; and they were delighting their hearts by dancing with liquid feet. And he saw his father's dear wife,

august ox-eyed Amphitrite, in the lovely house; she put a purple cloak about him and set on his thick hair the faultless garland which once at her marriage guileful Aphrodite had given her, dark with roses. Nothing that the gods wish is beyond the belief of sane mortals: he appeared beside the slender-sterned ship.[65]

This near-death experience is a kind of initiation for the hero, and for Peter Wilson, 'the Athenian youths "who shouted a paean with lovely voice"... are virtually indistinguishable from the youths of the Kean chorus.'[66] There is a political statement here along with the praise of Apollo.

Bacchylides 18 is also on the subject of Theseus. Composed in dialogue form, it tells the story of Theseus' arrival in Athens, slaying monsters along the road as he goes. These exploits were contrived to make him an Ionian counterpart to the Doric Heracles, and to give the Athenians a depth of mythical past that they otherwise lacked. So here, and also in Bacchylides 19, 'For the Athenians', Bacchylides follows a rather different path in search of patronage from that of Pindar.

Heroes belong to cities while gods belong to all the Greeks. So the choice of heroes is, almost, a partisan choice. Some heroes belong pre-eminently to the Games, but Bacchylides does not even have much to say of Heracles. If we had more of his poetry we might be able to say with more certainty what led his choices of mythological themes. But the contrast with Pindar, and between Pindar's paeans and his epinicians, is enough to suggest how important the choice of heroes is. In the poems for athletes, the deified hero Heracles remains a model to aspire to but, perhaps, never to equal. Bacchylides, in his more straightforward and conventional way, avoids the deep question of how divinity can suffuse a human life. Pindar never stops reflecting on it.

V

THE PRACTICE
OF PRAISE

In the prison of his days
Teach the free man how to praise

W.H. AUDEN

WHEN PINDAR WROTE ODES in celebration of humans, his job was to praise the addressee fitly; in the poems for divinities it was to fulfil the commission of a city or clan to celebrate their patron god or hero. Failure to recognise this role, which is so at odds with the Romantic conception of the poet as a free spirit, speaking as inspiration commands, bedevilled nineteenth and early twentieth-century criticism of the poet. For M.I. Finley it made the poet into a hired hack no better than an advertising copywriter;[1] and it led other critics to interpret obscure passages as supposed references to the poet's own considerations and problems rather than the circumstances of the victor. These approaches found some justification in the language Pindar uses to describe his own inspiration, and further support from the annotations of ancient scholiasts, who themselves resorted to 'biographical' explanations when they could not understand something.

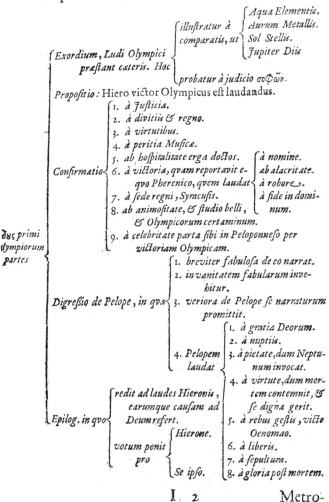

ΟΛΥΜΠ: Α.

ΣΥΝΟΨΙΣ

Dispositionis primi εἶδος Olympiorum.

δὺς primi Olympiorum partes

- Exordium, Ludi Olympici præstant cæteris. Hoc
  - illustratur à comparatis, ut
    - Aqua Elementis.
    - Aurum Metallis.
    - Sol Stellis.
    - Jupiter Diis
  - probatur à judicio σοφῶν.
- Propositio : Hiero victor Olympicus est laudandus.
- Confirmatio
  1. à Justicia.
  2. à divitiis & regno.
  3. à virtutibus.
  4. à peritia Musicæ.
  5. ab hospitalitate erga doctos.
  6. à victoria, qvam reportavit e- qvo Pherenico, qvem laudat
     - à nomine.
     - ab alacritate.
     - à robore.
     - à fide in dominum.
  7. à sede regni, Syracusis.
  8. ab animositate, & studio belli, & Olympicorum certaminum.
  9. à celebritate parta sibi in Peloponneso per victoriam Olympicam.
- Digressio de Pelope, in qva
  1. breviter fabulosa de eo narrat.
  2. in vanitatem fabularum invehitur.
  3. veriora de Pelope se narraturum promittit.
  4. Pelopem laudat
     1. à gratia Deorum.
     2. à nuptiis.
     3. à pietate, dum Neptunum invocat.
     4. à virtute, dum mortem contemnit, & se digna gerit.
     5. à rebus gestis, victo Oenomao.
     6. à liberis.
     7. à sepultura.
     8. à gloria post mortem.
- Epilog. in qvo
  - redit ad laudes Hieronis, earumque causam ad Deum refert.
  - votum ponit pro
    - Hierone.
    - Se ipso.

I. 2.   Metro-

5.1   Erasmus Schmid's analysis of *Olympian 1.*

But already in 1616 Erasmus Schmid had understood that the poet's prime purpose was praise, and in 1962 Pindaric scholarship was revolutionised by the publication of two short studies by Elroy L. Bundy: *Studia Pindarica*, in which he demonstrated

> That the Epinikion must adhere to those principles that have governed encomia from Homer to Lincoln's *Gettysburg Address*, so that when Pindar speaks pridefully in the first person this is less likely to be the personal Pindar of Thebes than the Pindar privileged to praise the worthiest of men.[2]

Some traditional scholars were shocked by this new approach, and perhaps not least by the rebarbative terminology Bundy devised to discuss the rhetorical structure of the odes – '*laudandus*', 'foil', 'vaunt' and so on – but the basic insight has prevailed and scholarship now takes for granted the laudatory purpose of the surviving odes. The case was eloquently restated by Hugh Lloyd-Jones in an article applying Bundy's insight to two problem odes, *Pythian* 2 and *Nemean* 7, in 1973.[3] In this chapter I propose to outline the way in which the rhetoric of praise is constructed: the themes that demand praise, the methods employed (including the problems that praise evokes) and the imagery that expresses praise.

All three of these correspond to traditional divisions of the rhetorician's art, expressed in the handbooks, both Greek and Latin, as 'invention, disposition and diction'. The earliest rhetorical theory seems to have been developed in Syracuse, about the time of Pindar's visit there, by Corax and his pupil Tisias; Pindar, though, will not have needed a theoretician's help to write according to the implicit norms of praise poetry. Later theory codified the rules into forms that were often overly mechanical and could become deadening if not employed by a skilled artist. Erasmus Schmid, being a humanist steeped in ancient rhetoric, employs this kind of terminology in his tabular analyses of every ode. In *Olympian* 1, for example, he divides the whole ode (with subdivisions) into: '*exordium*', on the pre-eminence of the Olympic Games; '*propositio*', the job in hand, ('*Hiero victor Olympicus est laudandus*'); '*confirmatio*', the reasons for praise; a '*digressio*' about Pelops;

an '*epilogus*' in which he returns to the matter of praise; and a prayer for the addressee. Such a dissection is valuable if, inevitably, mechanical; the only term with which one might wish to take issue is 'digression'. The idea that the myths, and other matter in the odes, constitute digressions and are therefore in many cases irrelevant, is a prime reason why Pindar's trains of thought have often been found obscure (as, for example, in the famous judgement of Abraham Cowley that he writes like a 'madman'). The terminology goes back to the scholiasts; along with 'biographical' explanations, it was one of their ways of dealing with what they could not understand. If the strong form of Bundy's thesis is to be upheld, that 'everything in an ode conduces to praise of the victor', then 'digression' is the wrong word. It may often be difficult to see why a passage, or a myth, is there, but the explanation is to be sought in the affairs of the *laudandus*. It may indeed remain ever obscure to us, but methodologically this is the right approach; it is not just the inspired poet wandering off on whatever topic he chooses.

Before Bundy, Wolfgang Schadewaldt had developed the concept of the Pindaric *Programm*: that every ode had to contain reference to a certain number of specified topics, namely the victor, his family, his city; the nature of his victory; a myth; gnomic utterance; prayers to the gods. Clearly this does not go as far as Bundy, but it is a helpful way of considering the essence of a Pindaric ode. In a way, each ode is a set of variations on this 'programme', and one waits for the inventive way in which each topic is handled with a connoisseur's eagerness.

We must add to Schadewaldt's insight the principle that Pindar clearly states, that an ode should have an arresting beginning: see by way of illustration *Olympian* 6.3–4, 'When a work is begun, it is necessary to make its front shine from afar.' Almost every poem has an example to offer: the lyre in *Pythian* 1, the Homeric address to the Muse in *Pythian* 4, the address to 'hymns, lords of the lyre' in *Olympian* 2; often, too, the opening is a prayer (*Paean* 2, *Paean* 6 and *Pythian* 12) or a gnome (*Olympian* 1, 'Water is best'; *Nemean* 6, 'the race of men and of the gods is one').

It can be illuminating to set Pindar's practice alongside a text from antiquity that discusses methods of praise. This is Menander Rhetor's *On Epideictic*,[4] a handbook for the practitioner on how to make '*epideictic*' speeches, 'namely those which people call encomiastic or invective'. Menander was writing probably in the late third century CE, some seven hundred years after Pindar's death, but the prescriptions he provides are remarkably pertinent. Like Mr Micawber who spoke prose without knowing it, Pindar composed rhetorical encomium before any of the terminology had been invented; the terminology arose out of the practice of orators who in turn had learnt from the poets.

Menander begins his discussion in his first treatise by saying:

> 'Praise' of some kind occurs sometimes in relation to gods, sometimes in relation to mortal objects.[5] When it relates to gods, we speak of 'hymns' and we divide these in turn according to the god concerned. Thus hymns to Apollo are called *paeans* and *huporchemata*, hymns to Dionysus *dithyrambs*, and *iobacchi* and the like, those to Aphrodite 'erotic hymns', while those appropriate to other gods are either called by the generic title 'hymns' or, more specifically, e.g. 'to Zeus'.[6]

He goes on to subdivide praise of mortal objects into that of cities and countries and that of living creatures, both men and animals. Unfortunately, from our point of view, he announces that he is going to pass over 'man'. After dividing hymns to the gods into *cletic* ('summoning'), *apopemptic* ('sending off'), scientific and mythical, genealogical and fictitious, deprecatory and precatory hymns, he passes on to praise of countries and cities. Here we can find many pointers to the way praise is structured in Pindar's odes. Cities are praised by their positions (as in *Pythian* 12, on Acragas, quoted in Chapter 2 of the present volume), their seasons and products: 'If the city is by the sea, or is an island [think of Aegina], you will speak ill of continental areas and continental settlements, and enumerate all the good things that come from the sea,' says Menander.[7] Next come relations with neighbours, harbours and so on. Next, importantly, origins, comprising 'founders, settlers, date, changes, causes of foundation' – all topics that are likely to arise in a Pindaric ode. Cities may then be praised for their accomplishments, their social organisation, their festivals and so on. Later encomia often clearly follow the patterns laid down by Pindar,[8] and the pattern is perhaps most easily seen in a comparison of Athenian *epitaphioi logoi*, funeral speeches, with these checklists and with what is known of Pindar's, and other poets', laments.[9]

Clearly this kind of prescription is quite mechanical but, like Schadewaldt's 'programme', it draws attention to the things that have to be there, and it suggests ways of dealing with the generically required topics. What is needed is a more dynamic analysis that shows how the topics are interwoven and build into crescendos, as Bundy called them. This is a task that can only be undertaken through analysis of individual odes,[10] but in the following pages I attempt to draw together some of the main argumentative structures that enable Pindar to move from one topic to the next.

What Do You Praise?

In an epinician ode, you praise the victor and his success in the event in question. In broad terms, you praise his *arete*, or virtue. Simonides provides the locus classicus in his poem for Scopas, which was discussed by Socrates in Plato's *Protagoras*.[11] The poem is about virtue, about what it is to be a good man, 'four-square in hands, in feet and in mind, fashioned without flaw'. About three further stanzas of the poem survive, in which Simonides meditates on how hard it is to be good:

> I shall never throw away my span of life on an empty, vain hope in quest
> of the impossible, the completely blameless man... I am not a fault-finder:
> I am satisfied with the man who is not bad nor too shiftless, one who
> understands the justice that helps his city, a sound man. I shall not find
> fault with him; for the generation of fools is numberless.

The poem lent itself to excerption since it provides a short moral essay without obvious reference to its purpose – praise of Scopas. But in praising Scopas as being 'realistically' good it introduces us to a couple of motifs that are prominent in Pindar too: the refusal to go for what is impossible, and the refusal to find fault. Blame, or malice, is for fools, not the wise poet.

In most cases the praise in Pindar is specifically for athletic *arete*, which, as we saw in the previous chapter, emerges from the high value the Greeks placed on athletic achievement. The job of the poet is to record virtue and provide its owner with fame; that is the contractual exchange in writing an epinician poem. However, there are plenty of other kinds of excellence that are also praised, perhaps the most notable being erotic appeal and beauty. Pindar's Fragment 123 (actually a complete poem) for Theoxenus of Tenedos is a perfect example:

> anyone who sees the shafts of light flashing from
> Theoxenus' eyes
> and does not swell up with desire,
> has a dark heart, forged of steel or adamant
> in a cold fire....
> For myself, [Aphrodite's] influence makes me
> soft as the wax of holy bees,
> when I see a shapely youth.
> Persuasion and Grace
> have taken up residence
> with the son of Agesilas in Tenedos.[12]

The justice of Pindar's praise is given added authority by his reference to his 'personal feelings',[13] and the poem ends with a straightforward utterance of the praiseworthy qualities of the subject. (The intriguing metaphor of 'cold fire' will be discussed below.) A fragmentary poem by Ibycus, who wrote about a century before Pindar, describes in a similar way a lovely youth:

> Among lovely buds (of roses), Charis, you nurtured him about the
> temple (of Aphrodite)... And the goddesses bestowed tender (beauty).
> But Justice (fled from the choir) of goddesses, and my limbs are weighed
> down, and passing sleepless (nights) I ponder (many things) in my heart.[14]

The 'life' of Ibycus given by the Byzantine encyclopaedia, the Suda, calls Ibycus 'completely crazed with love for boys'. It is true that many of his poems speak in such terms, but among them are also proto-epinicia such as Fragment 282A and encomia such as Fragment 282. Again, the metaphor in a fragment of Pindar's older contemporary Anacreon, Fragment 360 – 'Boy with the girlish glance, I seek you, but you do not notice, not knowing that you hold the reins of my soul' – might suggest that the boy in question is an athlete, or a charioteer, glimpsed on the sports field.[15]

Lacking a context for Ibycus Fragment 282C, one might interpret these lines equally as part of a poem of praise on another theme, in which erotic appeal is simply one of the terms of praise: A.P. Burnett shows how such motifs are woven into many of the poems for Aeginetan boy victors, not all of whom Pindar can have been in love with (I suppose): 'Hora, the opening figure of *Nemean* 8, is strongly eroticized. She rests on the eyelids of desirable youths (2), tells of their readiness for love (1), and decides when a suitor may be successful.'[16] Such poetry of physical praise is frequently found in drinking songs (*skolia*), and a piece like Pindar's Theoxenus poem was ideally suited to become a party piece long after Theoxenus (like Sweet Georgia Brown, or Long Tall Sally) was forgotten. Again, *Pythian* 10.54–60 praises Hippocleas as 'the darling of unmarried girls', and continues enigmatically, 'desires for various things stir the minds of various men, and each one who wins what he strives for may gain the coveted object...' Attractiveness to girls is congruent with attractiveness to older men.

Beauty always deserves admiration, but for Aristotle praise was due only to moral qualities: we do not praise men for things they can take no credit for (physique, good looks and so on) but only for the use of these gifts for some good and serious purpose.[17] Pindar reflects on the same antithesis: 'What comes by nature is altogether best. Many men strive to win fame with abilities that are taught, but when god takes no part, each deed is no worse for being left in silence.'[18] Natural endowment is vitally important for Pindar, and without it training is useless. Excellence can never be just a learned skill. Stesichorus had said the same in Fragment 64: 'There is no excellence and honour of mortals contrary to the dispensation of the god and Lachesis.' But one must allow the god to take a part in the exercise of one's gifts in order to achieve the heights. The victor must recognise the grace given him and not be puffed up: 'If a man fosters a sound prosperity by having sufficient possessions and adding praise thereto, let him not seek to become a god.'[19]

On the other hand, he must not hide what gives him his chance of immortality, he must make it permanent by having a poet celebrate it in lasting words. Renown is no good unless it is apparent and permanent. The statement at the beginning of *Nemean* 5 that words are more lasting even than statues is a commonplace of ancient Greek thought, and the danger of not spending to ensure lasting fame is vividly expressed in *Isthmian* 1.67–8: 'Now should a man store hidden wealth in his halls, and upon other fall with mocking laughter, little thinks he his soul shall fare to Hades with not a shred of glory.' Right use of achievement, right attitude to success, is crucial. Wealth itself may be praised, but like natural gifts it must be rightly used. Like beauty, wealth is not a virtue in itself. The poet's praise is made all the more heartfelt and honest by being tempered with warning.

But there is also the suggestion that wealth must be used to commission a suitable ode, which will immortalise the achievement in appropriate terms and avoid the shame of oblivion. As Stephen Instone has put it apropos *Pythian* 11.54–8:

> Athletic success, though the crowning achievement, requires a successful life afterwards, a life free from *hybris*; if you can achieve all that, then you will not meet a dark death, i.e. oblivion, the fate of the unsuccessful; rather, the successful and peaceable victor even when dead provides honour to future members of his family.[20]

How Do You Praise? Muses and Graces

The relationship of poet and addressee is crucial to adequate praise. There is an epinician etiquette, which requires that the poet prove himself adequate to the task of illuminating the victor's achievement. In doing this the poet lays claim not so much to divine inspiration (though the Muses are invoked as guarantors of the 'facts' he purveys) as to 'the right to be trusted' (the Greek word is *axiopistia*, and it is very important in forensic rhetoric). This is the reason for the very frequent first-person statements in the odes, which are introduced not simply as *sphragides*, seals, assertions of authorship like the cameo appearances of Alfred Hitchcock in each of his films. Authorship, as Gregory Nagy has gracefully put it, implies authority, and the poet must establish his authority to praise. This is relatively easily done in the odes for aristocrats, where Pindar can speak as an equal to equals, and may sometimes set up relationships of *proxeny* (as in *Nemean* 7) or kinship (as in *Pythian* 5) to emphasise the link. It is much harder in the poems for autocrats, the Sicilian 'tyrants'; the special means by which Pindar sets himself up as adequate to the task of praising such great men has been discussed in Chapter 2 above.

The use of the first person in the epinicians is thus quite different from that in the paeans and other genres of 'god-directed' poetry. In the paeans 'I' is frequently spoken in the person of the chorus (for further discussion, see the end of Chapter 4). There has been some dispute about whether this is a universal rule, since in *Pythian* 5.72–6, 'I' has been thought to suit only the singers of the Cyrenean chorus: 'Mine it is to proclaim the delightful glory that comes from Sparta, whence men born as Aigeidai, my forefathers, came to Thera, not without divine favour, but some Fate led them.' At first glance it is Cyrene, founded from Thera, which was itself colonised from Sparta, that should make this claim. A more subtle argument holds that Pindar's tribe of Theban Aegeidai claimed consanguinity with the Spartan Aegeidai, and thus the poet is claiming a family relationship with his addressee – another way of establishing his *axiopistia*.[21]

The poet, like any Greek poet, claims special abilities by virtue of the favour of the Muses, goddesses of poetry, from whom he receives his inspiration. The Muses' responsibility is to provide the 'matter' of a song (the '*inventio*', in rhetorical terms) and to ensure that it is accurate. In poetry like Pindar's, what the Muses mainly give is *kleos,* (undying) fame. The matter had become more complicated since Homer called on the Muse to 'sing the wrath of Achilles', or the Muses called on Hesiod to become a poet.[22] In Homer, the Muses know all that is, and has been, and is to come,[23] but Hesiod knew that the Muses might sometimes lie: they told him when they made him a poet, 'We know how to tell many lies, similar to real things; and we know, when we wish, how to utter things that are true.'[24] Lies here may mean no more than fiction, and the Muses would then be boasting of their ability to make up attractive stories for entertainment. But fiction might lead the unwary into tactless falsehood, and an invented story might insult its subject, as we are told that Stesichorus insulted Helen in a poem and was blinded for his crime, only recovering his sight when he wrote a second poem recanting everything he had said in the first. Pindar is very aware of the danger of false tales and false traditions, as we shall see when we discuss his narratives. *Kleos* must correspond to some reality. Pindar insists that the praise he has to offer is true. A fragment of an unidentified poem states this explicitly: 'Starting point for great achievement, Queen Truth, do not make my understanding stumble against rough falsehood'.[25]

Olympian 10 begins with a statement of confidence in the Muse: 'O Muse, but you and Zeus' daughter, Truth, with a correcting hand ward off from me the charge of harming a guest friend with broken promises'.[26] Truth is an important theme in this ode, which moves from Augeas' fraudulent behaviour towards strangers to an account of Heracles' foundation of the Olympic Games: 'At that founding ceremony the Fates stood near at hand, as did the sole assayer of genuine truth, Time, which in its onward march clearly revealed how Herakles divided up that gift of war [the booty taken from Augeas]'.[27] The assertion is followed by a rather Homeric list of victors at those first Games. Pindar places himself in the tradition of the poets who recorded them by offering similarly undeniable glory to Hagesidamos: 'The Pierian daughters of Zeus are fostering your widespread fame. And I have earnestly joined in... I have praised the lovely son of Archestratos, whom I saw winning...'[28] Pindar's presence at the victory guarantees, with the Muses' participation, a truth value for his assertion as great as that which attaches to those long-dead athletes of the days of Heracles.

His Muse inspires him and he is her prophet,[29] but he also has the judgement to know when what the Muse is telling him is adequate to the occasion. Like Homer, he can summon the Muse when needed: see *Pythian* 1.58, and *Isthmian* 8.5, 'I am asked to invoke the golden Muse'. He can give her orders, as at *Nemean* 6.32: 'Come, Muse, direct to that house a glorious wind of verses'; but he has to hit the 'target of the Muses' with accuracy, as at *Nemean* 9.55.

Many other passages show Pindar's insistence on the role of the Muse or Muses in truthful praise. Sometimes he also suggests a special relationship with Pan, who brought him a song in a dream; Pan was, moreover, once observed singing one of Pindar's paeans as he danced between Helicon and Cithaeron.[30] Simonides (perhaps),[31] in a frustratingly lacunose papyrus, seems to make Pan behave like the Muses in telling the subject of song: 'goat-legged divinity!... keeps mouth closed and uttering no sound... (sleep?)... he sang about famous...; and to us... truth... the god at once... clear notes... divine... whenever I... undefiled sacrifices... sweet... pouring libation....'[32]

Almost as important as the Muses to successful celebration are the Graces. Worshipped as goddesses in their own right at Orchomenos in Boeotia,[33] the Graces also have a symbolic role to play as guarantors of the beauty of poetry and of celebration.[34] Grace in theology is a free gift that cannot be striven for, and as a literary concept Alexander Pope spoke of 'a grace beyond the reach of art', so the Greek Graces are the deities that turn the technical mastery of the poet into something with a touch of magic. (Though sometimes they can also lead you astray, if their charm is not allied to truth: see *Olympian* 1.27–34, and the discussion of *Olympian* 1 in Chapter 6.) As Pindar wrote in *Olympian* 14:

> Hear my prayer. For with your help all things pleasant
> And sweet come about for mortals,
> Whether a man be wise, handsome, or illustrious.
> Yes, not even the gods arrange
> Choruses or feasts
> Without the august Graces.[35]

And at the beginning of *Pythian* 9 (in line 3), Pindar proclaims the victor 'with the aid of the deep-bosomed Graces'. Bacchylides speaks of the Graces in a similar way at the beginning of his ninth ode: 'Graces of the golden distaff, may ye grant the charm that wins mortal ears; for the inspired prophet of the violet-eyed Muses is ready to sing.' And at *Nemean* 4.6–8, 'the word lives longer than deeds, which, with the Graces' blessing, the tongue draws from the depths of the mind.' Grace is what makes a poem truly memorable.

And the Graces shed lustre not only on the poet's work, but on the victor himself, as, for example, in *Nemean* 10: 'Theaios, honor for athletic success often attends the famous race of your mother's ancestors with the help of the Graces and the Tyndaridai,'[36] and *Nemean* 6: 'In the evening by the Kastalian spring he was ablaze with the clamor of the Graces.'[37]

In this second passage, the Graces are bound up with the 'radiance' that characterises the victor – not the fact of victory but the brightness of it. The beauty they give is what makes the victory visible from afar, broadcasts its *kleos*.

Nature Imagery

The Graces are also involved in a second complex of imagery: that drawn from the processes of Nature. Men, gods and the natural world are all bound together in what sometimes seems like a holistic universe.[38]

> The race of men and of the gods is one.
> For from one mother have we both
>   The life we breathe.
> And yet the whole discrete endowment of power sets us apart;
> For man is naught, but the bronze vault of heaven
> Remains for ever a throne immutable.
> Nevertheless some likeness still
> May we with the immortals claim, whether
> Of mind's nobility or body's grace.[39]

How is it that men may become godlike? The Graces, besides their task of shedding radiance on the victor, also nurture it:

> The dewdrops of the Graces
> They shower in gleaming beauty
> On the Psaluchid clan.[40]

Such metaphors of watering, of vegetable growth and of plucking and harvesting are very common in Pindar. The Graces are gardeners.[41] Not only are addressees frequently urged to 'pluck' the fruits of victory, but, more importantly, human achievement is seen as part of the organic process of Nature. The lines of *Nemean* 6 that follow those just quoted make this very clear:

> Alcimidas makes it clear to see that his inherited
> Nature is like crop-bearing fields, which alternate
> And at one time give men abundant sustenance from the plains,
> But at another rest to gather strength.[42]

Alcimidas follows his grandfather, not his father, in achieving a victory: a generation has lain fallow like a field, or perhaps like an olive tree that bears only in alternate years.

Man is not a wild growth but a cultivated one. Central to this set of ideas is that of *phya*, the Doric equivalent of the Attic *physis*, nature. *Phya* is what you are born with, and it cannot be altered, but it can and must be nurtured, cultivated, like a thoroughbred horse or a fine strain of rose. No amount of training will get exceptional results from inferior raw material. It is Pindar's belief that such nature is hereditary. There is an aristocracy of achievement.

Connected with this idea is the frequent appearance of the related words *aotos* and *anthos*. *Anthos* means a flower or bloom; *aotos* is strictly speaking a fleece, but it comes to mean something like the 'bloom' of a peach or a plum, the nap that is the sign of perfect ripeness. Both words are frequently applied to the victor's achievement. *Anthos* is often the literal flowers with which the successful athlete is pelted or crowned: see, for example, *Olympian* 8.76, when the Blepsiadai have won 'a sixth crown from the leaf-bearing Games.'[43] At *Pythian* 4.159 it is used of 'the flower of youth', at *Nemean* 7.53 of the 'flowers of Aphrodite', while at *Olympian* 6.105 and *Olympian* 9.48 there are 'flowers of hymns': in the former Pindar prays to the god, 'Cause my hymns' pleasing flower to burgeon.' *Aotos* is rather different. Again it can be used of poems: 'A man raised in seven-gated Thebes must offer to Aigina the bloom of the Graces';[44] but at *Nemean* 2.6–9 the victor Timodemus also has a duty 'to reap over and over the most beautiful *aotos* of the Isthmian Games.'[45] The lexica show many examples where *aotos* stands for something like 'acme'.[46] If the word meant 'fleece', it seems from *Nemean* 2.6–9 that Pindar felt it to mean some kind of perfection of plant life. The victor wins not just the literal garlands of victory, but the perfections that the natural world offers. *Isthmian* 5.12–13 states this with a remarkable change of metaphor: 'Two things alone shepherd the *aotos* of life along with finely flowering [*euanthei*] prosperity: being successful and hearing good words of himself.' (Have those blooming peaches become a fleecy flock? We shall return to the matter of Pindar's metaphors.)

Lion, Eagle and Dolphin

The animal world too has a part to play in Pindar's encomiastic vocabulary. The dolphin is a type of speed in its element,[47] and by extension of excellence in its field; see, for example, *Nemean* 6.64–6: 'As swift as a dolphin through the sea would I say that Melesias is, that charioteer of hands and strength.'[48] The lion, king of land beasts, also appears in comparison to the victor at *Isthmian* 3.65 and *Olympian* 11.19f. But the beast Pindar most commonly refers to is the eagle, and many interpreters have regarded the eagle as a symbol for the poet's soaring art; Thomas Gray expressed it vividly in his famous Pindaric Ode (see Chapter 7). But excellence belongs above all to the *laudandus*, so at *Pythian* 2.50–2, mentioned above, the eagle and dolphin represent similar excellences. The point is made very clearly at *Pythian* 5.107–15:

> On all men's tongues
> these words I hear: that in the wisdom of his mind
>   and of his speech
> he far surpasses all men of his age: in courage
> a broad-winged eagle amongst birds; in combat
> a tower of strength: to share the Muses' gift, he soared
> even from his mother's arms aloft: in racing chariots
>   his skill is now revealed.[49]

It should be remembered that a mechanical bronze eagle and dolphin were mounted at the starting gate of the stadium at Olympia, which respectively flew up and dived down when the mechanism of the gate was operated.[50] The victor takes flight as a result of his victory, and every passage where the eagle has been said to be the poet can better be interpreted as referring to the victor.

Two passages have militated against this natural interpretation. The first is *Olympian* 2.83–8:

> I have many swift arrows
> under my arm
> in their quiver
> that speak to those who understand, but in general, they need
> interpreters. Wise is he who knows many things
> by nature, whereas learners who are boisterous
> and long-winded are like a pair of crows that cry in vain
> against the divine bird of Zeus.

The scholiast read this as self-praise by Pindar and a swipe at his two supposed rivals Simonides and Bacchylides.[51] If this piece of pseudo-historical deduction is ignored, it is easy to see that the eagle must be the addressee, Theron, whose city of Acragas was dominated by the temple of Zeus with the eagle on his arm, and on whose coins the eagle of Zeus was portrayed. The crows are the spirits of envy that must regularly be discounted in order to achieve unsullied praise (on which more later, see pp. 126–33). *Nemean* 3.76–84 is a similar case, where the eagle is contrasted with jackdaws that pester it, and has a similar explanation.[52]

Symposium

Aristocratic culture lies at the root of another important complex of imagery: that drawn from the symposium. The poem is often described as a drink, or compared to one: *Olympian* 7.1–8 is perhaps the locus classicus:

As when a man takes from his rich hand a bowl
foaming inside with dew of the vine
and presents it
to his young son-in-law with a toast from one home
to another – an all-golden bowl, crown of possessions –
as he honours the joy of the symposium
and his own alliance, and thereby with his friends
present makes him envied for his harmonious marriage,
so I too, by sending the poured nectar, gift of the Muses...[53]

The Graces are the special deities of the symposium, as their names indicate: Thalia (festivity), Aglaia (radiance) and Euphrosyna (good spirits). *Nemean* 9.48–55 pulls together many of these themes in a fine set piece:

Peace loves the symposium, but victory increases
with new bloom to the accompaniment of gentle song,
and the voice becomes confident beside the winebowl.
Let someone mix that sweet prompter of the revel,
and let him serve the powerful child of the vine in the
silver bowls which his horses once won...
I pray that with the Graces' aid I may celebrate that
achievement and surpass many in honouring victory
in words, casting my javelin nearest the target of the Muses.

The symposiac context is also important for the purpose of establishing a relationship between poet and addressee. The poem is presented as a gift, deserving a reward: see, for example, *Pythian* 2.74. Thus the poet who, as we saw in Chapter 2, presents himself as a *xenos* or guest friend, becomes the ideal party companion.

Metaphor

It is hard to discuss the texture of a poet's language through the medium of translations, but something needs to be said about the extraordinary quality of

Pindar's expression. When Cowley accused Pindar of writing like a madman, he was largely thinking of his abrupt transitions and trains of thought, but trains of thought on a smaller scale are evident in Pindar's often unusual figures of speech. He shares with other archaic poets a fondness for kenning, riddle and paradox.[54] But most striking are his metaphors. We have already discussed the word *aotos* and its range of connotations, and noted in passing the phrase in his poem for Theoxenus, 'a dark heart forged in a cold fire'. Consider also *Nemean* 4.88, which states that the victor's uncle Callicles 'blossomed with Corinthian parsley' at the Isthmus. This last is not difficult to disentangle in view of the nature imagery discussed above, and with the knowledge that the victor's crown at the Isthmus was made of parsley. The 'cold fire' also has an intuitive truth. But in many cases the image conjured up is wildly incongruous, as in *Nemean* 10.25–6, where Theaeus 'came with good fortune upon both the Isthmian and the Nemean crown and gave it to the Muses to plough'.[55] Or again at *Olympian* 6.82–3: 'Upon my tongue I have the sensation of a clear-sounding whetstone, which I welcome as it comes over me with lovely streams of breath.' There are many such examples of 'mixed metaphors' in Pindar, and it is notable that Bacchylides never uses expressions of this kind. It is a key feature of the *Kunstsprache* in which Pindar writes.[56]

In an article published in 1981 I compared this style to that of some metaphysical poets, citing Thomas Carew's lines:

> Nor can your snow (though you should take
> Alps into your bosom) slake
> The heat of my enamour'd heart...[57]

Rosemond Tuve stresses the incorrectness of letting modern, Romantic or any other associations of the Alps deflect us from recognition of the function of the image in this passage: 'To define this image by its formal cause is to realise that all we know from it is that Carew picked up somewhere that Alps were large, numerous, and snowy.'[58] Carew's readers were trained to recognise the rhetorical purpose of imagery; Pindar's audience too would recognise the succinct heightening of style and attend to the surface associations of individual words. We are not looking at symbolism here, but at metonymy.

The manner is not confined to the metaphysicals. In Shakespeare's *Troilus and Cressida*, Act I Scene 3, 64–8, we have:

> And such again
> As venerable Nestor, hatched in silver,
> Should, with a bond of air strong as the axle-tree
> On which heaven rides, knit all the Greekish ears
> To his experienced tongue...

A recent editor speaks of 'abstract metaphor'.[59] Hafiz is a good source of examples: for instance, 'The kindler of the lamp of our eye is the breeze from beauties' tresses',[60] (breezes do not normally kindle anything). Words become tokens: a pistachio nut connotes 'mouth', a narcissus, 'the beloved'. This is not slovenly writing. Pindar's metaphors work on a basis of substitution, not combination. They behave, that is, like dead metaphors, but by their juxtaposition they are foregrounded. In the theory of the Czech critic Jan Mukařovský, foregrounded motifs can either be motifs that were already in the tradition but were of secondary importance, or precisely those that were of first importance and had thereby become thoroughly conventional, 'automatised'; by a distancing of attitude they are 'de-automatised' and recover their power to catch the reader's attention. 'Garland' for victory is automatised, but in conjunction with the quite different metaphor of ploughing, it brings us up with a start: both terms are foregrounded. The mannered quality of the verse is brought to our attention, but having given our attention we are also invited to probe more deeply the resonances of what is being said. The metaphor adds depth to a conventional statement and reminds us that the gods are involved.

Foil and Climax

It was Basil Gildersleeve's insight that 'much in Pindar is foil' that Bundy built on to form his theory of the single purpose of Pindar's odes. 'Foil' is a phrase, expression or story that contrasts with, or leads into, and thus throws into relief, the main point. It is related to the archaic Greek habit of think-ing in polar opposites.[61] But what is important to recognize is that foil adds meaning to its context; it is not simply there to make the main point visible. One approachable form of foil is the priamel, also called the tricolon crescendo. A well-known example is the opening of *Olympian* 1, but it may be better to approach it through a simpler example, Fragment 221:

> Some take pleasure in the prizes and garlands
> of storm-footed horses,
> others in treasure-chambers full of gold;
> yet others enjoy embarking on the waves of the sea in a swift ship.

The passage will have gone on to focus on the subject Pindar actually wishes to adorn with his praise, as did the rather similar lines of Sappho in Fragment 16:

> Some say that the most beautiful thing on the black earth
> is an army of horsemen;
> others, an army of foot soldiers;
> others, a fleet of ships;
> but I say, it is whoever one is in love with.

In Sappho's lines, there is no obvious similarity of category between the items in the priamel and the climax; in the Pindar fragment, we do not know what the climax was; but in the opening of *Olympian* 1 the two terms of water and gold – which is itself compared to fire – offer two opposing types of elemental perfection. The mention of the Games introduces the third term of the crescendo, the sun, which in turns brings the focus on to the ultimate climax of the priamel, the Olympic Games; so the three terms of the crescendo emphasise the idea of brightness (and the gold that is associated with divinity in Greek thought), which is one of the key images of Pindar's poetry, and give a context of divine radiance to the subject. The tricolon is imbued with a symbolic significance as well.

(Attentive readers will have noticed that this paragraph on the priamel is structured as a tricolon crescendo, in the hope that it will thus be persuasive: priamel is, in a sense, a form of inductive argument.)

An interesting example of priamel is Fragment 128c, which we know from the text accompanying it in the papyrus is the beginning of one of Pindar's laments:

> There are paean-songs in due season belonging to the children
> of Leto with the golden distaff; there are also songs
> ... Dionysos' crown of flourishing ivy...
> others... put to sleep
> three sons of Kalliope, so that memorials of the dead might be set up for her.
> The one sang *ailinon* for long-haired Linus;
> another sang of Hymenaios, whom the last of hymns took
> when at night his skin was first touched in marriage;
> and another sang of Ialemos, whose strength
> was fettered by a flesh-rending disease;
> and the son of Oiagros... Orpheus of the golden lyre.

The text is corrupt, lacunose and obscure, but enough is visible to see that a double tricolon crescendo is at work here. The first colon goes through three types of hymns for the gods: the paean for Apollo and Artemis, the song for Dionysos and the songs devised by the three sons of Calliope. These are two types of lament, *linos* and *ialemos*, with a wedding-song sandwiched between. Calliope is usually known as the mother of Linus and Orpheus, and perhaps of Rhesus;[62] so the three heroes also form a tricolon climaxing in the most famous, Orpheus. Altogether six types of ritual song lead in to focus on the matter in hand, namely lament.

A less natural form of foil for us to understand is the following foil, where a statement or assertion of a value is immediately followed by its polar opposite. This is a very characteristic pattern of archaic thought, found for example in some of the pre-Socratic philosophers who were wont to analyse the substance of the universe in terms of opposites: light and dark, wet and dry, and so on. Often in archaic poetry such polar expressions are used to modify very positive statements that may call down the jealousy of the gods. The trope is common in Theognis as well as Pindar. The reason is made clear in a well-known story. When Croesus asked Solon whether he was not the happiest of all men, Solon counselled him to 'call no man happy until he is dead'; life's mutability may bring down even the greatest. One does well not to forget that nothing mortal endures except by the grace of the gods. Some of the most surprising instances of this form of thought occur at the end of odes, where a climactic statement of praise is offset by a warning. A good example is the end of *Isthmian* 1: the Muses are asked to raise the addressee's name high, and to do so again in future, but the poet goes on: 'But if a man keeps wealth hidden inside and attacks others with laughter, he does not consider that he is paying up his soul to Hades devoid of fame.'[63] Other examples of the trope are at the ends of *Olympians* 5 and 7, and *Nemean* 11, as well as Bacchylides 5. In all these cases the positive statement of praise calls forth the cautionary thought, but the thought is linked to the purpose of epinician in that it reminds the achiever that the achievement is not his alone, that a god has allowed it. To us it seems strange to conclude praise with sober warning, but the polarity expresses a religious position that is no less profound and firm for not being openly articulated.

The Achievement of Praise

When it comes at the end of these crescendos, praise is usually a simple ringing announcement of the victor's achievement. What this means is vividly expressed at the end of *Pythian* 8:

> When there comes to men
> A gleam of splendour given of heaven,
> Then rests on them a light of glory
> And blessed are their days.[64]

This is one of the strongest statements in Pindar's poetry of the 'transfiguration' that comes on the victor who is blessed by the gods with success. A.P. Burnett often draws attention to the importance of the repeated insistence on the *aigla*, the 'radiance', that, as in this passage, comes on the victors.[65] Bruno Currie has developed a detailed case for this being more than a metaphor: the victors are literally heroised.[66] This would be a step beyond what is claimed by other poets who immortalise their subjects.

The moment of actual praise in the odes is usually brief: in *Nemean* 8, we have, 'I am glad to cast a fitting vaunt upon your accomplishment, and many a man has with healing songs made hard toil painless. Yes, truly the hymn of victory existed long ago, even before that strife arose between Adrastus and the Kadmeans.'[67] Here, as often, it comes in the final lines of the ode, with a brief shadow cast by the last phrase to throw the celebration into relief.[68]

The radiance of achievement comes from the gods. It is by putting the victor in a relationship to the gods that Pindar validates his achievement and gives it an imperishable significance. This explains the frequency of prayers in the odes. *Pythian* 1 alone contains seven prayers, and Bacchylides 5 casts the concluding praise in the form of a prayer:

> I am easily persuaded to send Hiero speech to bring him glory, without (straying from) the path (of justice); for such speech makes the tree-stocks of blessings flourish: may Zeus, the greatest father, (preserve) them unshaken in peace.[69]

Problems of Praise

SATIETY

Pindar is very conscious that praise can make the hearer jaded if it is not directed at him. This danger is encapsulated in the word *koros*, meaning excess or satiety, which can lead to distaste or boredom.[70] It can be avoided by the poet's judicious exercise of *kairos*, a word that is often translated as 'opportunity' but really means 'the right amount' (of time or of anything else).[71] Brevity is one of the laws of epinician; as Pindar says at *Nemean* 4.32ff.: 'The law of song keeps me from telling the long tale, and the pressing hours.'

The late rhetorician Menander shows an awareness of this issue, though he is willing to indulge poets more than prose orators:

> In [the poet's] case the licence to speak at leisure and wrap up the subject in poetical ornament and elaboration produces no satiety or disgust – though I am not unaware that some of the poets themselves introduce untimely expansions of their themes – whereas prose-writers and orators have very little licence.[72]

ENVY

> The splendid work is crown'd today,
> On which Oblivion ne'er shall prey,
> Nor Envy make her spoil.[73]

A much greater danger in praise is that it can arouse envy and destructive malice. Envy was omnipresent in Greek public life. A generation before Pindar was born, Cimon the Athenian had been driven into exile by the tyrant Pisistratus. While in exile he won a victory with the four-horse chariot at Olympia. When he repeated the feat at the next Olympiad (probably 528 BCE) with the same team of horses, he relinquished his prize and allowed Pisistratus to be declared the winner, as a result of which Pisistratus allowed him to return from exile. The same horses again won him victory at the next Olympic Games (524 BCE) after the death of Pisistratus:

> But then, as it happened, he was killed by Pisistratus' sons... The Pisistratidae killed him by getting some assassins to surprise him one night in the town hall. Cimon is buried outside Athens, on the far side of the road called "Through Coele". The mares which won him three victories at Olympia are buried opposite him.'[74]

That 'as it happened' archly conceals a causal connection: it was no coincidence; rather Cimon's racing success – with those remarkable horses – was an overt expression of his continuing social dominance that made his rivals think him too big for his boots. Excess of success led to a form of intolerant hatred that the Greeks called *phthonos*, commonly translated 'envy'.

> Envy is pain at the sight of such good fortune as consists of the good things already mentioned [office, power, wealth, friends, a fine family]; we feel it towards equals; not with the idea of getting something for ourselves, but because the other people have it.[75]

Aristotle's definition, written a hundred years after Pindar's death, is applicable to the world of archaic Greek aristocracy. Plutarch was even more forthright: 'We tend to hate those who lean more towards wickedness, but envy is aroused rather by those who tend to virtue.'[76] Where Aristotle limited envy's objects to 'external' goods (and even excluded, surprisingly, such attributes as beauty),[77] Plutarch includes even good moral qualities as inspiring envy. Anyone who achieves success as radiant as that of a victor in the Panhellenic Games is bound to become the object of envy. Scholars sometimes write as if it were the lower orders who felt envy of the success of the aristocrats, so the point Aristotle makes, that envy is between equals, needs to be borne in mind. (The envy of the gods, so prominent in tragedy, is a different matter, and is a moral indignation against those whose achievements have made them over-proud and ready for a fall.) Envy could even be seen as the motivating factor behind the Athenian institution of ostracism, voting for the exile of whoever seemed to be too big for his community.

From a certain point of view, to be envied is a state to be desired: one becomes 'enviable'. So the archaic Sicilian poet Epicharmus, no doubt with the tyrants of his native island in mind, wrote: 'Who would not wish to become envied, friends? It is clear that the man who is not envied is as nothing. When you see a blind man you pity him, but not a single person envies him.'[78] It is almost a proverb that 'to be envied is better than to be pitied': so says Herodotus at 3.52.5, echoed by Pindar at *Pythian* 1.85. The Sicilian tyrants may have revelled in the envy of others: Hieron's brother was named Polyzalus, which means 'much envied' or perhaps 'much emulated'.

But more often Pindar speaks of the danger that *phthonos* poses to the victor. Interestingly, Bacchylides lays much less emphasis on the matter; however, some fragmentary lines of Ibycus in a poem entitled 'Callias' seem also to be discounting envy: 'Let this labour [of praise] always be mine; and if some mortal upbraids me... I make a still greater boast about these things...'[79] Here are two examples from Pindar:

> Prosperity sustains a matching envy
> whereas the din of a man of low ambition goes unnoticed.[80]

> Blame coming from
> others who are envious hangs over
> those who ever drive first round the twelve-lap course
> and on whom Charis sheds
> a glorious appearance.[81]

The matter is important to Pindar for two reasons: firstly, he must discount the danger of envy before he can embark on a clear statement of the victor's glory, since praise that appears to be excessive will draw the attention of enemies; secondly, if his praise appears to be excessive, critics may be displeased with the poet for praising incompetently. Envy may be aroused by the success itself or by the poet's praise of it. 'Praise of other people is tolerable only up to a certain point,' said Pericles in the Funeral Oration, 'the point where one still believes that one could do oneself some of the things one is hearing about. Once you get beyond this point, you will find people becoming jealous and incredulous.'[82]

As Hugh Lloyd-Jones expressed it in an eloquent passage:

> Envy is the force against which the poet who would praise his patron
> has to struggle, and in order to assure his patron's fame the poet must do
> battle against his detractors; this battle is a common theme of Pindar's
> poetry, and the mention of it serves to guard against the greater danger
> of divine envy of his patrons' greatness.[83]

So in the passage from *Olympian* 6 above, the poet immediately goes on to build to a new climax of praise by stating that the gods have forwarded Agesias' victory:

> [Hermes] it is, O son of Sostratos, who
> with his loudly thundering father fulfils your success.[84]

For Pindar envy is always ultimately futile; it gets the envier nowhere:

> Another man, with envy in his eye,
> rolls an empty thought in the dark
> that falls to the ground.[85]

> Purveyors of slander are a deadly evil to both parties,[86]
> with temperaments just like those of foxes.
> But what profit really results from that cunning?
> None...[87]

Sometimes the train of thought is hard to follow, as at *Nemean* 1.24f.:

> It is his [the victor's] lot to bring
> good men against his detractors as water
> against smoke. Various men have various skills,
> but one must travel in straight paths and strive by
> means of natural talent.

Much scholarly energy has been expended on the interpretation of the metaphor here: does throwing water on smoke extinguish it or make it worse? If we recognise the generic requirements of the passage as 'foil to praise', it is clear that the victor is quenching his detractors, not stirring them up. Water quenches fire, and the smoke generated is quickly dissipated. Simonides Fragment 541 refers to 'futile smoke' as a metaphor for malicious talk, and it is this metaphor that reappears here in 'frozen' form. In other cases historicist critics have assumed that envy is being directed at the poet, not the victor (as apparently at Ibycus Fragment 282B, above). *Olympian* 2.86–8 is a case in point:

> Wise is he who knows many things
> by nature, whereas learners who are boisterous
> and long-winded are like a pair of crows that cry in vain
> against the divine bird of Zeus.

The scholiasts state that the two crows are Pindar's rival poets, Simonides and Bacchylides, but the run of the passage demands that the 'divine bird of Zeus' be the victor, not Pindar;[88] so the crows are the envious who try to achieve success by learning rather than through their inborn excellence.

PYTHIAN 2

The test case for our understanding of the role of discounting envy in praise is *Pythian* 2. In this difficult poem, Pindar has a great deal to say about envy and malice. The earliest occurrence is in 52–6: 'But I must flee the persistent bite of censure, for standing at a far remove I have seen Archilochos the blamer often in straits as he fed on dire words of hatred.' Pindar must avoid vituperation, but this is really a litotic way of saying that he has to praise – but not excessively. Kings, it seems, always liked to surround themselves with wise men to add lustre to their courts: in his essay on flattery, Plutarch mentions the pairs of Solon and Croesus, Plato and Dion, while Pausanias states that in the old days, 'poets lived at the courts of kings... Anacreon lived with Polycrates, tyrant of Samos, and Aeschylus and Simonides made their way to Hiero in Syracuse.'[89] Xenophon wrote a dialogue entitled 'Hieron' in which he cast Simonides in conversation with the king: in it, Hieron insists on the loneliness and pain that attend absolute power, but Simonides' contention is that envy can easily be deflected by appropriate use of wealth, and generosity. For Pindar, buying popularity is not the easy option. Pindar is more concerned with his own task: if he gets praise right, there will be no risk of envy. The poet's authority is the leitmotif of this meditation.

In this poem the advice to Hieron implies that the king is such as Pindar exhorts him to be; as the philosophers say, 'ought' implies 'can'.[90] But advice is mere presumption if it is not delivered by an equal, so Pindar has to establish himself as an equal and an intimate of the king. Plato saw the problem in his second letter to Dionysius:

> Any marks of respect you show me, if you take the lead, will be evidence that you think highly of philosophy... On the other hand any marks of respect that I show you, unless you return them, will be interpreted as evidence of my admiration of and desire for wealth... To put it in a nutshell, if you do homage to me, we both rise in men's esteem; if I do homage to you, we both sink.[91]

Pindar is not expecting homage from Hieron, but he is counting on his respect, so that Hieron will pay attention to what he has to say. The good king is not fooled by flatterers and can take Pindar's discourse at its true worth. Having rejected the vituperative stance of Archilochus at line 55, Pindar will now avoid the opposite trap of flattery:

> Pretty is an ape in the eyes of children, always
> pretty, but Rhadamanthys has fared well because
> he was allotted the blameless fruit of good judgment
> and within his heart takes no delight in deceptions,
> such as ever attend a mortal through whisperers' wiles.[92]

In plain English: 'Simple people are fooled by flatterers, but wise kings have good judgement and don't fall for flattery.'[93]

Pindar does not try to establish his truthfulness by virtue of his status as a poet, as divinely inspired: he looks forward rather to the Aristotelian idea of the orator, whose words are believed because he is a good man.[94]

Pindar now goes on to discount the power of envy and malicious gossip. The lines are obscurely expressed in a series of metaphors, and have elicited pseudo-biographical interpretations in the past,[95] but the key point is that the envy is attendant upon the glory of Hieron, as was recognised by Erasmus

Schmid in his commentary of 1616, in which he labelled the passage '*par-aeneses ad Hieronem de cavendis obtrectatoribus*';[96] it has nothing to do with supposed enemies of Pindar for his association with tyrants. Some 20 lines (76–95) are devoted to discounting envious slander, a remarkably long passage. Pindar has to labour hard to clear away the suspicions with which a tyrant will view his courtiers. Again a parallel with the poem of Hafiz quoted above is relevant:

> ... by the tress of your lasso
> The ill-wisher's neck has become captive in chains.
> The wheeling of the heavens all at once is on the course of justice.
> Rejoice, because the tyrant gets nowhere.[97]

Pindar then concludes the ode with a reassertion of his own integrity, which is enhanced by association with the just king: 'May it be mine to find favour with the good and keep their company.'[98] A man is known by the company he keeps. Pindar has fitted himself into the tyrant's world by using the *topoi* of a genre that normally celebrates aristocrats and their families.

In general, the more difficult a poem, the more inclined the ancient scholars were to find explanations in supposed biographical details about Pindar himself. A notable case is the intervening passage from *Pythian* 2:

> What profit really results from that cunning [of the ape]?
> None, for just as when the rest of the tackle labours
>   in the depths of the sea, like a cork I shall go undipped
> over the surface of the brine.
>   The deceitful citizen cannot utter an effective word
>   among good men, but nonetheless he fawns on all
>   and weaves his utter ruin.
>   I have no part in his impudence.[99]

Here, too, many critics have supposed that Pindar is writing about himself and defending himself against – variously – rival poets, false friends, mali-cious slanderers at Hieron's court or aristocrats indignant at his cultivation of princes. But Erasmus Schmid in 1616 had no doubt that the reference was to Hieron, who is being advised to ignore his detractors. The poet speaks in the first person, but in order to give advice: 'If I were you', as we say. Hieron is strong enough to survive the buffets of slander and envy, and so the way is open for Pindar to offer unstinting praise.[100] The trope reappears in *Olympian* 3.43–5: 'Theron has reached the furthest point with his achievements and from his home now grasps the pillars of Herakles. What lies beyond neither wise men nor fools can tread. I will not pursue it; I would be foolish.' This was recognised by one of Pindar's greatest editors, Georg Dissen, in the early nineteenth century, as advice couched as praise: *'Suavius dicit de se quae Theroni dicere vult'* – 'He makes what he wants to say to Theron more palatable by saying it about himself.'[101]

Rather than ending the chapter on a negative note, let us consider how Bacchylides sets about praising the wealthy and powerful Hieron. Not for him this agonising about whether he is fulfilling his bardic duty correctly. In Bacchylides 3 he has no qualms about praising Hieron simply for his wealth:

> Of all men who dwell in Greece there is none, illustrious Hieron, who will be ready to claim that he sent more gold to Loxias [Apollo] than you. Anyone who does not fatten himself on envy[102] may praise this (flourishing?) horse-loving warrior who holds the sceptre of Zeus..., and has his share in the violet-haired Muses.[103]

These lines follow the narration of the myth (really a legend) about the king of Lydia, Croesus, who believed that he had earned his prosperity by his generosity to Apollo of Delphi. Yet when Cyrus the Mede conquered his city of Sardis, Croesus found himself facing death by burning and complained that all his piety to the gods had been of no avail. The pyre was already alight when Zeus sent a shower of rain and the pyre was extinguished:

> Nothing that the planning of the gods brings about is past belief: Delos-born Apollo carried the old man then to the Hyperboreans and settled him there with his slim-ankled daughters by reason of his piety, since he had sent up to holy Pytho greater gifts than any other mortal.[104]

The story is also told by Herodotus with far greater complexity, and drawing the moral that no man can be sure of happiness until he is dead.[105] For Bacchylides, the message is simple: Croesus won his lucky escape by dishing out gold to the gods, and Hieron can similarly assure himself deathless fame by dishing out gold. Pindar would never say anything so crude. But perhaps it is true, as the scholiasts liked to fantasise, that Hieron found Bacchylides' pretty poetry easier to understand.

VI

TELLING STORIES

The Myths in the Odes

FEW PEOPLES HAVE had a richer repertory of stories about their gods and heroes than the Greeks, and Pindar is one of our most prolific sources for the Greek myths. Almost every ode contains a myth, if not several, and this is as true of the poems for human addressees as it is of those for gods and heroes. Like the tragedians, Pindar scarcely ever turns to historical themes for his narratives,[1] and never in the epinician odes. The gods and heroes are there to evoke another world of timeless excellence, which the human victor temporarily touches through his achievement, or with which the ritual song brings its performers and audience into contact.

It may seem surprising that praise of a human should entail the telling of myths. Menander Rhetor, in his third century CE handbook of rhetoric, is uneasy about the inclusion of myths in speeches of encomium:

> Myths, nakedly set out, pain and distress the hearer very much; they
> should therefore be as brief as possible. Antidotes need to be applied,
> for the sake of brevity and charm; e.g. not introducing every detail in
> a direct form, but omitting some points, conceding some, introducing

135

some by combination, sometimes claiming to give explanations, or not committing oneself to belief or disbelief.[2]

Most of these stratagems can be found in Pindar, making due allowance for the difference between *polis* poetry of the fifth century B C E and international epideictic rhetoric of the third century C E. In many cases it is reasonably obvious why a particular myth has been included, at least in general terms: an ode for an Aeginetan tells a myth about the heroes of Aegina; an Olympian ode (for example *Olympian* 8) may tell of the origin of the Olympic Games; an ode for a Cyrenean (such as *Pythian* 9) may tell a story of the nymph Cyrene. Family and city are praised through the gods and heroes associated with them. Myths often emerge from a gnomic statement and seem to act as a general example: this is most obvious in the case of the athlete–heroes Heracles and the Dioscuri. But it is not always so simple, and even in such cases the choice of a particular episode in a particular poem raises questions. The ancient scholars were often bewildered and resorted to classifying myths as 'digressions'. *Nemean* 1 offers a radiant and unforgettable account of the first of Heracles' labours, when as an infant in his cradle he strangled the two snakes sent by Hera to kill him; the prophet Tiresias then tells of his future apotheosis, 'that he himself in continual peace for all time would be allotted tranquillity as the choicest recompense for his great labours in a blissful home… receiving flourishing Hebe as his wife'.[3] The poem ends with no further allusion to the victor, Chromius, and the ancients struggled to discern the relevance of the myth to the *laudandus*. The scholiast writes:

> There is debate about the motivation for this embarkation on a story about Heracles; for Heracles seems to have nothing to do with the present situation. Aristarchus says that some think that the poet was given a commission to mention the god; this is, as Aristarchus says, implausible. Perhaps it is because Pindar always praises those who achieve success by their nature rather than by training, and Heracles is such a person… But Chaeris says that Chromios, after working with Hieron to gain his ascendancy received a reward from him… But why should Pindar pick on just this moment in Heracles' life to demonstrate his

love of labour? He ought rather to have mentioned all his labours as a whole, and how he cleansed the land and sea and became a god. But Chrysippus says the labour is a Nemean one and so is the victory, and Heracles has been brought into the praise of the victor because of the Nemean lion. Didymus' view is better... that now that Chromius has begun to enter competitions and has won a victory right away, there is hope that he will win other garlands as well.[4]

This long quotation gives a flavour of the kind of speculation that the scholiasts indulged in, and the difficulties they faced in explaining some of the myths. A brief example is the introduction to *Pythian* 5: 'Because the story in the preceding poem [*Pythian* 4] was a narrative digression about Jason, Pindar had to write a second epinician.'[5]

Another form of use of 'digression' as an explanatory category occurs in the scholiast on *Nemean* 4, where Pindar writes (in lines 33–8):

> The law of song keeps me from telling the long tale [the story of Heracles],
> and the pressing hours:
> and by a love charm I am drawn to touch
>   upon the new-moon festival.
> Nevertheless, although the deep salt sea holds you
> by the waist, resist its treachery: we shall be seen
> to enter the contest in the light, far superior to our foes.[6]

By any standards this is an obscure passage. The scholiast's comment is, 'This seems to be directed at Simonides, since he is accustomed to use digressions.'[7] A historicist explanation is sought for a passage that needs to be explained in terms of generic constraints (brevity), and the foregoing myth is characterised as a 'digression'.

The bad practice of thinking of parts of the odes as digressions, as if the poet were unable to control his material, even appears in the terminology of Erasmus Schmid, who uses it to describe every myth, even when there is no obscurity of purpose. Thus, for example, he divides *Olympian* 1 into *exordium* (introduction), *praepositio* (statement of purpose), *confirmatio* (terms of praise), *digressio* on Pelops and *epilogus* (return to praise of Hieron). Extreme cases in the twentieth century were the commentator Erich Thummer, whose view is that all the myths in the odes are merely 'decorative', and C.M. Bowra, for whom the odes became 'a panorama of irrelevant observations on topical questions'.[8] Bowra does concede that:

> Pindar attaches importance both to the choice of a myth and to the actual treatment of it and that he thinks of it as much more than mere decoration, but he rather masks his intentions by the apparent insouci-ance with which he sometimes introduces a myth.[9]

Later: 'The universal character of Pindar's myths, and his skill at embodying it in a dramatic form, make it difficult at times to decide whether he directs his message to an individual or a city.'[10]

In fact every myth has a clear role in the structure of an ode that leads to praise. Furthermore, it has at least two roles: a rhetorical and an ideological one. The rhetorical role of myth is not just that of deepening the context of the victory praised, but also of delaying praise to make the climax more intense. A myth may thus very often be introduced precisely as an outgrowth of a 'break-off' formula, or one of the gnomic statements that can also act as 'joints' of the epinician ode. The ideological role is perhaps most clearly expressed in a case like *Pythian* 9, where Pindar asserts a wish to praise a Pythian victory and then launches straight into a myth as a way of building up to praise. The structural function of myth is illustrated in *Pythian* 9.78–81:

> Great themes briefly to embroider
> wins the ear of the wise; yet, above all, true timing
> achieves the furthest goal. This precept
> Iolaos long ago was seen to honour.

Conway's translation of *kairos* as 'true timing' is preferable to Race's 'deft selection'. The passage is difficult, and the *nin* that Conway interprets as 'this precept' may in fact refer to the *laudandus*, Telesicrates. The point seems to be that Iolaus somehow exemplifies the skill of 'getting it right':

after his killing of Eurystheus he wins himself a place in his ancestral tomb. So the myth illustrates the gnome. In *Pythian* 11 the myth of Agamemnon is broken off with a gnomic statement about envy attending the great, and is then resumed in a form more appropriate to the poet's purpose of praise:

> Can it be, O my friends, that I got confused where the way forked,
> when before I was going on the straight road?[11]

Lyric Narrative

This use of the break-off, as Chris Carey has argued, is integral to the constraints of narrative in lyric, rather than epic. All Greek poets recount myths. The epic tradition of Homer and the Epic Cycle allowed virtually unlimited space for telling the chosen tale, but few lyric poets have so much space at their disposal. The exception is Stesichorus of Himera, whose lyric narratives, as far as we can tell from the surviving fragments, are so generous in scale as to virtually be short epics. Their metre is not far removed from the dactylic hexameter, and much less complex than that of Pindar or the monodic poets. Stesichorus is said to have died in 556 BCE, some 40 years before Pindar's birth. His poetry was widely known in Greece, and Pindar may have had a particularly good opportunity to become acquainted with it on his visit to Sicily in the 470s. Certainly the older poet's influence is very apparent in *Pythian* 4, the longest of Pindar's odes, which narrates a large part of the tale of the Argonauts as background to the colonisation of Cyrene; as we shall see, though, Pindar's narrative approach is much more complex. Ibycus too seems to have devoted much space to myths, as is evident from the long *praeteritio* in Fragment 282:

> But now it was not my heart's wish to sing of Paris, deceiver of his host,
> or of slim-ankled Cassandra and Priam's other children and the unmen-
> tionable day of the capture of high-gated Troy, nor shall I recount the
> proud valour of the heroes whom hollow, many-bolted ships brought
> to be an evil for Troy, fine heroes... On these themes the skilled Muses

of Helicon might embark in story, but no mortal man (untaught?) could tell each detail... [a list of heroes] These have a share in beauty always: you too, Polycrates, will have undying fame as song and my fame can give it.

Other choral poets, like Alcman and Bacchylides as well as the monodic poets Sappho and Alcaeus, have to suggest myths rather than narrate them in full. They could rely on an audience's familiarity with the myths, and a snippet was enough to evoke a whole complex tale. Bacchylides, likewise, often chooses to recount a single episode: Heracles in the Underworld in *Ode* 5, Croesus on the pyre in *Ode* 3, Theseus' visit to the depths of the sea in *Ode* 17. Pindar too does this, though here too he is more complex since he often makes explicit changes to the known forms of the myths.

The art of narrative in Homer has already reached a high degree of artistry. The *Iliad* does not set out to tell the entire story of the Trojan War, but evokes the whole war by concentrating on a period of a few weeks in the final year, which are told more or less consecutively. The *Odyssey* has a more expansive canvas, with a narrative of ten years of Odysseus' wanderings. The danger of an 'and then... and then...' type of narrative is averted by placing the adventures of Odysseus in a frame narrative about Telemachus in Ithaca and his quest to find his father, and by making Odysseus recount a large part of his adventures as a first person narrative to his hosts in Phaeacia. The Iliad also knows this kind of embedded tale – on a smaller scale – when Glaucus in Book 6 recounts his ancestry and the myth of Bellerophon to his opponent, Diomedes. The Homeric Hymns, too, give largely linear narratives of their myths, though these are embedded in a framework of celebration of the god in question.

But in Pindar, the construction of narrative becomes much more complex. The problem of selection of material becomes more acute with the emergence of shorter forms, lyric and even tragedy, which always selects a particular episode from the vast body of stories available. The visual arts must perforce concentrate on a single episode, or series of moments; words can structure a story in a way that has more depth and resonance. So Pindar employs numerous techniques, one of the most common of which in his poetry has conventionally been termed 'ring composition': when a story is introduced by its conclusion and then returns to it at the end. But Pindar's narratives can swing back and forth between different chronological moments. He can even tell a story backwards. He can evoke a whole myth through a single brief action. He can employ flashbacks; and, importantly, he can use prophecy to deepen the chronological range of a story as well as to draw out its wider or divine significance.[12] Let us look at some examples.

In *Nemean* 3 Pindar praises the victory of Aristocleidas:

> If the son of Aristophanes has embarked on utmost
> deeds of manhood, it is no easy task to go yet further
> across the untracked sea beyond the pillars of Herakles,
> which that hero-god established as famed witnesses
> of his furthermost voyage. He subdued monstrous beasts
> in the sea, and on his own explored the streams of the shallows,
> where he reached the limit that sent him back home,
> and he made known the land. My heart, to what alien
> headland are you turning aside my ship's course?
> To Aiakos and his race I bid you bring the Muse.
> The essence of justice attends the precept 'praise the good',
> but longings for foreign themes are not better for a man to bear.
> Search at home...[13]

Pindar elegantly provides his *laudandus* with the extreme of praise by comparing him to the greatest of heroes, Heracles, the 'hero–god', and in one sentence he evokes the whole of Heracles' labours on land and sea, including the marking of the Straits of Gibraltar. But he turns away from this theme: his pretext is that he must praise a hero local to Aegina, but the implication is that comparison of the young victor to the lifetime achievement of the mature Heracles is going a bit too far. Propriety demands the correct measure of praise (the concept elsewhere expressed by *kairos*).

If one seeks a straightforward linear narrative in Pindar, one could hardly choose better than that in *Pythian* 3. This ode is commonly interpreted as a consolation for Hieron on the occasion of an illness, rather than a regular epinician (though a chariot victory is briefly alluded to). Pindar begins with a prayer that the wise centaur Chiron were still alive, and this leads straight into the story of the birth of one of Chiron's most famous pupils, the healing god Asclepios, son of Apollo. Asclepios' mother, Coronis, slept with a stranger even though 'she was carrying the god's pure seed':

> But she could not wait for the marriage feast to come...
> No, she was in love with things
> remote...
> chasing the impossible with hopes unfulfilled.
> Indeed, headstrong Koronis of the beautiful robes
> fell victim to that great delusion, for she slept
> in the bed of a stranger
> who came from Arcadia.
> But she did not elude the watching god...[14]

Apollo, who knows everything that comes to pass, sent plague on her and her neighbours, but when her body was placed on the pyre, Apollo determined to save his unborn son, and seized him from the womb of his dead mother. Asclepios was given to Chiron to be educated, and became a great healer, until he too overstepped the mark and raised a man from the dead, so that Zeus struck him down. The main stages of the story are thus told in consecutive order, though very allusively, and both of the main episodes illustrate the folly of overstepping the mark, of seeking what one should not have – Coronis in taking a second lover, Asclepios in defying death.

The story is not known from other poets than Pindar, though of course all of his myths are gathered together in the comprehensive handbook of Apollodorus; we have to fill in the gaps from later sources. But the tale was doubtless known to his audience, and the selection of episodes to illustrate a point is transparent: Hieron should not expect immortality either, and should not long for what is impossible. A later portion of the ode reminds him to count his blessings:

An untroubled life
did not abide with Aiakos' son Peleus
or with godike Kadmos: yet they are said to have attained
the highest happiness of any men, for they even heard
the golden-crowned Muses singing on the mountain and
in seven-gated Thebes.[15]

Another poem that tells its myth in linear manner, though in fragmented episodes, is *Pythian* 9, where Pindar recounts the myth of the nymph Cyrene, the virgin huntress. Again the ode introduces Apollo and Chiron. Cyrene catches Apollo's eye while she is wrestling with a lion, and he turns to Chiron to ask who she is. Chiron sees the funny side of this,[16] and points out that he is only telling the omniscient god what he must know already, that 'you have come to this glen to be her husband'.[17]

Chiron continues with a prophecy of the career of Cyrene as the origin of the Libyan city of Cyrene. The poet goes on: 'Swift is the accomplishment once gods are in haste, and short are the ways. That very day settled the matter. They joined together in love in the gold-rich chamber of Libya.'[18] There is no need for detailed narrative since the ways of the gods are so swift. The story is a series of moments, but it is given temporal extension as well as significance by Chiron's prophecy about the future.

Another story that is told in order but includes a prophecy, in this case as the final moment, is that of the infant Heracles in *Nemean* 1. Jealous Hera sent snakes to attack him in his cradle, but he sat straight up and strangled them both. The maids and warriors came running in alarm, but when the father arrived and saw 'the extraordinary determination and power of his son' he summoned the prophet Tiresias, 'who declared to him and to all the people what fortunes Heracles would encounter: all the lawless beasts he would slay on land, and all those in the sea' (*Nemean* 1.61–4), as well as Heracles' eventual welcome to Olympus, where the goddess Hebe becomes his bride.[19] This myth does indeed pose puzzles, both in determining its relevance to the victor Chromius and in the fact that the ode concludes with Tiresias' prophecy: there is no return to the subject of the victor. But as a narrative it is clear and

6.1   The infant Heracles strangling the snakes. Attic
red-figure hydria by the Nausicaa painter, from Capua.
c.450 BCE. New York, Metropolitan Museum of Art.

offers a remarkably economical way of reminding hearers of the whole
of the hero's career, while recounting just one episode – which happens
to be the first.

Compare this lapidary sketch of the essentials with Theocritus' narrative of the same events in Idyll 24. The Hellenistic poet clearly follows
Pindar's poem, since he has the same events in the same order: Heracles in
the cradle, the snakes arrive, the family awakes in alarm, Heracles kills the
snakes, Alcmene calls Amphitryon – 'Hurry! Don't wait to put on your san-
dals; I'm scared' – Amphitryon arrives with a sword, at dawn Alcmene calls
Tiresias in to prophesy Heracles' future. Then there is a coda on Heracles'
later childhood. The manner of this epyllion is discursive, even bland. The
scene is a domestic crisis, even with Tiresias' intervention when he 'rose
from his ivory seat and hurried off, unhindered by the weight of years'. The
comparison shows vividly the virtues of lyric narrative, in its tight focus on
a moment of meaning.

A more complex mode of narration meets us very often. It is sometimes referred to as ring composition, a method with epic pedigree,[20] where the narrator begins with a particular moment, then goes back in time to the beginnings of the story and returns to the original moment by regular stages. The story Glaucus tells Diomede in *Iliad* 6 takes this form, though the central narrative about Bellerophon is very long and only comes back right at the end to explaining Glaucus' pedigree. *Nemean* 10 provides an excellent example of this kind of narration. Castor and Polydeuces, the twin sons of Zeus, are introduced at line 49 as ancestral guests of the addressee's family, and as an explanation of the family's athletic prowess: 'Truly the race of gods is faithful.' Then Pindar explains that the twin gods spend alternate days under the earth in Therapnae and in heaven with their father, because the one who was immortal could not bear to be parted from his mortal brother when Castor was killed. This sentence crystallises the 'ethical moment' of choice. Pindar continues: 'For Idas, somehow angry about cattle, wounded him with the point of his bronze spear.'[21] The introduction of the beginning of the story is abrupt. Who is Idas? Why were he and his brother Lynceus angry about cattle? Pindar assumes knowledge of the story in his audience, and also passes over the differing versions of the quarrel between the Dioscuri and the brothers Idas and Lynceus. (One version had it that they fell out over cattle rustling, as depicted on the Sicyonian Treasury at Delphi; another version, told in the *Cypria*, and also by Lycophron, was that they quarrelled over the daughters of Leucippus whom they had abducted. Pindar has even been accused of referring to the ladies as 'cows'.) The story is told in three 'loops' of narrative, each longer than the last. The first sentence, just quoted, introduces the beginning of the story (Idas), an earlier stage (the quarrel) and a later one (the wounding of Castor). Then comes, 'Watching from Taygetos, Lynceus had seen them sitting in the hollow trunk of an oak tree, for of all mortals he had the sharpest eyes.' The moment follows the quarrel but precedes the wounding. The narrative continues forward in chronological time to the suffering of the brothers at the hands of the Dioscuri (chronologically prior to the wounding of Castor) and is then elaborated by a description of the attack that caused the suffering: 'Polydeukes attacked them with his swift javelin and drove the bronze into Lynkeus' side. Zeus

6.2 Castor and Polydeuces, Idas and Lynceus (one figure is lost) rustling cattle. Relief from the Sicyonian treasury, Delphi; sixth century BCE.

hurled against Idas a smoldering thunderbolt of fire.'[22] This second loop of narrative concludes with a *gnome*. The third and final moment of narrative is Polydeuces finding his brother gasping his last, and his prayer to Zeus, which the god answers with the gift of a shared immortality. (The god's words are quoted in Chapter 4, p. 94.)

And, with the 'unloosing of the eye and the voice of bronze-belted Castor', the poem ends. (See Diagram A.)

Another complex narrative is that of *Nemean* 3: the myth of Achilles, which occupies exactly one triad of its ode (perhaps a sign of relatively late date). See Diagram B for the structure of this ode. Lewis Farnell complained in *Pindar: A Commentary* (1932) that the myth was 'disorganised', but in fact it can be interpreted as a spiral progression through three main themes:

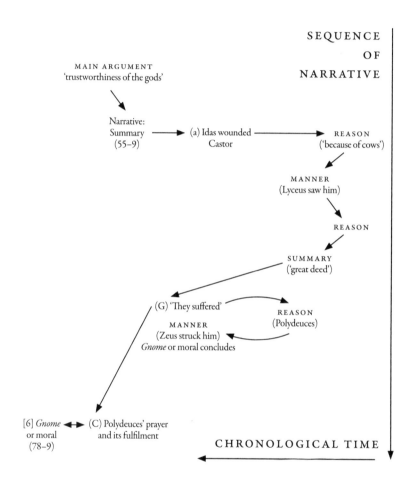

6.3 The Dioscuri myth in *Nemean* 10.

PINDAR

(1) Achilles' natural ability and its expression in his childish play while being educated by Chiron, which evokes the admiration of the gods;

(2) Chiron's earlier pupils, including Jason in the distant past, leading back to Achilles and his education, which was the point of departure;

(3) a leap forward in time to Achilles' later career, from which a single episode is selected: his slaying of Memnon, son of the Dawn, before Troy.

The final section can be compared with the fragment of Bacchylides 27.34–8, where Chiron prophesies Achilles' future deeds: 'What the wise son of

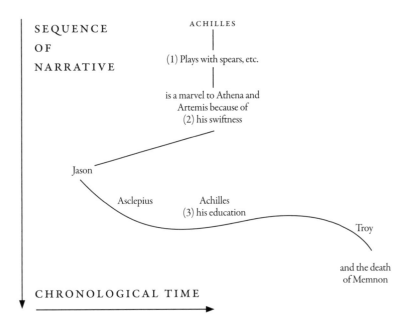

6.4   The Achilles myth in *Nemean* 3.

148

Philyra often says of him, touching his blond head: he declares that he will crimson the eddying Scamander as he kills the battle-loving Trojans.' In the case of *Nemean* 3, it is Pindar himself who provides the prophecy (as it were).

Nemean 4 offers yet another way of deepening mythical chronology, with a myth that swings back and forth through time. First Timasarchus is brought to Thebes, and to the 'blessed hall of Herakles' – which evokes the story of the hero's exploits at Troy, against the Meropes and the giant Alcyoneus. Pindar now drops this story and continues to a second one, more directly related to Aegina:

> Thetis rules
> over Phthia, Neoptolemos over the far-reaching mainland
> where high cattle-grazing forelands descend,
> beginning from Dodona, to the Ionian Sea.
> But at the foot of Pelion, Peleus subdued Iolkos...
> after he had experienced the treacherous wiles
> of Akastos' wife Hippolyta.[23]

Thetis and Peleus are husband and wife (for a while), Neoptolemus is their grandson and the encounter with Hippolyta precedes Peleus' nuptials with Thetis. The fight with Acastus is briefly narrated and is immediately followed by the wrestling with the sea-nymph Thetis as she repeatedly changed form: 'After thwarting the all-powerful fire, the razor-sharp claws of boldly-devising lioness and the points of fiercest teeth, he married one of the lofty-throned Nereids'[24] – namely Thetis. Generations and chronology seem to blur as the narrative focuses in on the 'destiny fated by Zeus', which is the moment of extreme human bliss when Peleus 'beheld the fine circle of seats on which the lords of the sky and sea sat and revealed to him their gifts and his race's power'.[25] Here again, as in the earlier evocation of Heracles, Pindar breaks off: to evoke such blessedness will lead the addressee to overblown expectations. The narrative is highly allusive, which is the easier to take as the myths of this family are intensely familiar to everyone on Aegina.

Another highly familiar myth is that in *Olympian* 10, the foundation of the Olympic Games by Heracles, which can be regarded as so well known that Pindar takes no risk in, effectively, telling it backwards:

> The ordinances of Zeus have prompted me to sing
> of the choice contest, which Herakles founded
> with its six altars by the ancient tomb of Pelops,
> after he killed the son of Poseidon,
> goodly Kteatos, and killed Eurytos, so that he might exact the wage
> for his menial service from mighty Augeas.[26]

Each episode is chronologically prior to the one mentioned before it. From here Pindar starts to move forward again, first through the killing of the Moliones, Kteatos and Eurytos, and then through the sack of Augeas' kingdom. These enemies subdued, Heracles marks out the seat of contest at Olympia.

> And at that founding ceremony the Fates stood near at hand, as did the
> sole assayer of genuine truth, Time, which in its onward march clearly
> revealed how Heracles divided up that gift of war.

The form of narration both shows that everything that happened was pre-destined and reveals the importance of Time in revealing what was always fated. This is one of the ways in which the timeless world of the gods intersects with the mutable and always degenerating experience of humans.[27]

The story of the foundation of the Olympic Games is also told at *Olympian* 3.11–38, and here too it is told backwards before circling again to the present:

> A[1] Heracles establishes the Games
> A[2] He brings the olive tree from the Danube
> B *because* he was able to persuade the Hyperboreans who dwelt there
> C *because* there were no trees at Olympia at that time
> B *So* he went from Arcadia to the Hyperboreans, where he saw trees
> that were
> A[2] suitable to plant at Olympia
> A[1] and he *now* presides at Olympia

It is worth emphasising again how different this style of narrative is from that of epic and even from the other lyric poets. Not only Stesichorus but even Sappho tend to tell their stories straight, in linear fashion. Pindar enfolds different levels of mythological time in order to set the timeless moment of heroic achievement (of the victor) in a golden glow of radiance from the gods.

Even *Pythian* 4, Pindar's longest narrative, in his longest poem, of the tale of the Argonauts, is nothing like epic. The premise is the colonisation of Libya, and the narrative leaps back in time in order to show how that colonisation arose out of predestined events: Medea's prophecy, given 17 generations before, begins the story and shows that everything that happened was what had to happen (as Herodotus was wont to put it). It alludes to one Euphamos (Latin Euphemus) receiving a clod of earth from a god disguised as a man, and the prophecy seems thoroughly enigmatic, though no doubt the hearers knew well what it was about. (The story of the clod that washed up on Libya is also told by Herodotus.[28]) The story of Jason and the quest for the Golden Fleece is then told, more or less in linear fashion, though it, too, is shown as predestined because at the beginning (in lines 71–8) King Pelias is told by an oracle to beware of a man with one sandal. From lines 171 to 246 the story of the voyage and the arrival in Colchis, where Medea assists Jason in carrying out the dangerous tasks set by her father, are straightforwardly told. King Aeëtes reveals the location of the fire-breathing serpent who guards the golden fleece. Pindar skips over what a Homer or Stesichorus would have made the climactic episode of the tale: the slaying of the dragon and the seizing of the fleece; he now leaps forward to the encounter of the Argonauts with the Lemnian women on the journey home, which introduces the mention of Euphamos, sprung from one of those unions, who is the ancestor of the addressee Arcesilaus. So in a sense, the whole long and enthralling narrative was only there to bring about the conclusion (told at the outset) of the story of Euphamos and his clod. The ways of the gods are hidden from men, but they always lead to the desired end.

The use of speeches in this long ode is more extensive than is usual in Pindar, but speeches, like prophecies, are often used to focus or expand a narrative.[29] Bacchylides is much more given to leisurely epic-type speeches, as

in Ode 5; Ode 18 is largely constructed from speeches in dialogue, bringing
the poem closer to drama.

False Tales

In *Olympian* 1 Pindar tells the story of Pelops, the ancestral hero of Olympia,
where the games were held. Poseidon had fallen in love with Pelops, and carried him off to Olympus. How, then, did Pelops come to be under the earth
at Olympia? In order to explain this, Pindar takes issue with the traditional
tale about Pelops – that his father, Tantalus, king of Sipylus, prepared a
banquet at which the gods were to be guests, and in a fit of insane pride, or
a desire to test the gods' omniscience, killed and cut up his young son Pelops
and put him in a stew to feed them. Clotho, one of the three Fates, rescued
Pelops from the cauldron and put his body together again, but a part of his
shoulder was missing as Demeter had already bitten into it, and this was
replaced with a piece of ivory. Pindar dismisses this tale as a false invention
of malicious neighbours: 'But for my part, I cannot call any of the blessed
gods a glutton – I stand back.'[30] When he first introduces the story of the
feast and the ivory shoulder at line 25ff., Pindar comments:

> Yes, wonders are many, but then too, I think, in men's talk
> stories are embellished beyond the true account
> and deceive by means of
> elaborate lies. For Charis [Grace], who fashions all things pleasant for mortals,
> by bestowing honor makes even what is unbelievable
> often believed:
> yet days to come
> are the wisest witnesses.
> It is proper for a man to speak
> well of the gods, for less is the blame.
> Son of Tantalos, of you I shall say, contrary to my predecessors,
> that when your father invited the gods
> to his most orderly feast...

then it was that the Lord of the Splendid Trident seized you,
his mind overcome by desire.

It was later, when Tantalus became arrogant as a result of the favour of the gods, that they punished him by, among other things, sending his son back to earth.

So the refashioning of the myth results in Pelops being back on earth, where he is needed as hero. As for the theology, there is no reason to doubt that Pindar means what he says, that one should speak well of the gods; but the new version of the story also increases Pelops' glory (and Pindar also conceals his murder of Oenomaus, by which he won the chariot race at Olympia) and makes him a more suitable example for praise of the victor.[31]

In this story the sources of the traditional version that Pindar rejects are not easy to identify. In other cases it is clear that he prefers versions from the non-Homeric tradition rather than those sanctified by Homer. At *Nemean* 7.21, Pindar clearly says: 'I believe that Odysseus' story has become greater than his actual suffering because of Homer's sweet verse, for upon his fictions and soaring craft rests great majesty, and his skill deceives with misleading tales.' The immediate occasion of this outburst is praise of Ajax (Aias), whose reputation, Pindar claims, has been eclipsed by that of Achilles as hero of the *Iliad*. The case is made at greater length at *Nemean* 8.22ff., where Pindar places the blame on envy:

> Envy fastens
> always on the good, but has no quarrel with lesser men.
> It was that which feasted on the son of Telamon
> when it rolled him onto his sword.
> Truly, oblivion overwhelms many a man whose tongue
> is speechless, but heart is bold,
> in a grievous quarrel; and the greatest prize
> has been offered up to shifty falsehood.
> For with secret votes
> the Danaans favoured Odysseus, while Aias,
> stripped of the golden armor, wrestled with a gory death.[32]

6.5 The vote over the arms of Achilles; Athena presiding.
Attic red-figure vase by Douris, ARV² 429.26.

It is readily to be understood not only that Pindar supports the Aeginetan
hero Ajax against the smooth talker Odysseus, but furthermore that Odysseus
represents for him many of the characteristics of the democratic government
of Aegina's great enemy, Athens. Odysseus' facility with words seems to
recall the readiness of the sophists to argue any case, good or bad, with equal
aplomb; moreover, the use of secret voting is characteristic of the Athenian
law courts. The voting over the allocation of the dead Achilles' arms was in
the tradition, though it is not in the *Iliad*. It was told in the *Aethiopis*, and is
also depicted in vase paintings, though the vote does not seem to be secret
there. (Some authors, for example Sophocles at *Ajax* 1135, said the voting
was rigged.) In Aeschylus' *Judgement of Arms* the victory was again won by
deceit;[33] Pindar's portrayal of the trickster Odysseus is the beginning of a
long anti-Odyssean tradition in antiquity, which was still to the fore when
Shakespeare wrote *Troilus and Cressida*.[34]

The mention of the *Aethiopis* here raises an important point about
Pindar's choice of myths. As stated above, he rarely follows the versions

of 'Homer', that is of the *Iliad* and the *Odyssey*. Perhaps the fact that these had become a kind of Athenian cultural property after their codification by Pisistratus made them anathema to him. It can often be shown that he is making use of other poems from the Epic Cycle of which we now have only fragments.[35] It might be that he wished to avoid treading where a supreme poet had already trodden – 'Not going on the trodden highway of Homer, but on another's horses, since... winged chariot [of the] Muses I [ride?]'[36] – but there might also be a hint in these unfortunately fragmentary lines that Pindar, travelling with the Muses, has the better version.

The marriage of Peleus and Thetis is a good example. Pindar tells parts of this story in five different odes: *Nemeans* 3, 4 and 5; *Isthmian* 8; *Pythian* 3.[37] A composite narrative would be as follows: after escaping the treachery of Astydameia/Hippolyta and sacking Iolcus, Peleus won Thetis as a bride by wrestling with her. This match was arranged by Zeus, either as a reward for Peleus' piety or because Themis warned him of the danger if he himself married Thetis, as he wished (because Thetis was fated to bear a son who would be greater than his father – in the event, Achilles). Chiron made the detailed wedding arrangements, and the marriage took place in his cave on Mount Pelion; it was attended by the gods, who brought wedding gifts, and the Muses sang. But, as Pindar implies though never explicitly says, the marriage did not last: the story conforms to the folk-tale pattern of the human prince who marries a mermaid but can only keep her as long as they never speak to each other.[38] Peleus' moment of bliss was, as is inevitable for mortals, only a moment.

There are two inconsistencies in this tale: Was Zeus' decision a reward for Peleus or an act of self-preservation for himself? And did Peleus win his bride by wrestling with her, or receive her at a grand wedding? There is no absolute contradiction in these versions, though some scholars have found various parts of them incompatible. Apollodorus 3.13.5 seems to suggest that different parts of the story were found in different poems, but besides Hesiod's *Catalogue of Women* the main poem to treat the saga was the lost *Cypria*, and it seems reasonable to suppose that this is what Pindar followed. At any rate, we can say for sure that he takes no cognisance of the version in the *Iliad*, where Thetis is apparently still leading a happy married life with Peleus.

6.6 Peleus wrestles with Thetis, who transforms herself into a lion and a snake, among other things. Attic red-figure cup, signed by Peithinus. From Vulci. Berlin, Staatliche Museen.

Another example of Pindar's predilection for the Epic Cycle over (our) Homer is his use of the *Thebais*. That he did use it can be stated with some confidence, for his account of the flight of Adrastus after the sack of Thebes *Olympian* 6.2–17[39] and also for the account of the foundation of the Nemean Games. Most of the foundation legends of the Panhellenic Games were created in the sixth century, but the story around which the Nemean Games' origin revolves was in the *Thebais*. They were founded by the Seven against Thebes in commemoration of the dead hero Opheltes, who was bitten by a snake there. The mythographer Apollodorus explains:

> When Adrastus and his party appeared on the scene, they slew the serpent and buried the boy; but Amphiaraus told them that the sign foreboded the future, and they called the boy Archemorus ['beginning of doom']. They celebrated the Nemean games in his honour.[40]

Apollodorus lists the victors in the various events. Because such a recital is very much in the epic manner as we know it from the *Iliad*, and because we know that Homer borrowed material from the *Thebais*, it is likely that this whole account comes from the *Thebais*. The story is also in Bacchylides 9.10–13:

> There demigods with red shields, distinguished Argives, held contests
> for the very first time in honour of Archemorus, whom a monstrous
> fiery-eyed serpent killed as he slept, an omen of bloodshed to come.

(See also Simonides 553 P and Aeschylus' *Nemea*, but the theme does not appear in vase-painting until well into the fifth century.) It is most likely that the existing story of Opheltes' death was adapted in the sixth century, when the foundation legends were being created. The story in the *Thebais* was of course grist to Pindar's mill.

Pindar does not only reject or ignore Homeric versions of the myths; he also rejects other traditional versions. We have already seen this in the case of the myth of Pelops in *Olympian* 1. Another clear example is the treatment of the death of Phocus in *Nemean* 5. Phocus was the brother of the Aeginetan heroes Peleus and Telamon, son of Aeacus by the Nereid Psamathe. His name means 'Seal' (and his mother's name is 'Sand') and it is likely that he was some kind of fishy half-human. In *Nemean* 5.11–18, the three brothers

> Stood by the altar of father Hellanios
> and together stretched their hands toward the sky.
> I shrink from telling of a mighty deed,
> one ventured not in accord with justice,
> how in fact they left the glorious island
> and what fortune drove the brave men
> from Oinona [Aegina].
> I will halt, for not every exact truth
> is better for showing its face,
> and silence is often the wisest thing
> for a man to observe.

Pindar steers clear of mentioning the murder of Phocus by his brothers, as a result of which they were exiled, Telamon to Salamis and Peleus to Iolcus. The decorum of not mentioning a discreditable tale combines with the rhetorical move to the next subject (which happens to be the marriage of Peleus and Thetis), but it is notable that Pindar does not reject the tale as he does that of Pelops: the events are necessary to the story of Peleus and Telamon as he tells it here and elsewhere, so he simply passes over them.

Innovation in stories was not uncommon in the lyric poets. Stesichorus was famous for it. The story went that he had slandered Helen in a poem about Troy, making her into a minx who brought about the war; as a result he was blinded by the gods, so he wrote a second poem, a palinode, in which he stated, 'That story is not true, and you did not go on the well-benched ships and you did not reach the citadel of Troy.'[41] Instead, it was a phantom Helen who went to Troy, while the real Helen spent the war years in Egypt. This was the story that Euripides dramatised in his *Helen*.[42]

Stesichorus also changed a number of other myths, as a commentary found on papyrus makes clear,[43] but what reasons lay behind the changes we cannot say.

The most notorious case of alteration of a myth in Pindar is his treatment of Neoptolemus in *Nemean* 7, for Sogenes of Aegina,[44] and *Paean* 6, which has become a test case for the validity of the kind of historicising arguments put forward by the scholiasts. The ancient scholars Aristodemus and Aristarchus stated that in *Nemean* 7 Pindar was defending himself against a charge of slanderous treatment of the myth of Neoptolemus in a paean. With the publication of the paeans in 1908, it became evident that *Paean* 6 was what they had in mind.

Neoptolemus, the son of Achilles, has the dubious honour of being the first great war criminal in myth: at the sack of Troy, he killed King Priam even though the latter had taken refuge at the altar of Zeus, and he hurled the young child Astyanax from the city walls. Apollo's vengeance was to ensure his death when he visited Delphi, in a quarrel over the sacred meats. Despite this, Neoptolemus became a protecting hero at Delphi and was regarded as responsible for the good conduct of sacrifices. His cult was maintained there by the Aenianes from Dodona, in Neoptolemus' legendary kingdom of Molossia.[45]

In *Paean* 6 Pindar describes his killing of Priam, and how the god 'slew him as he was quarrelling with the attendants over countless honours in his own sanctuary at the broad navel of the earth. Iē sing now, young men, sing the measures of paeans.'[46] According to the scholiasts this passage offended the Aeginetans, and he had to apologise for it when he wrote *Nemean* 7 for the young Sogenes.

This historicising explanation is problematic. As A.P. Burnett says, the scholiasts' idea would destroy the poem as an act of praise, and raises the question of why the Aeginetans would have employed Pindar at all on the occasion of Sogenes' victory. There is, furthermore, no evidence for the date of either poem: *Paean* 6 might well be later. There is a groundswell of opinion that the scholiasts' is the wrong way to interpret the poem, but it still poses real difficulties. Let us begin by quoting the passage in *Nemean* 7 in full.

Honor belongs to those
whose fair story a god exalts after they die.
As a helper, then, I have come to the great navel
of the broad-bosomed earth. For in Pytho's holy ground
lies Neoptolemos, after he sacked Priam's city,
where the Danaans also toiled. When he sailed away,
he missed Skyros, but, after wandering,
he and his men reached Ephyra. In Molossia he was king for a short
time, but his offspring have forever held
that privilege of his. He then went to visit the god,
bringing with him items from the finest spoils of Troy.
There, when he became involved in a quarrel over
sacrificial meats, a man struck him with a sword.
The hospitable Delphians were exceedingly grieved,
but he had paid his debt to destiny, for it was necessary
that within the most ancient precinct
one of the royal Aiakidai remain ever after
beside the god's well-walled temple, to dwell there
as a rightful overseer of processions honouring heroes with many sacrifices.

When it comes to just renown, three words will suffice:
no lying witness presides over his accomplishments.[47]

So far, so good. The narrative is transparent and linear. The presentation of Neoptolemus undoubtedly glosses over any part he might have had in the origin of the quarrel at Delphi and treats him as a great hero of Aegina. Pindar now goes on to state his ties to Aegina as a *xenos* and his duty to praise the victor: 'Keeping away dark blame, like streams of water I shall bring genuine fame... If any Achaian man is nearby, one dwelling beyond the Ionian Sea, he will not blame me; I also trust in the proxeny.'[48]

The references here can be unpacked as follows: the Achaean man is a descendant of Neoptolemus, who will approve of Pindar's treatment of the hero. Bruno Currie has argued that there were cultic links between Aegina and Molossia, and that the addressee's father, Thearion, is likely also to have been a member of a hereditary guild of officials at the institution in Aegina known as the Thearion, which would have been responsible for arranging sacred embassies to Delphi.[49] (Sacred ambassadors were known as *theoroi*, or in the dialect of Aegina *thearoi*.)

The choice of Neoptolemus rather than another hero as an example for Sogenes might be explained in terms of the performance context of *Nemean* 7. The occasion for the ode might have been a sacrifice followed by feasting at the Aeginetan *thearion*, perhaps a sacrifice preliminary to the Delphic Theoxenia, where Neoptolemus received cult honours.[50]

There is no space here to recapitulate Currie's detailed arguments, which occupy over 40 pages of his book. Suffice it to say that this approach gives meaning to the myth and the *gnomai* as acts of praise. Currie's proposal for the association of the hero with the victor is consonant with the rest of his book, which argues that victorious athletes do, or may, become heroes and receive cult in their own right: 'Although Sogenes is a boy victor and his victory is in the lowest-ranking of the Panhellenic Games, he has broken into the company of athletes who might aspire to heroization.'[51] More simply, Burnett suggests that Neoptolemus is a suitable myth for Sogenes simply because of the extreme youth of both characters: Neoptolemus, as son of the young Achilles, is always envisaged as an impetuous youth.[52]

A problem remains: the concluding lines of the poem are by any interpretation puzzling. After the myth, Pindar has returned to praise of Nemea,
invocation of its presiding deity, Zeus, and prayers for Sogenes' future and
the prosperity of his descendants. Then: 'My heart will never say that it has
treated Neoptolemos with unyielding words, but to plow the same ruts
three and four times is pointless, like someone yapping at children, "Corinth
belongs to Zeus".'[53]

Why does Pindar return to Neoptolemus, and why does he sound so
defensive? For Lloyd-Jones, these lines were the sticking point that meant
the one poem must be an apology.[54] Currie's approach is subtle.[55]

There is a logical connection between the laudator's denial that he has dis-
honoured the hero and his comparison of the *laudandus* to the hero through
the parallels developed in lines 93–101, the prayers for Zeus and Athena to
protect Sogenes. While the comparison of Sogenes to Neoptolemus elevates
the former, it runs the risk of degrading the latter.

Currie goes on to cite some pertinent parallels where 'to put humans
on a par with the gods is to devalue the latter'. The argument is cogent and
may well be right. Controversy will continue to affect this poem until, *per
impossibile*, concrete historical evidence emerges to explain all the apparent
allusions. Whether one is convinced by all their arguments or no, Currie
and Burnett have both shown that it is possible to interpret the poem, and
its myth, consistently as a continuous act of praise for the boy Sogenes.

Conclusion

Pindar is one of the great storytellers of antiquity. The myths, which he
evokes more often than narrating them in full, shed a god-given radiance on
the victor who for his moment of glory steps into the world of the heroes.
Behind every human act there lies the favour of the gods or a parallel with
the heroes. These are not just stories about a legendary past; they are ever-
present religious truths. Pindar's manner of narration, which cancels, reverses
or coalesces chronological time, sets the victors in a timeless world that, in
modern terms, might be called heaven on earth.

A final example shows Pindar adapting this approach to the particular beliefs of an addressee, in this case Theron, whose adherence to the mystery religion of Demeter and Persephone, presiding deities of Sicily, is plain. The myth in *Olympian* 2 is Pindar's most unusual, as it describes not the actions of heroes but the fate that awaits the blessed dead who have been initiated into the mysteries. Included among them is Peleus, who in other poems is an epitome of human bliss because of his wedding on Olympus, where the Muses sang for him.

> Those with the courage to have lived
> three times in either realm, while keeping their souls
> free from all unjust deeds, travel the road of Zeus
> to the tower of Kronos, where ocean breezes
> blow round
> the Isle of the Blessed, and flowers of gold are ablaze,
> some from radiant trees on land, while the water
> nurtures others; with these they weave
> garlands for their hands and crowns for their heads,
> in obedience to the just counsels of Rhadamanthys,
> whom the great father keeps ever seated at his side,
> the husband of Rhea, she who has
> the highest throne of all.
> Peleus and Kadmos are numbered among them,
> and Achilles too...[56]

Scholars have debated whether Pindar himself may have been an initiate, drawing attention to mystery religions in Boeotia;[57] but there is no need to assume this to explain this passage, a myth chosen for its applicability to the addressee. Greek polytheism is non-exclusive and all the gods are there to be called on when need arises. Pindar's poetic 'wisdom' is the channel of communication that brings the gods closer to men.

VII

RECEPTION

AFTER THE WORK OF THE Alexandrian grammarians, we find little awareness of the poetry of Pindar and other lyric poets until the rebirth of lyric poetry in Rome with Catullus and then Horace. Bound to a social context and made inaccessible by their use of dialects that became unfamiliar as the koine form of Greek dominated the Hellenistic world, the lyric poets had become writers of interest mainly to scholars.[1] A major exception to this generalisation is Theocritus, who took Pindar as a kind of model in three of his idylls written in the third century BCE: *Id.*17, 'Encomium to Ptolemy II', *Id.*22, 'The Dioscuri' and *Id.*24, 'The Childhood of Heracles'.[2] The third of these has already been discussed in the preceding chapter on narrative. 'The Dioscuri', like 'Heracles', is an epyllion, or mini-epic, that concentrates on relating two episodes from the life of Castor and Pollux with epic breadth. The second of these is the conflict with Idas and Lynceus narrated by Pindar in *Nemean* 10, but Theocritus stops at the killing of Idas by Zeus with his thunderbolt, and does not allude to the magical moment of Castor's reanimation that concludes Pindar's poem. Theocritus' conclusion is in entirely conventional hymnic style, like many of the Homeric Hymns:

> The man who fights Tyndareus' sons is the loser.
> Their power is not to be challenged. It comes from heaven.
> Goodbye now, children of Leda, and may you send
> My hymns long-lasting fame![3]

The 'Encomium to Ptolemy' is Theocritus' most Pindaric poem, though the differences are still immense. Theocritus begins with two lines of praise of Zeus before turning to Ptolemy, 'the noblest man', and asserting the value of praise in song. He gives details of Ptolemy's genealogy, praises his uxorious love of his wife Berenice (without mentioning that she is also his sister). A brief mythic allusion to Achilles' birth from Thetis paves the way for a mythicised account of Berenice's bearing their son, Ptolemy. Praise of Egypt's prosperity follows, and then of Ptolemy's personal wealth and his piety to the gods. In the praise of his wealth is embedded the usual hint from poet to patron:

> Proudly the servants of the Muse record
> The patron's bounty, and exalt his name,
> Ptolemy the Generous! What nobler aim
> Can wealth achieve than honour in the world?[4]

The poet's ability to provide *kleos* has come a long way from Homer, and Pindar's 'mercenary Muse' has now lost all shame. The poem reflects the circumstances of poetry at the court of an autocrat whose power ranged far wider than even that of the tyrants of Sicily to whom Pindar strove to measure his poetry. Theocritus' commonplace toadying shows by contrast how great an achievement is Pindar's stance as inspired prophetic bard, and link between gods and men.

Horace

Theocritus' poems are in hexameters. The habit of lyric composition fell largely into abeyance in the Hellenistic period in favour of hexameters and elegiacs. But when Catullus in the late first century BCE revived the simpler lyric metres of the Greeks along with elegiac verse, he was soon followed by Horace, who explored for the first time the richness of archaic Greek lyric metre. Horace concentrated on the metres of the monodic poets Sappho and Alcaeus. He gave his reasons for eschewing the grandeur of Pindaric verse in his poem *Odes* IV.2, *Pindarum quisquis studet aemulari*:[5]

> He, who to Pindar's height attempts to rise,
> Like Icarus, with waxen pinions tries
> His pathless way, and from the venturous theme
> Shall leave to azure seas his falling name.
>
> As when a river, swollen by sudden showers
> O'er its known banks, from some steep mountain pours,
> So in profound, unmeasurable song
> The deep-mouth'd Pindar, foaming, pours along.
>
> Well he deserves Apollo's laurel'd crown,
> Whether new words he rolls enraptur'd down
> Impetuous through the dithyrambic strains,
> Free from all laws, but what himself ordains;
>
> Whether in lofty tone sublime he sings
> The deathless gods, or God-descended kings,
> With death deserv'd who smote the centaurs dire,
> And quench'd the fierce Chimaera's breath of fire
>
> Or whom th'Olympic palm, victorious prize!
> Immortal crowns, and raises to the skies,
> Wrestler or steed – with honours that outlive
> The mortal fame, which thousand statues give,
>
> Or mourns some hapless youth in plaintive lay,
> From his fond, weeping bride, ah! torn away...
> Thus when the Theban swan attempts the skies,
> A nobler gale of rapture bids him rise.[6]

Horace goes on to contrast Pindar's grandeur with his own poetic practice, which he compares to a bee flitting from flower to flower. The image of

Pindar's inimitable splendour is filled out with a number of references to the odes: Bellerophon's encounter with the Chimaera in *Olympian* 13; the odes for the Sicilian tyrants or 'kings'; the Olympian victory odes; and the laments, now largely lost to us but known from a few fragments (128–37). An important point is Horace's description of Pindar's poetry as 'profound, unmeasurable song', *numeris lege solutis*, which literally means 'in metres with no laws, no regularity'. The complex metres of Pindar's poetry were not understood, and his verse was thought to be, if not free verse, exactly, at least so irregular in its line lengths and metrical patterns as to be virtually unintelligible as verse. This opinion continued to hold sway as late as the seventeenth century, when Abraham Cowley wrote in the preface to his translation of *Olympian* 2:

> We must consider that our ears are strangers to the musick of his num-
> bers, which sometimes (especially in Songs and Odes) almost without
> anything else, make an excellent poet; for though the grammarians
> and criticks have laboured to reduce his verses into regular feet and
> measures (as they have also those of the Greek and Latine Comedies)
> yet in effect they are little better than prose to our ears.

This poem sets a tone for Horace's fourth book of odes, in which two others – 4 and 14 – are conspicuously Pindaric praise poems. *Odes* 4.4 celebrates the victories of the two sons of Augustus, Drusus and Tiberius, north of the Danube in 15 BCE. Like Pindar, Horace insists that inborn ability counts for at least as much as education and training. The second part of the ode celebrates the strength of Roman arms through a long speech placed in the mouth of Hannibal, Rome's greatest enemy, at last defeated in the Punic Wars 200 years before. A piece of republican history takes the place of a myth, as so often happens in Roman writing.[7] The poem opens with an extended Pindaric simile comparing the heroes to an eagle, before homing in on the Raetian and Vindelican campaigns. In lines 18 to 22, Horace shows his Pindaric credentials with a mannered break-off formula about the Amazons, which unlike Pindar's originals does not signal any unease about the direction in which the praise is going; it is simply a way of moving on to the next subject – *fortes creantur fortibus et bonis*, the praise of inborn virtue – which continues to line 36. Now comes the 'myth': Hannibal asserts that it is victory simply to escape the Romans, and ends with lamentation for his dead brother.

The last four lines are a crux. On the Pindaric model (*Nemean* 1, *Nemean* 10) one might expect the poem to end where the speech ends. But does Hannibal really, in the commentator Richard Thomas' words, 'praise the sagacity of the man who delivered his dead brother's decapitated head to him'?[8] The matter has been disputed since antiquity and is unlikely ever to be resolved: whichever solution the reader prefers, it does not detract from the profoundly Pindaric meaning and structure of the ode.

Much of Horace's Book 4 is in fact Pindaric in conception. Ode 5 is also for Augustus. It uses a symposiastic trope in the reference to serving wine (see lines 33–5) but is otherwise straightforward in conception: 'We miss you, welcome back.' Ode 6 is hymnic/encomiastic in plan. It begins from Apollo, and offers a kind of 'hymn to Achilles' like a Paean;[9] and it ends by establishing Horace's credentials through a *sphragis*, a 'seal', that establishes the author's authority, though in less ringing tones than *Odes* 3.30. Odes 7 and 8 break the pattern, but 9 is praise for Lollius: in it, Horace avers that all heroes need a *vates*, a poet–prophet, and in the course of doing so invokes all the lyric poets as precedents.[10] Lines 34 to 44 detail all the vices that Lollius avoids, but if this is supposed to be Pindaric 'advice', the actual praise never seems to arrive, and the ending is thoroughly downbeat. Following foil is pushed beyond what Pindar would have done. Even Ode 11, an invitation, has a Pindaric moment at line 29 where the recipient is warned to 'know his limits', while Ode 12 has a Pindaric metaphor at line 26: *nigrorum ignium*, 'black fires'.

The last of the encomiastic odes, 4.14, for Augustus, is more straightforward than 4.4. As Fraenkel put it:

> By writing the epinikion for Drusus in his grandest style, Horace had made it exceedingly difficult for himself to produce a poem to match

this ode when he was soon afterwards called upon to celebrate the victories won by Tiberius in the course of the same campaign in which his younger brother had distinguished himself.[11]

The structure is again Pindaric, with extended periods and similes, but no myth and no reliance on vatic statements or tropes like the break-off. But neither is there the slightest hint of the poet's relation to the victor(s), neither as prophet nor as hireling. Horace knows his own value as a poet[12] and is secure in the *princeps'* favour.

The Renaissance

Though there were no further significant imitators of Pindar (to my knowledge) in the millennium that followed Horace, his poetry began to be regarded highly as a model with the rediscovery of antiquity in the Italian Renaissance. The first poet to model himself on Pindar was Francesco Filelfo (1398–1481), the leading humanist of the quattrocento. Most of his odes (written in Latin) are addressed to the great men of the day, and many of them take the form of encomium, though he covers a wide range of themes including war, patronage, friendship and how to be a good ruler. His metres are all taken from Horace, but structurally they are on what Filelfo conceived to be a Pindaric model. In fact they lack the concision and elegance of Horace as well as the startling metaphors and juxtapositions of Pindar. Above all one sees the influence of rhetorical theory in their composition, and many of them are much longer than even Pindar's epinicians, let alone Horace's odes. Filelfo's Ode II.10, *Quem tibi pulchris capias canendum*,[13] to Gaspar da Vimercate, wears its Pindaric affiliations clearly on its sleeve:

> Of what great man worthy of praises, beautiful and well-deserved, do
> you think you should sing, O Clio? What man would you hymn with
> a lofty poem? For time does not permit you to celebrate a star of the
> highest goodness refulgent with every title and honor – King Charles.

For he flies throughout the whole world, like the sun shimmering with wondrous rays, which shining piety spreads over all the lands. Among high kings, a poem awaits Charles, which all peoples will throng to hear and which neither time nor tempests will efface.

But now, O Clio, give satisfaction to a tired poet. If you could celebrate a man in song, who alone would be first in glory among all the Milanese? The Milanese have brought forth no one in our time with as much virtue as Gaspar possesses.[14]

The opening echoes Pindar's *Olympian* 2, 'What man, god or hero...?', and employs an address to the Muse in the Pindaric manner. The reference to King Charles as a star echoes the comparison of the Olympic Games to a star in *Olympian* 1, while the whole opening 'paragraph' is structured as a tricolon, leading to the celebration of Charles; the whole paragraph in praise of Charles then acts as foil to his real subject, the lesser hero Gaspar, introduced by a 'break-off' and turn to a new subject with 'But now, O Clio'. Filelfo has absorbed the rhetorical structure of the ode but not the unique qualities of its poetry.

Many other Renaissance poets composed Latin Pindaric odes, as well as odes that followed a Horatian model. Among them may be counted Giovanni Pontano, Benedetto Lampridio, Julius Caesar Scaliger, Luigi Alamanni, Antonio Minturno and Giovanni Chiabrera.[15] None of these are of particularly high quality (Pontano is perhaps the best as a poet), but it is worth mentioning the poems of Maffeo Barberini (later Pope Urban VIII), who composed several odes, both secular and sacred, in a triadic Pindaric manner: 'Hymn to the Holy Spirit', 'Ode on John the Baptist', 'Ode on Mary Magdalene', 'Ode on St Laurence' and 'Ode on St Louis, King of France'. The ode on (or to) Mary Magdalene, after a grand opening describing the nature of *blanda voluptas* (seductive pleasure), swooping down on her many-coloured wings (*pennis innixa versicoloribus*), recounts to the unhappy saint her own past history:

But [at line 109] Magdalene safely passed through the Sicilian straits and the rage of Charybdis, passed through the borders of Italy, and arrived at the cities of Gaul. Here by the approval of God and led by the heavenly powers she settled in the port of Marseille, and spread the name of Christ to the gentiles. Here she dwelt in seclusion in a cave high in the mountains, which was almost touched by the stars. Here she lamented and wept; here she is attended by the watches of angels singing; here she meditated on Christ with no thought of herself. 'O how soiled I am by my crimes! O see me lying prone!' – sweet leader of all penitents. Christ heard you... Hail, rock dear to God, hail, famous spring; now the very peaks of Pindus seem shabby to me.

The Latin is almost as prosy as my translation, and the succession of metrical elements is bewildering and lacks the harmony of Pindar, but there is no doubt that Pindar is the model behind this remarkable celebration of Christian salvation.

A greater poet by far, Pierre Ronsard (1524–85) also sought inspiration in Pindar and adapted some very Pindaric techniques in his odes. The second poem of Book I closely echoes the movement of the opening of Pindar's *Olympian* 7:

> *Comme un qui prend une coupe*
> *Seul honneur de son trésor,*
> *Et de rang verse à la troupe*
> *Du vin qui rit dedans de l'or,*
> *Ainsi versant la rousee,*
> *Dont ma langue est arrousee,*
> *Sur la race des Valois,*
> *En son doux Nectar j'abreuve*
> *Le plus grand Roy qui se treuve*
> *Soit en armes, ou en lois.*[16]

The praise (or flattery) is straightforward, but the poet places himself in the same relation to his addressee as does Pindar in his ode for Diagoras, though he does not evoke the further level of comparison with the wedding-guest toasting a bridegroom. So rarely do Pindar's imitators pack as much into a few words as does their original.[17]

Ronsard adopted what he thought was an explicitly Pindaric stance in *Odes* I.11, where he writes of '*Le bon poète endoctriné/ par le seul naturel bien-né*' and contrasts him with '*ces rimeurs qui ont appris/ Avec travail peines et ruses*'.[18] Echoing the famous lines of *Olympian* 2 in which Pindar compares the eagle to the chattering crows who try to do him down, and adopting the conventional interpretation that it is Pindar contrasting himself with his 'rivals' Bacchylides and Simonides, Ronsard goes on:

> *Eux comparez à nos chants beaux,*
> *Sont faits semblables aux corbeaux*
> *Qui dessous les feuilles caquettent*
> *Contre deux Aigles, qui aguettent*
> *Aupres du throne de leur Roy.*[19]

And Ronsard proudly states his own mission:

> *L'ayant prise* [sc. *la Muse*] *pour ma guide*
> *Avec le chant incognu*
> *De mon luth, je suis venu*
> *Où Loire en flotant se ride*
> *Contre les champs plantureux*
> *De tes ancestres heureux.*[20]

The rhetorical structure of the Pindaric ode was elaborated in great detail by the great scholar Erasmus Schmid of Wittenberg in his edition of 1616, making use of the principles of the French humanist Peter Ramus (1515–72), who rejected Ciceronian models of rhetoric for a more dialectical approach that unpicks the chains of arguments in a piece of writing. Thus Schmid already anticipated the work of Bundy in the twentieth century in showing how everything in a Pindaric ode tends to the single end of praise. The short ode *Olympian* 5 offers a good example of his method of analysis:

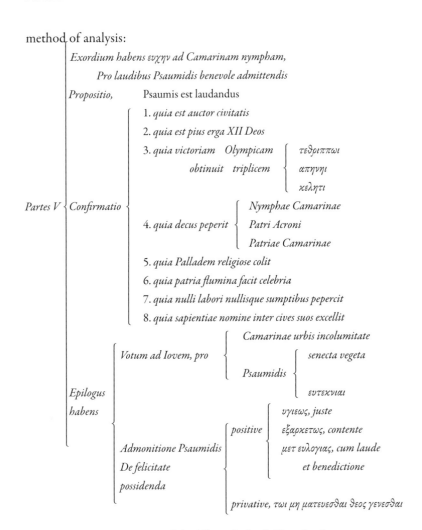

7.1   Erasmus Schmid's analysis of *Olympian* 5.

This elaborate diagram (p. 139 of his edition) divides the ode into five sections, the *exordium*, or opening sally; the proposition or statement of the theme (Psaumis is to be praised); the confirmation, giving eight reasons for his praise; and the epilogue, further divided into two parts – a prayer to Zeus and advice to Psaumis. At first sight bewildering and complex, it is in fact a very workable analysis of the train of thought in the ode. If the model sometimes became shaky or excessively complex when applied to a longer or more elaborate ode, it still provided a system for analysis that completely belied the charge of rambling. It even helps with such notorious problem poems as *Pythian* 2 and *Nemean* 7.

The edition was prefaced by a number of Latin epigrams in praise of Schmid's work; one of them, by M. Justus Grisius of Tübingen, is itself a short Pindaric ode in form, with strophe, antistrophe and epode. The antistrophe begins with the turn to the *laudandus, culte o Schmidi* ('O cultivated Schmid'), and praises him, *sic modos sermonis adsiduus imbibisti*: 'Thus you have thoroughly swallowed down the methods of construction of his argument'.

In the year that the cultivated Schmid's edition was published, the poet Andreas Gryphius (1616–64) was born. Some of his poems use the Pindaric model of strophe–antistrophe–epode ('*Satz–Gegensatz–Zusatz*'), and a rather irregular metrical structure though strophic response is observed. An example is his reworking of Psalm 71:20, which begins, '*Reiss Erde! Reiss entzwey!*' ('Break open, earth, break asunder!') a very un-Pindaric beginning. Apart from metre and form the poem has little in common with Pindar. After the opening address to Earth, most of the poem is an anguished out-pouring of emotion to God. There is no myth, no gnomic moralising, and of course no *laudandus*. There are, then, none of the elements that give a Pindaric ode its complex levels of meaning.

The English Pindarists

Ben Jonson (1572–1637) had an instinctive understanding of the poet's method of discourse. In his poem 'To the Immortal Memory and Friendship of that Immortal Pair, Sir Lucius Cary and Sir H. Morison', he created for the first time a poem that can stand beside Pindar's own as an example of the Pindaric ode. It uses triadic structure (Turn–Counter-turn–Stand) and strophic response. It is a poem of praise and also of lament, since the heroes he celebrates are dead. It *opens* with a 'digression',[21] a 'myth' from Roman history about a child that refused to stay in the world into which he was born and retreated into his mother's womb to die. This leads to moralising about the difference between longevity and value in a life, and thence to the direct praise of Morison and his deeds, summed up in the famous lines:

> It is not growing like a tree
> In bulk, doth make man better be;
> Or standing long an oak, three hundred year,
> To fall a log, at last, dry, bold and sere:
> A lily of a day,
> Is fairer far, in May,
> Although it fall, and die that night;
> It was the plant, and flower of light.
> In small proportions, we just beauties see:
> And in short measures, life may perfect be.[22]

These lines occupy the third strophe (or 'Turn') and continue with direct address to Cary, asserting Morison's immortality and his own authority to assert this:

> And there he lives with memory; and Ben
> Jonson!

He now has the power to assert the greatness of both his living and his dead addressee, who are compared with the Dioscuri. At the same time, the imagery of the tree seems to owe something to Pindar's lines in *Nemean* 8.40ff.: 'Excellence grows like a tree that springs up to fresh dew, when lifted among wise and just men to liquid heaven,' though Jonson takes the trope a stage further.

Jonson's poem shows a thorough internalisation of the Pindaric rhetoric, from the use of myth to make a moral point to the need to establish the poet's own authority to make praise permanent. How different this is from Abraham Cowley's remarks about Pindar's seeming madness. But Cowley (1618–67) did go on to defend the poet:

We must consider in Pindar the great difference betwixt his age and
ours, which changes, as in pictures, at least the colours of poetry, the
no less difference betwixt the religions and customs of our countries,
and a thousand particularities of places, persons and manners, which
do but confusedly appear to our eyes at so great a distance. And lastly,
we must consider that our ears are strangers to the musick of his numbers, which sometimes (especially in songs and odes) almost without
anything else, makes an excellent poet.[23]

This effort of historical imagination ensured that Cowley's were the first
effective translations of Pindar's poems; he terms them 'imitations', but in
general they stick closely to their models, and we may regret that he only
attempted two: *Olympian* 2 and *Nemean* 1. He shows, however, no awareness of metrical and strophic response.

The Pindaric model was important to Cowley; he also translated Horace's
ode about Pindar in four stanzas of irregular metre. The same free structure
is apparent in his other 'Pindarique Odes', which include a poem of praise
of Thomas Hobbes, an encomium of the Roman hero Brutus, a rhapsodic
'Of Life and Fame', and a version of Isaiah I.34, as well as a narrative about
'The Plagues of Egypt'. The style seems to give the poet licence for a kind of
fervid, ecstatic effusion of ideas, which was to characterise the ode thereafter:
think of Keats and Wordsworth. He neatly imitates various Pindaric tricks,
such as the break-off:

> Stop, stop, my Muse, allay thy vig'rous heat,
> > Kindled at a Hint so Great.
> Hold thy Pindarique Pegasus closely in,
> > Which does to rage begin...[24]

... in a poem he describes as 'truly Pindarical, falling from one thing into
another, after his Enthusiastical manner'.

Cowley's manner in the translations is to smooth out the angularities of
Pindar's speech by increased wordiness. His *Olympian* 2 begins:

Queen of all Harmonious things,
Dancing words, and speaking strings,
What God, what Hero wilt thou sing?
What happy man to equal glories bring?
     Begin, begin thy noble choice,
And let the hills around reflect the image of thy voice.
     Pisa does to Jove belong,
     Jove and Pisa claim thy song.

Several contemporaries of Cowley also made use of the Pindaric mode, though not in so overt a manner. Richard Crashaw (1613–49) sometimes Pindarises in his Latin dithyrambs as well as his English odes. As Carol Maddison writes, 'As in Pindar the style is paratactic, but, unlike Pindar's, most of these odes are static, there is no action or story, only wit and highly refined emotion.'[25] Crashaw's love of metaphysical conceits may possibly have taken a cue from some of Pindar's more startling metaphors: in 'To the Name above Every Name, the Name of Jesus. A Hymn' they tumble one upon another:

O, see so many worlds of barren years
Melted and measured out in seas of tears!
O, see the weary lids of wakeful hope,
Love's eastern windows, all wide ope,
          With curtains drawn
To catch the day-break of thy dawn!...
Lo, where it comes, upon the snowy dove's
Soft back, and brings a bosom big with loves![26]

The 'Ode on the Morning of Christ's Nativity' of John Milton (1608–74) is Pindaric in its stanzaic form, though his language works very differently; likewise 'Alexander's Feast' by John Dryden (1631–1700) follows the form, though not much else, in an essentially narrative poem, though it is nominally in praise of music.

     In the next century, Gilbert West (1703–56) used similar diction in his translation of a selection of 12 of Pindar's odes, but his historical understanding represented an advance over Cowley. In his own preface he cites the preface of William Congreve to a translation of two odes, in which he emphasises the regularity of Pindar's metrical structures: 'On the contrary (adds he) there is nothing more regular than the Odes of Pindar, both as to the exact observation of the measures and numbers of his stanzas and verses, and the perpetual coherence of his thoughts.'[27] West goes on to explain the nature of strophic responsion and its connection with dance. He also argues that the reason for the wide range of topics covered in a Pindaric ode is that the victory itself

> could rarely furnish out matter sufficient for an ode of any length, so
> would it have been an indecency unknown to the civil equality and
> freedom, as well as to the simplicity of the age in which Pindar lived,
> to have filled a poem intended to be sung in publick, and even at the
> altars of the gods, with the praises of one man only.[28]

This assertion, alas, is just the reverse of the truth, and the vision of the uncorrupted and democratic Greek past is one that does not apply to Pindar's milieu. But West had also done extensive research on the Olympic Games and added to his translation a valuable 'Dissertation on the Olympick Games', to demonstrate the importance of athletic excellence in Greek culture.

West's translations strive consciously for sublimity and are often effective, despite a tendency to rococo decor. In *Isthmian* 2 he evokes the old days when:

> As yet the Muse, despising sordid gain,
> > Strung not for gold her mercenary lyre:
> Nor did Terpsichore adorn her strain
> > In gilded courtesy and gay attire,
> > With fair appearances to move the heart,
> And recommend to Sale her prostituted art.

> (Epode I)
> But now she suffers all her tuneful train
> > Far other principles to hold;

And with the Spartan Sage maintain,
> That man is worthless without gold.
This Truth himself by sad experience prov'd,
Deserted in his Need by those he lov'd.
Nor to thy wisdom is this truth unknown,
No longer therefore shall the Muse delay
To sing the rapid steeds, and Isthmian Crown,
Which the great Monarch of the briny Flood
> On lov'd Xenocrates bestow'd,
His gen'rous Care with Honour to repay.

(Strophe II)
Him too, his Agrigentum's brightest Star,
> Latona's son with favourable Eyes
At Crisa view'd, and bless'd his conqu'ring Carr...

Thomas Gray (1716–71) was a little younger than West. His Pindaric odes, 'The Progress of Poesy' and 'The Bard', consciously follow the triadic model, but they have no addressee or encomiastic purpose: they are outpourings of the poet's own ideas. 'The Progress of Poesy' contains the famous lines:

Oh lyre divine, what daring spirit
Wakes thee now? Tho' he inherit
Nor the pride, nor ample pinion,
That the Theban Eagle bear
Sailing with supreme dominion
Through the azure deep of air:
Yet oft before his infant eyes would run
Such forms, as glitter in the Muse's ray
With orient hues, unborrow'd of the Sun:
Yet shall he mount, and keep his distant way
Beyond the limits of a vulgar fate,
Beneath the good how far – but far above the great.[29]

The Pindaric imagery here is borrowed from the lines at the end of *Olympian* 2, of which Ronsard (above) also made use, and which have made the term 'The Theban Eagle' a familiar metonymy for Pindar himself.[30]

The German Enlightenment and Hölderlin

Goethe's discovery of classical antiquity led him to Pindar, but for him, as for Cowley, he was a 'god-intoxicated dithyrambist',[31] as he makes clear in 'Wanderers Sturmlied'. Trevelyan cites Wilamowitz: 'In the harsh word-order, that breaks every grammatical rule, he imagined himself to be following Pindar, perhaps also in the rhythms. In fact no greater contrast could exist than that between the lawless style of this unschooled revolutionary and Pindar's rigid technique.'

Goethe's younger contemporary Friedrich Hölderlin (1770–1845) might have earned similar criticism from that great philologist, but his harshness represents a genuine engagement with the style of Pindar and, even more, with the spirit of Pindar. Hölderlin's response to Pindar is the most poetically creative of any of his imitators, and sheds light on its original as well. In 1800 he translated most of the Pythian and Olympian odes, word for word, perhaps simply for himself, partly as a crib, but mostly as an exploration of the poet's mind. Pindar's spirit is then infused into many of his own long poems. In a letter to Böhlendorff of 4 December 1801, he writes:

> I have laboured at this for a long time [sc. the Pindar translation] and know now that apart from what must be the supreme thing with the Greeks and with us, that is, living craft and proportion, we cannot properly have anything in common with them. But what is our own has to be learnt just as much as what is foreign. For this reason the Greeks are indispensable to us.

His first editor, Norbert von Hellingrath, eloquently summed up his view:

He said to himself: why did Pindar write poems? To honour a victor who was his friend / the games of the gods and the deities of the city / in order that festive choruses should go around and make the festival more glorious with his songs / that a pious people might receive their god-given wisdom / and finally that the bustle of the festival, the blooming youth of the victor, the blooming here-and-now of the Hellenic people / that the living moment should become eternal, captured in immortal words. With this he may have compared his own poetic activity / how he found words for the setting of the eternal sun, for the miserable up-and-down of the mortal soul, and thus had them printed in a volume and perhaps moved the heart of one who read them quietly, in his quiet home. And then it seemed to him as if he was not in the right poetic climate, and asked 'Wherefore a poet in time of want?' [*Wozu Dichter in dürftiger Zeit?*] And he thought that his poetry lacked the real existence and the right life, here where everyone endures his life alone.[32]

For Hölderlin, the gods have retreated from the earth and it is the poet's job to bring them back.[33] He expresses this idea through a very Pindaric myth (though it is not one that Pindar used) in '*Wie wenn am Feiertage*' ('As on a festival day'):

So once, the poets tell, when she desired to see
The god in person, visible, did his lightning fall
On Semele's house, and the divinely struck gave birth to
The thunder-storm's fruit, to holy Bacchus.
And hence it is that without danger now
The sons of Earth drink heavenly fire.
Yet, fellow-poets, us it behoves to stand
Bareheaded beneath God's thunder-storms,
To grasp the Father's ray...[34]

Hölderlin takes at face value Pindar's self-presentation as a prophet,[35] and sees the potential regeneration of Germany through 'the mythical celebration of the higher life of individual and community'.[36] Such a celebration, a *Göttertag*, is a necessity for the full civic life. In '*Am Quell der Donau*' ('At the source of the Danube') he looks back to a time when men and heroes mingled on earth:

> And often, you citizens
> Of beautiful towns, they walked among you contented,
> At Games, where once in secret the hero
> Invisible sat with poets, watched the wrestlers and smiling
> Praised – he, the recipient of praise – those idly serious children.
> An endless loving it was, and is.[37]

Hölderlin's very style often derives from Pindar. The opening of '*Wie wenn am Feiertage*' closely follows the structure of the opening of *Olympian* 7:

> As on a holiday, to see the field
> A countryman goes out, at morning, when
> Out of hot night the cooling flashes had fallen
> For hours on end, and thunder still rumbles afar,
> The river enters its banks once more,
> New verdure sprouts from the soil,
> And with the gladdening rain of heaven
> The grapevine drips, and gleaming
> In tranquil sunlight stand the trees of the grove;
> So now in favourable weather they stand
> Whom no mere master teaches, but in
> A light embrace, miraculously omnipresent,
> God-like in power and beauty, Nature brings up.[38]

Hölderlin's last poetic work before the onset of his madness was his Pindar fragments of 1805. In Pindar he found a vision of the golden world infused by the gods, though he responded little to the specifics of the victor's deeds. See, for example, 'The Sanctuaries':

At first the
Heavenly led well-advising
Themis, on golden horses, next to
The ocean's salt,
The ages to the ladder,
The holy, of Olympos, to
The shining return,
To be the rescuer's
Ancient daughter, of Zeus,
But she, the good, gave birth to
The gold-riveted,
The shiningly fertilised places of rest.[39]

The poet's commentary sees here an evocation of the moment when 'the god and the man recognize each other... Themis, the order-giving, gave birth to the human sanctuaries... and something around them that divines, as though remembering, experiences that which they experienced formerly.'

A plain translation of this fragment (30; hymn 1) would read:

> [the Muses sing] how the Fates/ brought heavenly Themis of the wise counsel/ on golden horses from the springs of Ocean/ to the awesome stair that marks the shining way to Olympus,/ to the original wife of Zeus the Saviour:/ she gave birth to the Seasons with golden diadems,/ who never forget to bring forth brilliant fruit.

It may be argued that Hölderlin's Greek was inadequate and his translation inaccurate; but the 'slavish cleaving' to the letter and word order of the original represents not just a 'self-annihilation', but, as David Constantine says, 'appropriation, self-discovery, self-identification and in the end self-assertion.'[40] Hölderlin does not reproduce the purposes of Pindar's poetry, or its metres, but in the end we understand more of what Pindar *means* through the later poet's reaction. The choice of fragments is significant. Though in his translations of Sophocles' *Oedipus Tyrannus* and *Antigone* Hölderlin had identified the 'caesura' of the play as the moment when man and god come into irreconcilable conflict (and the man is destroyed, as he was by his madness, when he wrote '*Apollon hat mich geschlagen*' – 'Apollo has struck me a blow'),[41] he found himself unable in a discursive way to achieve his task of 'bringing back the gods'. Moments of vision, such as these fragments offer, are all that remain possible for him.

Fragments

The soaring ambition of Hölderlin's conception of Pindar has not been equalled by any later writer, though the model continues to be used occasion-ally: Tennyson's ode on the death of the Duke of Wellington is perhaps the most famous English example. Tennyson himself once remarked that 'Pindar is a manner of Australian poet; has long tracts of gravel with immensely large nuggets imbedded.'[42] Many of Pindar's phrases, though, have become quotable tags. 'What god, man, or hero shall I place a tin wreath upon,' wrote Ezra Pound facetiously in *Hugh Selwyn Mauberly*, echoing the sounds of *Olympian* 2's opening, '*tin' andra, tin' heroa, tina theon keladesomen?*' ('what god, what hero, and what man shall we celebrate?'). The style can easily become bombastic, and would be unsympathetic to a Modernist poet.

But let us conclude with a richer, if brief, response to Pindar by the Greek poet Odysseas Elytis (1911–96), whose surrealist imagination found something kindred in Pindar. In the section entitled 'What one loves' of his poem 'The Little Seafarer', he includes, alongside words evoking for him such poets as Homer, Sappho and Aeschylus and the philosopher Heraclitus, these three lines:

> PINDAR
> we are all swimming towards a false shore
> chill flame
> let him search for the bright light of manly Quietude.

The first phrase comes from the encomium for Thrasybulus of Acragas;[43] in full, the fragmentary sentence runs: 'On a sea of golden wealth we are all swimming towards a false shore: he who is destitute [will] then be rich, while those who are rich...'

These three phrases from Pindar's poems express the poet's sense of the uncertainty of human life, his intense and startling metaphors, and his desire for the peace of the cities of men, irradiated by the light of the gods. What better summary could there be?

GLOSSARY

AGORA: The public meeting place of the *polis*.

AULOS: A double-reed wind instrument.

AULETE: A player of the aulos.

BARBITOS: A lyre with a small sound box and very long curved arms.

DAPHNEPHORIKON: Laurel-bearing.

DEMOS: The people (as distinct from the aristocracy).

EPHEBOI: Beardless youths.

GENOS: Family, clan.

HYPORCHEME: A dance accompanied by song.

KAIROS: Literally 'the right amount'; often translated as 'opportunity' or 'the right time'.

KITHARA: A large box-shaped lyre supported on the left arm and plucked with the right hand.

KLEOS: Fame.

KORDAX: A fast, lively and perhaps obscene dance.

LAUDANDUS: The person to be praised.

LINOS: In legend, a primitive form of the lament, named after Linus, the son of a Muse, for whom it was originally sung in mourning. It was traditionally sung at harvest time.

MONODY: Solo performance.

OIKOS: Family or household.

PANKRATIAST: A competitor in the *pankration*.

PANKRATION: A form of wrestling with no holds barred other than biting and gouging.

PARTHENEIA: Maiden-songs.

PHORMINX: A lyre with curved arms, normally with a tortoise-shell as sound-box.

POLIS/POLEIS: City-state(s).

POLEMARCH: One of the nine Athenian archons ('rulers') originally reponsible for military affairs.

PRIAMEL: From Latin *praeambulum*, i.e. preamble, denotes a rhetorical form in which a series of terms leads up to a climax.

SKOLIA: Drinking songs.

SPHRAGIS: Literally 'seal'; refers to a passage in a poem where the author identifies himself.

THEOXENIA: A festival at which the gods were invited and entertained to dinner at table.

XENIA: 'Guest-friendship'; a bond of hospitality between citizens of two different *poleis*.

XENOS / XENOI: 'Guest-friend(s)', persons linked by reciprocal obligations of hospitality and respect.

ABBREVIATIONS

AJP	*American Journal of Philology*
BICS	*Bulletin of the Institute of Classical Studies*
CJ	*Classical Journal*
DK	*Diels-Kranz, Fragmente der Vorsokratiker*
JHS	*Journal of Hellenic Studies*
PCPS	*Proceedings of the Cambridge Philological Society*
POxy	*Oxyrhynchus Papyrus*
TAPA	*Transactions of the American Philological Association*
QUCC	*Quaderni Urbinati di Cultura Classica*

Pindar's poems are abbreviated as follows:

O.	Olympian
P.	Pythian
I.	Isthmian
N.	Nemean
Pa.	Paeans

'Fr.', used of Pindar's works and others, abbreviates 'Fragment'.

TEXTS AND TRANSLATIONS

The translation of Pindar used is that by W.H. Race in the Loeb Classical Library, except where otherwise indicated.

The translation of the other Greek lyric poets is that by David Campbell in the Loeb Classical Library, except where otherwise indicated.

I also make use of M.L. West's translation of the Greek Lyric Poets and my own translation of the fragments of Pindar in Stoneman 1997.

The most beautiful recent translation of Pindar, in my opinion, is that by Anne Pippin Burnett (Baltimore, MD, 2010: see my brief review in *JHS* 2012).

TRANSLITERATION

The transliteration of Greek words and names leads to the usual inconsistencies. I generally employ Latin spellings, with -c-, -ae- and -us in preference to -k-, -ai- and -os (epinician, Antaeus). Race however uses the 'Greek' forms in his translation, which means that spellings may vary within a single paragraph of discussion and citation. The island now known as Aigina (Éyina in modern Greek pronunciation) is in ancient Greek Aigina (hard g) and in its Latin form Aegina, usually pronounced in English Ee-JIE-na. The reader is free to use any or all of these at will.

TIMELINE OF
PINDAR'S CAREER

ALL DATES ARE CONJECTURAL, EXCEPT for those that are fixed by the known dates of the Olympic and Pythian victories. For the decisions regarding the uncertain dates, see the notes in Conway-Stoneman 1997.

All dates are BCE.

518	Birth of Pindar	478	I. 8 for Cleandrus of Aegina, *pankratiast*
498	P. 10 for Hippocleas of Thessaly, runner	477	I. 3 and 4 for Melissus of Thebes, chariot and *pankration*
497/6	a dithyrambic victory	476	O. 1 for Hieron of Syracuse, chariot
490	P. 6 for Xenocrates of Acragas, chariot		? N. 1 for Chromius of Aetna, chariot
	P. 12 for Midas of Acragas, piper		O. 2 for Theron of Acragas, chariot
488	? O. 14 for Asopichos of Orchomenos, runner		O. 3 for Theron of Acragas, chariot
487	? (or 483) N. 5 for Pytheas of Aegina, *pankratiast*		B. 5 for Hieron of Syracuse, chariot
486	P. 7 for Megacles of Athens, four-horse chariot		? Pa. 2 for the men of Abdera
485	? N. 2 for Timodemus of Acharnae, *pankratiast*	475	? P. 2 for Hieron of Syracuse, perhaps for some local games
	? N. 7 for Sogenes of Aegina, pentathlete		? N. 3 for Aristocleidas of Aegina, *pankratiast*
482	I. 6 for Phylacidas of Aegina, *pankratiast*		
480 / 78	I. 5 for Phylacidas of Aegina, *pankratiast*		

474	O. 11 (if not 476) for Hagesidamus of Epizephyrian Locris, boys' boxing
	O. 10 for Hagesidamus of Epizephyrian Locris, boys' boxing
	? P. 3 for Hieron of Syracuse; not an epinician
	? N. 9 for Chromius of Aetna, chariot
	P. 9 for Telesicrates of Cyrene, armoured race
	? P. 11 (if not 454) for Thrasydaeus of Thebes, boys' foot race
473	? N. 4 for Timasarchus of Aegina, wrestling
470	P. 1 for Hieron of Aetna, chariot
	? I. 2 for Xenocrates of Acragas, chariot
	B. 4 for Hieron of Aetna, Pythian victory, chariot
468	O. 6 for Hagesias of Syracuse, mule-cart
	B. 3 for Hieron of Syracuse, Olympian victory, chariot
466	O. 9 for Epharmostus of Opous, wrestling
	? O. 12 for Ergoteles of Himera, long foot race
465	? N. 6 for Alcimidas of Aegina, boys' wrestling
464	O. 7 for Diagoras of Rhodes, boxing
	O. 13 for Xenophon of Corinth, short foot race and pentathlon

After 464	N. 10 for Theaeus of Argos, wrestling
463	(or 478) Pa. 9 for the Thebans at the Ismenion
462	P. 4 for Arcesilas of Cyrene, chariot
	P. 5 for Arcesilas of Cyrene, chariot
460	O. 8 for Alcimedon of Aegina, boys' wrestling
	(or 456) O. 4 for Psaumis of Camarina, mule-cart
	O. 5 for Psaumis of Camarina, mule-cart; probably not by Pindar
459	? N. 8 for Deinis of Aegina, foot race
458	? I. 1 for Herodotus of Thebes, chariot
After 458	Pa. 4 for the Ceans at Delos
454	? P. 11 (see above, 474)
	? I. 7 for Strepsiades of Thebes, *pankration*
452	B. 6 for Lachon of Ceos, boys' sprint
446	P. 8 for Aristomenes of Aegina, boys' wrestling
	? N. 11 for Aristagoras of Tenedos, on his inauguration as prytanis (chief magistrate)
438	death of Pindar

The Odes of Bacchylides

Only those odes included in the timeline above are dateable.

1   Argeius of Ceos, boxer, Isthmia

2   Argeius of Ceos, boxer

3   Hieron of Syracuse – Olympic victory (468)

4   Hieron of Syracuse – Pythian victory (470)

5   Hieron of Syracuse – Olympic victory (476)

6   Lachon of Ceos, sprint, Olympia

7   Lachon of Ceos, sprint, Olympia

8   Liparion of Ceos?

9   Automedes of Phlius, pentathlon, Nemea

10   [X] of Athens, footrace, Isthmia

11   Alexidamus of Metapontion, boys' wrestling, Isthmia

12   Teisias of Aegina, wrestling, Nemea

13   Pytheas of Aegina, *pankration*, Nemea (cf. N. 5, 487)

14   Cleoptolemus of Thessaly, chariot, Petraean Games (Thessaly)

14B   Aristoteles of Larissa, unknown event and location

15   The Sons of Antenor (dithyramb)

16   Heracles: for Delphi

17   The Young Athenians *or* Theseus; for the Ceans to perform in Delos

18   Theseus; for the Athenians

19   Io; for the Athenians

20   Idas; for the Spartans

23   Cassandra (a few lines)

24   unidentified

25   Meleager: a few lines

26   Pasiphae? – a few lines

27   Chiron? – a few lines

28   Orpheus? – a few words

FESTIVALS, VICTORS, EVENTS AND MYTHS

Festivals at which victories mentioned in the epinician odes were won

1. PANHELLENIC GAMES

FESTIVAL	CITY	MONTH	PRIZE
Olympia	Olympia	July/August	olive wreath
Pythia	Delphi	July/August	laurel wreath
Nemea	Nemea	July/August	parsley wreath
Isthmia	Isthmus	April/May	wild parsley

Greek history was dated by Olympiads, periods of four years (five by the Greek inclusive reckoning) beginning with the first celebration in June/July (= Month 1) 776 BCE. The first Pythiad was almost certainly 582 BCE. The series of the Panhellenic Games was as follows (the Greek year begins in midsummer):

OLYMPIAD	DATE	MONTH	FESTIVAL
75.1	480/79	July/August (month 1)	Olympia
75.2	479/8	July/August	Nemea
75.3	478/7	April/May (month 10)	Isthmia
		July/August	Pythia
75.4	477/6	July/August	Nemea
	476/5	April/May	Isthmia
76.1	476/5	July/August	Olympia

2. LOCAL GAMES

FESTIVAL	CITY	DATE/ MONTH	PRIZE	REFERENCE
Adrasteia	Sicyon (or Sicyonian Pythia)		silver cups	N. 9
Agriania (Demeter)	Argos	(March?)		Fr. 70a
Aiaceia/ Delphinia	Aegina	new moon		N. 5.44, O. 7.83, P. 8.66, Farnell vol. II, p. 466; vol. IV, p. 147
Alcathoia	Megara			O. 7.83, N. 5.45, N. 3.84
Aleaia	Tegea			N. 10.47
Asclepieia	Epidaurus	annual		N. 3 (end), Paus. 2.26.7
Carneia	Sparta, Cyrene	July/August		P. 5.90
Daphnephoria	Thebes	nine-yearly (probably in spring)		Farnell, vol. 4, p. 284
Delphinia – see Aiaceia				
Dia	Pellene		woollen cloak	N. 10
Eleusinia	Eleusis	four-yearly, in second Olympic year		I. 1.57

FESTIVAL	CITY	DATE/ MONTH	PRIZE	REFERENCE
Ge and Nymphs	Athens	27 Boedromion		P. 9.101
Hecatombaea (Hera)	Aegina	Panemos (June); uneven years BCE		P. 8.78ff.
Hecatombaea / Heraea	Argos		bronze shield, myrtle wreath	O. 7.83, N. 10
Heliaea	Rhodes			
Hellotia (Athena)	Corinth			O. 13.40
Heracleia/ Iolaeia	Thebes	annual, two days	bronze tripod, myrtle crown	O. 7.83, N. 4.20, I. 4.61
Hydrophoria	Aegina	Delphinios		P. 8.64, N. 4.35. N. 5.44
Koriasia/ Koreia (Athena)	Cleitor			O. 7.153
Lycaea	Arcadia/ Parrhasia	winter	bronze armour	O. 7.83, O. 9.102, O. 13.108, N. 10.48, X Anab 1.2.10
Minyeia	Orchomenus			I. 1.56
Olympia	Athens	19th Munychion		P. 9.101
Panathenaea	Athens	28 Hecatombaeon = c.17 July	jars of oil	O. 13.38
Protesilaea	Phylake			I. 1.59
Theoxenia	Pellene			O. 9.98, N 10.44
Theoxenia	Acragas			O. 3
Theoxenia	Delphi			Pa. 6.62
uncertain	Achaea		bronze vases	N. 10.47
uncertain (Heracles?)	Marathon		silver cup	O. 9.89, P. 8.78; Parke, pp. 181ff.
uncertain	Euboea			I. 1.57

NOTES

I. PINDAR THE POET

1   O. 14.

2   See O. 6.3–4: 'When a work is begun, it is necessary to make its front shine from afar.'

3   N. 5.34–43, trans. G.S. Conway.

4   O. 6.46, 55–7.

5   O. 7.62–3.

6   O. 3.13–15.

7   The term was introduced by Walter Schadewaldt in *Der Aufbau des pindarischen Epinikion* (Tübingen, 1966).

8   See Bruno Currie, *Pindar and the Cult of Heroes* (Oxford, 2005).

9   Timosthenes: the brother of the victor.

10   O. 8.15–21.

11   Moses I. Finley, *Aspects of Antiquity* (Harmondsworth, 1968), pp. 45, 49.

12   David W. Fearn, 'Aeginetan epinician culture: Naming, ritual, and politics', in D. Fearn (ed.), *Aegina: Contexts for Choral Lyric Poetry: Myth, History, and Identity in the Fifth Century BC* (Oxford, 2011), pp. 175–226.

13   Leslie Kurke, *The Traffic in Praise: Pindar and the Poetics of Social Economy* (Ithaca, 1991). See also Mark Golden, *Greek Sport and Social Status* (Austin, 2008), p. 23.

14 Anne Burnett, *Pindar's Songs for Young Athletes of Aigina* (Oxford, 2005).
15 Stesichorus, fr. 212.
16 See Hugh Lloyd-Jones, introduction to Ulrich von Wilamowitz-Moellendorff, *History of Classical Scholarship* (Baltimore, MD, 1982), pp. xiii-xiv.
17 Ulrich von Wilamowitz-Moellendorff, *Pindaros* (Berlin, 1922), p. 463, trans. Richard Stoneman.
18 Basil L. Gildersleeve, *Selections from the Brief Mention of Basil Lanneau Gildersleeve* (Baltimore, 1930), p. 280.
19 Isaac Schapera, *Praise Poems of Tswana Chiefs* (Oxford, 1965), p. 245.
20 John A. Burrow, *The Poetry of Praise* (Cambridge, 2008), p. 131.
21 Kurke, *The Traffic in Praise*, pp. 18–20.
22 Elroy L. Bundy, *Studia Pindarica* (California, 1986), p. 35.
23 Wilamowitz, *Pindaros*, p. 441, trans. Stoneman.
24 C. Maurice Bowra, *Pindar* (Oxford, 1964), p. 335. It is fair to say that *any* interpretative approach comes to despair when faced with *Nemean 7*.
25 William Spencer Barrett, whose articles on Pindar definitively solved a number of historical problems, could see no value in Bundy's work at all.
26 'Pindar's Twelfth Olympian and the fall of the Deinomenidai', *JHS* 93 (1973), pp. 23–35; 'The Oligaithidai and their victories' in R.D. Dawe (ed.), *Dionysiaca: Studies in Honour of Sir Denys Page* (Cambridge, 1978), pp. 1–20.
27 Simon Hornblower, *Thucydides and Pindar: Historical Narrative and the World of Epinikian Poetry* (Oxford, 2004).
28 Collected and edited by Anders Bjørn Drachmann in *Scholia vetera in Pindari carmina*, 3 volumes (Leipzig, 1903–27).
29 Drachman, *Scholia vetera* (1903), vol. 1, pp. 1–7.
30 Translation from Mary Lefkowitz, *The Lives of the Greek Poets* (London, 1981), pp. 155–7.
31 *POxy* 2438; ed. Italo Gallo (Salerno, 1968).
32 Hornblower, *Thucydides and Pindar*, p. 253.
33 Claude Calame, *Choruses of Young Women in Ancient Greece* (Lanham, MD, 2001); and see Chapter 3.

II. PINDAR'S CAREER

1 Ar. *Ach* 863–6.
2 *Politics* 1274b1.
3 N. 6.8–12.
4 *Iliad* 6.146.
5 Fr. 104b.
6 Paus. 9.10.4, trans. Peter Levi. See Albert Schachter, *Cults of Boeotia* (London, 1981), vol. I, p. 83ff.
7 'Soft' or 'tender' would be better.
8 Pa. 2, fr. 94b.

9   Geoffrey S. Conway and Richard Stoneman, *Pindar: the Odes and Fragments* (London, 1997), p. 287.

10 I. 4.50.

11 I. 4.52–5.

12 Whether P. 5.72–6 means that he was himself a member of the Aegeid clan, or whether it is the persona of the chorus that is speaking, remains imponderable: see Mary Lefkowitz, 'ΤΩ ΚΑΙ ΕΓΩ: the first person in Pindar', *HSCP* 67 (1963), pp. 177–253, and my note in Conway-Stoneman, *Pindar: the Odes and Fragments*, ad loc.

13 Alcaeus fr. 130b.

14 For example, lines 31–8.

15 Polybius 4.8-12, trans. Evelyn S. Shuckburgh.

16 Plato, *Laws* 653d–654b, trans. Trevor J. Saunders.

17 Basil L. Gildersleeve, *Selections from 'Brief Mention'* (Baltimore, 1930), pp. 162–3.

18 David Campbell (ed. and trans.), *Greek Lyric* (Cambridge, MA and London, 1992), vol. IV, p. 1.

19 Cf. fr. 2.692.

20 O. 14 (488 B C ?).

21 P. 7.486.

22 I. 3 and 4.477.

23 See Moses I. Finley, *Aspects of Antiquity* (Harmondsworth, 1968), quoted in Chapter 1 of this volume.

24 Leslie Kurke, *The Traffic in Praise: Pindar and the Poetics of Social Economy* (Ithaca, 1991). Kurke was partially anticipated by Kevin Crotty in *Song and Action: The Victory Odes of Pindar* (Baltimore, 1982), pp. 108–20, where he wrote of the *nostos* ('return') of the victor, treating this return as a quasi-initiation.

25 David W. Fearn, 'Aeginetan epinician culture: naming, ritual, and politics', in D. Fearn (ed.), *Aegina: Contexts for Choral Lyric Poetry: Myth, History, and Identity in the Fifth Century BC* (Oxford, 2011), pp. 175–226.

26 Bruno Currie, 'Epinician choregia: funding a Pindaric chorus', in Lucia Athanassaki and Ewen Bowie (eds), *Archaic and Classical Choral Song: Performance, Politics and Dissemination* (Berlin, 2011), p. 277.

27 Alcman fr. 16.

28 Maria Stamatopoulou, 'Thessaly in the age of epinician', in Simon Hornblower and Catherine Morgan (eds), *Pindar's Poetry, Patrons and Festivals* (Oxford, 2007), p. 335.

29 Giovan Battista D'Alessio, 'Defining local identities in Greek lyric poetry', in Richard Hunter and Ian Rutherford (eds), *Wandering Poets in Ancient Greek Culture* (Cambridge, 2009); cf. Ewen Bowie, 'Wandering poets, archaic exile', in the same volume.

30 Geoffrey Lloyd, *The Ambitions of Curiosity: Understanding the World in Ancient Greece and China* (Cambridge, 2002).

31 Peter Avery (ed.), *The Collected Lyrics of Hafez of Shiraz* (Cambridge, 2007), p. 370.

32 Richard Seaford, *Money and the Early Greek Mind* (Cambridge, 2004).
33 Leonard Woodbury, 'Pindar and the mercenary muse: *Isthm.* 2.1–13'. *TAPA* 99 (1968), pp. 368–75.
34 *Life of Homer* 32 = Hesiod fr. 302 MW.
35 Scholiast on Aristophanes *Peace* 695ff.
36 *Rhetoric* 2.16.1391a.
37 Mary Renault, *The Praise Singer* (London, 1978), p. 227. See also Ps.-Plut. *Hipparchus* 228bc: 'gifts love Simonides'.
38 Simon. fr. 510 PMG.
39 Compare also P. 11.41–4.
40 Alcaeus fr. 69 LP; Theognis 189–92.
41 Kurke, *The Traffic in Praise*, p. 245.
42 Ibid., p. 259.
43 The description here is indebted to David W. Fearn, *Bacchylides: Politics, Performance, Poetic Tradition* (Oxford, 2007).
44 G. Aurelio Privitera, 'Pindaro, *Nem.* III 1–5 e l'acqua di Egina', *QUCC* 58 (1988).
45 The spring was often the scene of such celebrations, for some years later (in 475 perhaps), another *pankratiast*, Aristocleidas, was the honorand of Pindar's third Nemean ode.
46 N. 5.1–5.
47 R.R.R. Smith, 'Pindar, athletes, and the early Greek statue habit', in Hornblower and Morgan (eds), *Pindar's Poetry*.
48 Pliny, *NH* 34.9–10.
49 Anne Pippin Burnett, *Pindar's Songs for Young Athletes of Aigina* (Oxford, 2005), pp. 29–44.
50 Simon Hornblower, *Thucydides and Pindar: Historical Narrative and the World of Epinikian Poetry* (Oxford, 2004), p. 216.
51 Simonides fr. 581 PMG.
52 B. 13, 230 lines.
53 Burnett, *Pindar's Songs*, pp. 31–2; James Watson, 'Rethinking the Sanctuary of Aphaia', in Fearn (ed.), *Aegina: Contexts for Choral Lyric Poetry*, pp. 79–113.
54 B. 13.79–99.
55 See Fearn's discussion in *Bacchylides*, pp. 87–160.
56 N. 5.53–5.
57 Timothy Power, 'The Parthenoi of Bacchylides 13', Harvard Studies in Classical Philology 100 (2000), pp. 67–81; Eva Stehle, *Performance and Gender in Ancient Greece: Non-Dramatic Poetry in its Setting* (Princeton, 1997).
58 Burnett, *Pindar's Songs*, pp. 17–28.
59 Strabo 8.6.16.
60 Herodotus 6.88–91; Robin Waterfield translates the term 'the men of substance': Carolyn Dewald ad loc. in Herodotus, *The Histories*, trans. Waterfield, ed. Dewald (Oxford, 1998).
61 Pausanias 8.5.8.

62 Polyaenus 5.14.
63 Herodotus 7.147.2.
64 Thomas Figueira, *Aegina: Society and Politics* (New York, 1981), p. 199.
65 Carl Otfried Mueller, *Aegineticorum Liber* (Berlin, 1817).
66 The metaphor of seafaring in *Nemean* 6.30 does not prove that the family in question, the Bassidai, were seafarers: see Simon Hornblower, '"Dolphins in the Sea" (*Isthmian* 9.7): Pindar and the Aeginetans', in Hornblower and Morgan (eds), *Pindar's Poetry*, p. 296.
67 Geoffrey Ernest Maurice de Ste. Croix, *Athenian Democratic Origins*, ed. David Harvey and Robert Parker (Oxford, 2004).
68 Hornblower, *Thucydides and Pindar*, p. 212 suggests that they are all warships, but I do find this unlikely.
69 Hornblower, '"Dolphins in the Sea"', pp. 290–1.
70 Richard Stoneman, *Palmyra and its Empire: Zenobia's Revolt against Rome* (Ann Arbor, 1994), p. 59.
71 N. 4.14–21.
72 Herodotus 4.152.
73 P. 1.20–4.
74 The story's extensions are brilliantly evoked by Lane Fox in *Travelling Heroes: Greeks and their Myths in the Epic Age of Homer* (London, 2008), pp. 298–318.
75 P. 1.13–14.
76 P. 1.5–6.
77 Σ O. 6.162a and c.
78 Thuc. 6.2–6.
79 Herodotus 7.166; or Thermopylae: Diodorus Siculus 11.1.4–21, 24.1.
80 Diod. 11.25.
81 Polybius 9.27. The identifications of the temples are uncertain.
82 Diod. Sic. 9.12.3 = Alc. T8.
83 Alc. T. 429.
84 Alcaeus 129.
85 Diodorus 11.49.
86 Strabo 6.2.3.
87 Diod. 11.67.
88 David Asheri, 'Sicily 478–431 BC', in *Cambridge Ancient History*, 2nd edition (Cambridge, 1992), vol. V, p. 153.
89 Aelian, *Historical Miscellany* 9.1.
90 Xen. *Hieron* 6.12.
91 Xen. *Hieron* 11.11, 13, 15.
92 Aelian, *Historical Miscellany* 4.15.
93 Translation by Douglas Young, *Chasing an Ancient Greek* (London, 1950), p. 189. The Scots dialect reflects the translator's ebullience rather than anything in Theognis' standard epic diction.
94 Ibycus fr. 282B.
95 Macrobius 5.18.17.

96 P. 6.490.
97 P. 12.
98 The story is told by Strabo at 6.2.4.
99 O. 6.4.
100 O. 38–41.
101 P. 1.67–8.
102 P. 1.81–4.
103 P. 1.85–6.
104 P. 1.92–8.
105 Edward Augustus Freeman, *The History of Sicily from the Earliest Times*, 2 volumes (Oxford, 1891–4), p. 258.
106 Diodorus 11.67–8.
107 Fr. 129–30 and 131.
108 O. 2.19–20.
109 See Hugh Lloyd-Jones, 'Pindar and the afterlife', *Entretiens Hardt* 17 (1985) = Hugh Lloyd-Jones, *Greek Epic, Lyric and Tragedy: Academic Papers* (Oxford, 1990), pp. 80–105, with addendum at 105–9.
110 P. 9.36.
111 P. 9.44–9.
112 P. 9.111ff.
113 Leonard Woodbury, 'Cyrene and the *Teleuta* of marriage in Pindar's ninth Pythian ode', *TAPA* 112 (1982), pp. 245–58.
114 Kurke, *The Traffic in Praise*, p. 122ff.; Anne Carson, 'Wedding at noon in Pindar's ninth Pythian', *GRBS* 23 (1982), pp. 121–8.
115 P. 9.73–5.
116 P. 5.79–80: 'At your banquet, Carneian Apollo, we honor the well-built city of Cyrene.'
117 See further Chapter 6, esp. pp. 151–2.
118 P. 4.292.
119 Hornblower, *Thucydides and Pindar*, pp. 145–266 is an exhilarating exploration of what can be known of Pindar's contacts throughout the Greek world, including a paradoxical twelve pages (pp. 145–56) on 'Pindar and Chios'.
120 On Athenian victors who do not feature in Pindar, see Hornblower, *Thucydides*, p. 211.
121 On this last, see below, p. 100.
122 D. 2.8–14, trans. Richard Stoneman.
123 N. 11.37–8, 44–6.
124 The name of Arcesilas is given in some manuscripts as Hagesilas, which is the name of the father of Theoxenus, the young man in whose arms Pindar is supposed to have died. Aristagoras would thus be Theoxenus' older brother. But the metrical values of Hagesilas and Arcesilas are not the same, and the alternative reading seems impossible, so that the family link is removed.
125 P. 8.95–100.

III. THE RANGE OF PINDAR'S POETRY

1 Monica Negri, *Eustazio di Tessalonica: introduzione al commentario a Pindaro* (Brescia, 2000).
2 He certainly had more *Isthmians* than we do: see ibid., p. 12.
3 Eustathius, *Prooemium* 34, in Anders B. Drachmann (ed.), *Scholia vetera in Pindari carmina*, (Leipzig, 1927), vol. III, p. 303.
4 Pausanias 9.16.1.
5 Simonides 581P; quoted in Chapter 2.
6 N. 5.1–3.
7 Plutarch, *Nicias* 29.
8 Eupolis fr. 398 PCG.
9 Ar. *Birds* 924–5 quotes Pi. fr. 105, *Knights* 1264–6, 1329.
10 Plato, *Protagoras* 339a–346d.
11 Simonides 542P.
12 *Ion* 534d.
13 *Clouds* 1353–8, produced in 423.
14 Quoted in David Campbell (ed.), *Greek Lyric*, (Cambridge, MA: 1991), vol. III, p. 5. There has been a lively debate regarding choral or monodic performance of Pindar's odes since Mary Lefkowitz's 1988 article 'Who sang Pindar's Victory Odes?': see Malcolm Heath and Mary Lefkowitz, 'Epinician Performance', *CP* 86 (1991), pp. 173–91, supporting possible monodic performance, with Chris Carey in the succeeding pages (pp. 192–200) pointing out that choral performance is 'the unvarying assumption of hellenistic scholars'. Corinna 692 fr. 2 seems to be explicit in referring to 'the light step accompanying the voice'.
15 O. 2.58.
16 P. 8.99, 9.91.
17 N. 3.68, N. 6.46.
18 O. 5.14.
19 N. 2.3, I. 4.70.
20 In a paper delivered at the APA meeting, January 2011.
21 Eur. *Helen* 1.
22 Bruno Currie, 'Reperformance scenarios for Pindar's odes', in C.J. Mackie (ed.), *Oral Performance and Its Context* (Leiden, 2004), pp. 49–69 is a helpful characterisation of the possible scenarios.
23 The translation is odd. Conway has 'linking his lively lyre with my song'. Pindar uses the word *klino*, 'I lean', only twice; here it should mean something like 'applying himself to'.
24 The text is uncertain: it may say 'Euphanes will celebrate him...' (Race) or 'Euphanes used to celebrate him' (Conway), in which case both men are dead. The interpretative point will stand.
25 Euripides, *Alcestis,* 445–52.
26 Cf. Ar. *Knights* 1329 = Pi. F. 76.
27 *FGrH* 595F5.

28 It is remarkable that in this instance the paean, usually a song of celebration or battle, takes on some of the functions of the lament.

29 Ian Rutherford, *Pindar's Paeans: A Reading of the Fragments with a Survey of the Genre* (Oxford, 2001), p. 144.

30 Thomas Hubbard, 'The dissemination of Pindar's non-epinician choral lyric' in Lucia Athanassaki and Ewen Bowie (eds), *Archaic and Classical Choral Song: Performance, Politics and Dissemination* (Berlin, 2011), pp. 347–63.

31 Two variant lists are given in *POxy* 2438, basically the same in a different order, and in the Suda s.v. Pindaros. See Rutherford, *Pindar's Paeans*, p. 147n, and Monica Negri, *Pindaro ad Alessandria: le edizioni e gli editori* (Brescia, 2004).

32 Plato, *Laws* 700.

33 Rutherford, *Pindar's Paeans*.

34 Pa. 2 Abderus, Pa. 6 Neoptolemus.

35 Rutherford, *Pindar's Paeans*, p. 83.

36 Aristoxenos fr. 117W; see Peter Wilson, *The Athenian Institution of the Khoregia* (Cambridge, 2000), pp., 279–80.

37 Nick J. Lowe, 'Epinikian eidography', in Simon Hornblower and Catherine Morgan (eds), *Pindar's Poetry, Patrons and Festivals* (Oxford, 2007), p. 167.

38 Diodorus 13.82.

39 N. 1.7, O. 2.52, 10.77, 13.29.

40 P. 10.53.

41 Archilochus fr. 120 is the locus classicus for the dedication of dithyramb to Dionysus.

42 At Herodotus 1.23, followed by the *Suda*.

43 B. 15–29, according to the papyrus.

44 Rutherford, *Pindar's Paeans*, p. 98.

45 Dith 2, 6–8, 12–14, 20–1. Trans. R. Stoneman; see also the quotation at the end of Chapter 2, above, p. 48.

46 Claude Calame, *Choruses of Young Women in Ancient Greece* (Lanham, MD, 2001).

47 For recent interpretations see Gloria Ferrari, *Alcman and the Cosmos of Sparta* (Chicago, 2008); Ewen Bowie, 'Alcman's first Partheneion and the song the Sirens sang', in Lucia Athanassaki and Ewen Bowie (eds), *Archaic and Classical Choral Song: Performance, Politics and Dissemination* (Berlin, 2011), pp. 33–65.

48 Parth. 2.5–14. Trans. R. Stoneman.

49 See further Chapter 6, pp. 158–61.

50 Negri, *Pindaro ad Alessandria*, p. 39.

51 Kevin Crotty, *Song and Action: The Victory Odes of Pindar* (Baltimore, MD, 1982), pp. 115–6.

52 Rutherford, *Pindar's Paeans*, p. 106.

53 Lucian, *On Dance*, 61.

54 Athenaeus 14.29 (631a). This is also implied by Aeschylus *Choephori* 1024f.

55 Athenaeus 14.7 (617).

56 Richard Seaford, 'The "Hyporchema" of Pratinas', *Maia* 29–30 (1977–8), pp. 87–8.

57 See Ps-Plutarch, *De Musica* 9, 1134bd.

58 Fr. 128c.

59 The two contrasted clauses introduced by *men* and *de* would then refer to the sending and receiving of the poem; or the *kastoreion* would be the second part of the poem.

60 N. 1.7, O. 2.52, 10.77, 13.29; once it is an *enkomios hymnos*: P. 10.53.

61 See the discussion in Simon Hornblower, *Thucydides and Pindar: Historical Narrative and the World of Epinikian Poetry* (Oxford, 2004), pp. 19–20.

62 Fr. 128c, Lament 3.

63 See John P. Barron, 'Ibycus: *Gorgias* and other poems', *Bulletic of the Institute of Classical Studies* 31 (1984), pp. 13–24; and Hornblower, *Thucydides*, pp. 21, 237.

64 Barron, 'Ibycus', p. 20.

65 N. 8.50ff.

66 Campbell (ed.), *Greek Lyric*, vol. III, p. 373.

67 Sim. fr. 510; Cicero *de oratore* 2.86.351–3.

68 Joachim Ebert, *Griechische Epigramme auf Sieger an gymnischen und hippischen Agonen* (Berlin, 1972), no. 12.

69 Chris Carey, 'Prosopographica Pindarica', *CQ* 39 (1989), pp. 1–9. Conversely, 'to be preserved in song as an anonymous father, uncle or grandfather is not to be preserved at all': see Sappho fr. 55V.

70 *Anth. Plan.* 23. Pindar also wrote a poem for this man's victory at the Isthmus: see fr. 2, 3.

71 Ebert, *Griechische Epigramme*, 26; Denys L. Page, *Further Greek Epigrams* (Cambridge, 1981), 'Simonides', p. xliii.

72 Page, *Further Greek Epigrams*, compares Pi. O. 7.81ff. and O. 13.107ff.

73 Ibycus fr. 287, fr. 288.

74 For example, IG XII 3.543, 'Barbax danced well'; 546, 'Telecrates is a good dancer'; 536, 'Pheidippides ωιπhc. Timagoras and Eupheres and I εγωιπhομες [did something]; Empylos here is a tart; Empedocles inscribed [or, buggered?]... he danced here, by Apollo.' See Nigel B. Crowther, 'Male beauty contests in Greece: the Euandria and Euexia', *L'Antiquité Classique* 54 (1985), pp. 285–91 and Thomas Hubbard, 'Hieron and the Ape in Pi. P. 2.72–73', *TAPA* 120 (1990), pp. 73–83; in general, Thomas F. Scanlon, *Eros and Greek Athletics* (New York, 2002).

75 *Wasps* 578.

76 Fustel de Coulanges, *La Cité antique* and *Questions historiques*, cited in Arnaldo Momigliano, 'The ancient city of Fustel de Coulanges', in *Essays in Ancient and Modern Historiography* (Oxford, 1977), pp. 328, 334.

77 Simon. fr. 531.

78 Nicholas J. Richardson, 'Review of W.K. Pritchett, *The Greek State at War* and *Guerre et religion en Grèce à l'époque antique*', *JHS* 101 (1981), pp. 185–7.

79 See in general Deborah Boedeker and David Sider, *The New Simonides: Contexts of Praise and Desire* (New York, 2001).

80 *Life* of Aeschylus, 2.8.

81 John Boardman and Donna Kurtz, *Greek Burial Customs* (London, 1971), p. 202 refers to games being held to commemorate Miltiades in Thrace, Leonidas in Sparta and Timoleon in Sicily.

82 Plato, *Meno* 81B.
83 Fr. 178.
84 Emily Vermeule, *Aspects of Death in Early Greek Art* (California, 1979), p. 49, n. 14, citing Margaret Alexiou, *The Ritual Lament in Greek Tradition* (Cambridge, 1974), p. 41: 'A wise housewife, an orderly woman,/ has made up her mind and decided to go down to Hades./ If you have messages to send, give them to her to take,/ and if you have a son unarmed, send him weapons too.'
85 Cicero, *de legibus,* 2.26.59ff.; Plut. *Solon* 21. See also Plato *Laws* 12.958D–960B; Boardman and Kurtz, *Greek Burial Customs*, pp. 200-201, 363.
86 Dion. Halic. *Ant. Rom.* V.17.4, Diod XI.33.
87 Aristotle *AthPol* 58.1; Plut. *Arist.* 21.2.
88 Plut. *Per* 28.4.
89 Plato, *Menexenus* 249B; Lysias II.80.
90 Paus. 9.10.4.
91 Trans. Richard Stoneman.
92 Lucian, *On Dance*, 10.
93 See P. 12.
94 Pa. 3.94; fr. 70.
95 N. 9.8-9.
96 Lillian B. Lawler, *The Dance in Ancient Greece* (London, 1964.). But see Frits Naerebout, *Attractive Performances: Ancient Greek Dance: Three Preliminary Studies* (Amsterdam, 1997) for an attempt to clear the ground for a proper study, especially pp. 220–89 on the evidence for the physical performances of ancient dances.
97 *Iliad* 18, trans. George Chapman.
98 Lawler, *The Dance in Ancient Greece*, pp. 46–7, and Chapter 4.
99 Plut. *Mor.* 747ff.
100 Athenaeus 14.25–30 and 1.26.
101 *On Dance*, 7, trans. Richard Stoneman.
102 *Timaeus* 40c, trans. Benjamin Jowett.
103 Ferrari, *Alcman.*
104 Athenaeus 14.27.
105 Athenaeus 14.27–8.
106 Athenaeus 14.29.
107 *On Dance*, 33ff.
108 Ibid., 37–61.
109 Ibid., 63.
110 Statius, *Achilleis* 1.827–34: the girls raise and lower their *thyrsoi, multiplicantque gradus.*
111 Lucian, *On Dance*, 71.
112 Ibid., 72.
113 Naerebout, *Attractive Performances*, pp. 220–25, 280–83, 236.
114 William Mullen, *Choreia: Pindar and Dance* (Princeton, NJ, 1982), p. 142.

IV. ATHLETES AND HEROES

1 Simon Hornblower, *Thucydides and Pindar: Historical Narrative and the World of Epinikian Poetry* (Oxford, 2004), pp. 11–13; Martin P. Nilsson, *Griechische Feste* (Leipzig, 1906); Herbert W. Parke, *Festivals of the Athenians* (London, 1977).
2 *IG* I³, p. 131, cf. Plato *Apology* 36d.
3 See especially David Sansone, *Greek Athletics and the Genesis of Sport* (Berkeley, 1988).
4 Sansone, *Greek Athletics*; Gregory Nagy, *Pindar's Homer: The Lyric Possession of an Epic Past* (Baltimore, 1990), Chapter 5.
5 See Stephen G. Miller, *Ancient Greek Athletics* (New Haven, CT, 2004) – the source of the quotations.
6 *HhAp* 146–55, trans. George Chapman, 220ff.
7 Cicero *Tusculan Disputations* 5.3.8, quoted in Peter Gorman, *Pythagoras: A Life* (London, 1979).
8 Euripides, *Hippolytus*, 1016–20.
9 Thuc. 4.121.1.
10 Robert H. Brophy and Mary Brophy, 'Death in the Panhellenic Games II', *AJP* 106 (1985), pp. 171–98.
11 P. 1.42–5.
12 N. 7.70–4; Hugh M. Lee, 'The terma and the javelin in Pindar, *Nemean* vii 70–3, and Greek athletics', *JHS* 96 (1976), pp. 70–9; also Miller, *Ancient Greek Athletics*, pp. 71–3.
13 Miller, *Ancient Greek Athletics*, p. 17. There was a room for dust storage at Oenoanda, the *konisterion*. Philostratus offers a typology of dust in *Gymnasticus* 56: earthy dust is suitable for the majority, pottery dust is good to induce sweat, pitchy dust will soothe the chilly; yellow dust has a better appearance than black when a body is coated with it.
14 Ilya Pfeijffer, 'The images of the eagle in Pindar and Bacchylides', *Classical Philology* (1994), pp. 305–17.
15 Nigel B. Crowther, 'Male beauty contests in Greece: the Euandria and Euexia', *L'Antiquité Classique* 54 (1985), p. 289.
16 Paus. 5.9.2.
17 Fr. 515.
18 David C. Young, *The Olympic Myth of Greek Amateur Athletics* (Chicago, 1984). The problem of professionalism continued to bother Pliny as governor of Bithynia, however: see Miller, *Ancient Greek Athletics*, p. 207f.
19 Xenophanes fragment 2 DK.
20 Fr. 282 = Athenaeus 10.5, 413c.
21 See also *Contest of Homer and Hesiod* 64ff. for a similar contrast of athletes and wise men.
22 Diogenes Laertius 1.56.
23 Isocrates 16.32ff.

24 R.R.R. Smith, 'Pindar, athletes and the early Greek statue habit', in Simon Hornblower and Catherine Morgan (eds), *Pindar's Poetry: Patrons and Festivals* (Oxford, 2007), p. 137f.
25 Paus. 6.7.5, trans. Peter Levi.
26 *Inschriften von Olympia* 151.
27 O. 7.1–11. Pindar uses the symposiac metaphor again at I. 6.1–9.
28 O. 7, 62–3, 69–71.
29 Carol Dougherty, *The Poetics of Colonization* (Oxford, 1994), pp. 120–30.
30 O. 12.
31 O. 12.13–16, 19–20.
32 For a modern account of these stories see Miller, *Ancient Greek Athletics*, pp. 160–5.
33 Paus. 6.11.9.
34 Paus. 6.9.6–8.
35 Paus. 6.6.4.
36 *Inschriften von Olympia* 144. See also Miller, *Ancient Greek Athletics*, pp. 162–3.
37 Bruno Currie, *Pindar and the Cult of Heroes* (Oxford, 2005), p. 412.
38 Ibid., 218f.
39 Ibid., p. 284.
40 O. 3, 6, 9, 10; P. 9; N. 1, 3, 4, 7, 10; I. 4, 6, 7; also Ba. 5 and 9.
41 He won the boys' boxing in 520 BCE.
42 Simonides fr. 509.
43 I. 1.12–22.
44 I. 4.54–6.
45 N. 3.22.
46 N. 10.84–90.
47 N. 1.69–74.
48 O. 10.46–9.
49 O. 9.29–40.
50 Fr. S. 15; the papyrus breaks off here.
51 Fr. 169a.
52 Hugh Lloyd-Jones, 'Pindar fr. 169', *Harvard Studies in Classical Philology* 76 (1972), pp. 45–56 = Lloyd-Jones, *Greek Epic, Lyric and Tragedy: Academic Papers* (Oxford, 1990), pp. 154-65.
53 For a full discussion, see Laura Swift, *The Hidden Chorus* (Oxford, 2010).
54 Robert Parker, *On Greek Religion* (Ithaca, 2011), pp. 142–3. The fragmentary Paean 15 may refer to a Theoxenia. Bacchylides fr. 21 also alludes to a feast for the Dioscuri.
55 N. 10.49–54.
56 Friedrich Deneken, *De Theoxeniis*, diss. (Berlin, 1881), pp. 21–2.
57 Simon. fr. 555.
58 Pa. 4.21–4.
59 Plutarch, *Nicias*, trans. Thomas North. On the liturgy see Peter Wilson, *The Athenian Institution of the Khoregia* (Cambridge, 2000), pp. 44–6.
60 Pa. 2.28–30.
61 Herodotus 1.168.

62 Strabo 14.1.30. See Richard Stoneman, *Pindar: The Odes and Fragments*, re-edition of translation by Geoffrey S. Conway (London, 1997), p. 324; Hornblower, *Thucydides*, p. 181.

63 Plutarch, *Theseus*; Lillian B. Lawler, *The Dance in Ancient Greece* (London, 1964), pp. 46–7; Chapter 3 above, pp. 73–4.

64 B. 1.113–23.

65 B. 17.128–9.

66 B. 28–9; Wilson, *The Athenian Institution*, p. 46.

V. THE PRACTICE OF PRAISE

1 See Chapter 1, p. 6.

2 Elroy L. Bundy, *Studia Pindarica* (California, 1986; first published 1962), p. 3.

3 Hugh Lloyd-Jones, 'Modern interpretation of Pindar: The second Pythian and seventh Nemean odes', *JHS* 93 (1973), pp. 109–37.

4 Donald Andrew Russell and N.G. Wilson (eds and trans.), *Menander Rhetor*, (Oxford, 1981).

5 Here he echoes the scholiasts' division outlined in Chapter 3, and coincides with his contemporary Proclus' categorisation of lyric genres.

6 Russell and Wilson (eds and trans.), *Menander Rhetor* 331.18–332.2.

7 348.25.

8 William H. Race, 'Pindaric encomium and Isocrates' *Evagoras*', *TAPA* 117 (1987), pp. 131–55.

9 See Chapter 3 of the present volume.

10 Some classic examples may be found in: David C. Young, *Three Odes of Pindar* (Leiden, 1968); Lloyd-Jones, 'Modern interpretation of Pindar', pp. 109–37; Adolf Köhnken, 'Pindar as innovator: Poseidon Hippios and the relevance of the Pelops story in *Olympian* 1', *CQ* 24 (1974), pp. 199–206; Adolf Köhnken, 'Gods and descendants of Aiakos in Pindar's Eighth Isthmian Ode', *BICS* 22 (1975), pp. 25–36; Chris Carey, 'Pindar's Eighth Nemean Ode', *PCPS* 22 (1976), pp. 26–41; Gretchen Kromer, 'The value of time in Pindar's *Olympian* 10', *Hermes* 104 (1976), pp. 420–36; Mary Lefkowitz, 'Pindar's Pythian 8', *CJ* 72 (1977), pp. 209–21; Malcolm M. Willcock, 'Second Reading of Pindar: "The Fourth Nemean"', *Greece and Rome* 29 (1982), pp. 1–10; Anne Carson, 'Wedding at noon in Pindar's Ninth Pythian', *GRBS* 23 (1982), pp. 121–8; Stephen Instone, 'Pythian 11: Did Pindar err?', *CQ* 36 (1986), pp. 86–94; Kurke, Leslie, 'Pindar's Sixth Pythian and the Tradition of Archaic Poetry', *TAPA* 120 (1990), pp. 85–107; Ilya Pfeijffer, *Three Aeginetan Odes of Pindar: A Commentary on Nemean V, Nemean III and Pythian VIII* (Leiden, 1999).

11 339a-346d = fr. 542.

12 Fr. 123.2–6, 10–15.

13 Which need not be really 'personal' at all, *contra* Peter von der Mühll, 'Persönliche Verliebtheit des Dichters?', *Museum Helveticum* 21 (1964), pp. 168–72.

14 Ibycus fr. 282C, in David Campbell (ed.), *Greek Lyric* (Cambridge, MA, 1982–93), vol. III.

15 The fact that *gymnazein*, 'to exercise', means at root 'to be naked' is the key to two lines of Theognis, 1335–6: 'Happy is he who is in love and "exercises" when he gets home, sleeping all day with a beautiful boy.' On athletics and eros see in general Thomas F. Scanlon, *Eros and Greek Athletics* (New York, 2002), p. 211ff., and the images at pp. 236–49.

16 Anne Pippin Burnett, *Pindar's Songs for Young Athletes of Aigina* (Oxford, 2005), pp. 168–9.

17 *Nicomachean Ethics* 1101b12–18.

18 O. 9.100–4.

19 O. 5.22–4.

20 Stephen Instone, 'Pythian 11: Did Pindar err?', *CQ* 36 (1986), p. 93.

21 Fully argued by Mary Lefkowitz in both 'ΤΩ ΚΑΙ ΕΓΩ: the first person in Pindar', *HSCP* 67 (1963), pp. 177–253 and 'Pindar's *Pythian* 5', *Pindare, Entretiens sur l'antiquité classique* (Geneva, 1985), vol. 31, pp. 33–58; both are reprinted in Mary Lefkowitz, *First Person Fictions: Pindar's Poetic 'I'* (Oxford, 1991). The interpretation is accepted by William H. Race in his Loeb edition. Simon Hornblower, *Thucydides and Pindar: Historical Narrative and the World of Epinikian Poetry* (Oxford, 2004), pp. 240–1, is undecided.

22 *Theogony* 22–3.

23 *Iliad* 2.484–6.

24 *Theogony* 27–8.

25 Fr. 205.

26 O. 10.3–5. The reference to broken promises and, in the preceding lines, to a debt owed, have often been interpreted as referring to a promise made in the earlier *Olympian* 11, since these two odes are unique in both celebrating the same victory. Bundy has shown that *Olympian* 11 is sufficient to itself. The reference to delay may be literal; Pindar was busy in 476 with three great Sicilian odes; but the poet's debt is also an epinician convention and may not need explanation from outside the poem.

27 O. 10.52–6.

28 O. 10.95–6.

29 Fr. 150.

30 Σ Aristides iii Dindorf; Pi. fr. 95.

31 Simon. 519B fr. 1.

32 One may think of the Silenus of Virgil *Eclogue* 6, who reveals himself as a source of cosmic knowledge.

33 O. 14.

34 The Graces of Theocritus 16, who 'come home sulky, trailing their bare feet and blame me for sending them on a wasted journey' are a different matter. They can find no proper object for their adornment, since, Theocritus claims, no one is ready to pay the poet adequately. The poem presents itself as an importunate address to the ruler of Syracuse, Hieron II.

35 O. 14.5–9.

36 N. 10.37–8.

37 N. 6.36–8.

38 Gerard Manley Hopkins has a not dissimilar view: 'The world is charged with the grandeur of God' – but his metaphors are mineral ones, not vegetal like Pindar's: 'It will flame out, like shining from shook foil; It gathers to a greatness, like the ooze of oil crushed.' (From 'God's Grandeur'.)

39 N. 6.1–6. I here use Conway's translation because I believe that his, not Race's, interpretation of the much disputed opening line is correct. Literally, 'one is of men, one of gods the race', which Race interprets as 'there is one race of men, another of gods'.

40 I. 6.63–4.

41 See O. 9.27.

42 N. 6.8–11.

43 Race's 'games that award crowns of leaves' obscures the image.

44 I. 8.16. My own translation, as both Conway and Race obscure the sense.

45 My translation; Conway has 'cull flowers' which implies destroying them, and Race has 'pluck the prize'; but *drepesthai* is done with a sickle, not the fingers, and *aotos* certainly does not 'mean' 'prize'.

46 I. 6.4 and O. 0.19, '*aotoi* of garlands', P. 4.131 'reaping the holy *aotos* of good living', P. 4.188, 'the *aotos* of sailors (the Argonauts)', N. 8.9 'the *aotos* of heroes'.

47 P. 2.50–2; I.9.6f; fr. 234; cf. PMG 939.8.

48 Melesias is the victorious boy's trainer.

49 Trans. Geoffrey S. Conway.

50 The sanctuary of Artemidorus at Old Thera is adorned with reliefs of a lion, a dolphin and an eagle, apparently intended as symbols of eternal flourishing: *IG* XII Supp. 1345, 1346, 1347.

51 So also in the *Life* in *POxy* 2438, which crucially changes the words of the poet: 'He was accustomed to say, **the true poet** is he who knows many things by nature; but those who rely on learning, intemperate in their loquacity, are like crows squawking vainly against the divine bird of Zeus.'

52 See the fuller discussion in Richard Stoneman, 'The "Theban Eagle"', *CQ* 26 (1976), pp. 188–97. The argument was rebutted without any kind of counter-argument by Paola Angeli Bernardini in 'L'"aquila tebana" vola ancora', *QUCC* 26 (1977), pp. 121–6. Some later commentators have preferred to have their cake and eat it, making the eagle symbolise both poet and victor simultaneously: see, for example, Ilya Pfeijffer, 'The images of the eagle in Pindar and Bacchylides', *Classical Philology* (1994), pp. 305–17.

53 There is a similar, shorter simile at N. 3.76–8. See also fr. 124 ab.

54 See Hesiod *Works and Days* 742–3 with West's extensive note here and on 524; note Ingrid Waern, ΓΗΣ ΟΣΤΕΑ: *The Kenning in Pre-Christian Poetry* (Uppsala, 1951). Such forms are also characteristic of Old English poetry; see above, Chapter 3, p. 100 on Paean 2.

55 My translation.

56　For what follows, compare my article 'Ploughing a garland: metaphor and metonymy in Pindar', in *Maia* 33 (1981), pp. 125–36.
57　Thomas Carew, 'To My Mistress, I Burning in Love'.
58　Rosemond Tuve, *Elizabethan and Metaphysical Imagery* (Chicago, 1947), p. 261.
59　Shakespeare, *Troilus and Cressida*, ed. Anthony B. Dawson (Cambridge, 2003), p. 22.
60　Peter Avery (ed.), *The Collected Lyrics of Hafiz of Shiraz* (Cambridge, 2007), 456.
61　Geoffrey Ernest Richard Lloyd, *Polarity and Analogy: Two Types of Argumentation in Early Greek Thought* (Cambridge, 1966).
62　The fragment is preserved by a scholiast on Euripides' *Rhesus* 895, and confirmed as a lament by a smaller papyrus fragment: in the play, the Muse (unspecified) sings the *Ialemos* over the dead Rhesus.
63　I. 1.67–8.
64　P. 8.95–7.
65　Burnett, *Pindar's Songs*, p. 7: 'A choral song brought a touch of the eternal upon an earthly celebration.' For the term, see O. 13.36; P. 3.73.
66　Bruno Currie, *Pindar and the Cult of Heroes* (Oxford, 2005).
67　N. 8.48–52.
68　For this kind of dark foil, see also the surprise conclusion of Theognis' poem in praise of Cyrnus:

> Future men likewise, all who have an interest,
>> Will sing of you, while earth and sun exist.
> And yet from you I can not get some slight respect;
>> You lie to me as if I were a child.

(Theognis 237–54, trans. Martin Litchfield West).
69　B. 5.195–200.
70　See O. 2.95.
71　John R. Wilson, 'Kairos as "due measure"', *Glotta* 58 (1980), pp. 177–204.
72　Menander Rhetor 338.28ff. Spengel.
73　Mr Hayley's 'Occasional Stanzas on the Publication of Gibbon's Roman Empire'; from Edward Gibbon, *Autobiography* (London, 1911), p. 171.
74　Herodotus 6.103. See Rosalind Thomas, 'Fame, memorial, and choral poetry: The origins of epinikian poetry', in Simon Hornblower and Catherine Morgan (eds), *Pindar's Poetry: Patrons and Festivals* (Oxford, 2007), pp. 143–4.
75　Aristotle, *Rhetoric* 1387b23–5.
76　Plutarch, *On Envy and Hatred* 537a.
77　Aristotle, *Rhetoric* 1387a12–16.
78　Epicharmus fr. 285 Kaibel = Stob. 3.38.21. Quoted in Peter Walcot, *Envy and the Greeks* (Warminster, 1978), p. 39.
79　Ibycus fr. 282B.
80　P. 11.28–9.
81　O. 6.74–6. Patricia Bulman, *Phthonos in Pindar* (California, 1992), pp. 17–19 collects 16 of the most prominent examples of *phthonos* in Pindar.
82　Thucydides 2.35. On fifth- and fourth-century political envy, see Walcot, *Envy*, pp. 52–76.

83 Lloyd-Jones, 'Modern interpretation', p. 126. The matter is also succinctly covered by Walcot in *Envy*, pp. 41–3.
84 O. 6.81–2.
85 N. 4.39–41.
86 Race notes, 'i.e. to those who slander and to those who believe them'. They cannot harm the victims of their envy.
87 P. 2.76–8.
88 See p. 118 above in this chapter.
89 Paus. 1.2.3 = Simonides T. 18 Campbell; cf. Plato *Ep*. 2.311a = Simonides T. 17.
90 What follows summarises points from my article 'The ideal courtier: Pindar and Hieron in *Pythian* 2', in CQ 34 (1984), pp. 43–9.
91 Plato, *Ep*. 2. 312cd.
92 P. 2.73–5.
93 Thomas Hubbard, 'Hieron and the Ape in Pi. P. 2.72–73'. *TAPA* 120 (1990), pp. 73–83, reads this as the ape being fooled by the children, as Hieron avoids being fooled by flatterers. I find the interpretation contorted, but the general idea is right. Hieron is not fooled.
94 Aristotle, *Rh*. 1356a1–7.
95 See Lloyd-Jones' trenchant discussion in 'Modern interpretation'.
96 'Admonitions to Hieron that he should beware of slanderers.'
97 Avery (ed.), *Collected Lyrics of Hafiz*.
98 P. 2.96.
99 P. 2.79–83.
100 See my discussion in 'The ideal courtier', pp. 46–7.
101 Quoted in Carol Maddison, *Apollo and the Nine: A History of the Ode* (London, 1960), p. 17, from Basil L. Gildersleeve's edition of the *Olympians and Pythians*, ad loc.
102 The metaphor is the same as in Pindar's reference to Archilochus in P. 2, above. Does this suggest rivalry between the two poets? Lefkowitz, *First Person Fictions*, p. 99, shows how the scholiasts' interpretation of Pindar's position – that he was envious of Bacchylides because he was preferred by Hieron – turns Pindar's compliment into an insult: he criticises Hieron for liking the 'inferior' poet.
103 B. 3.63–71.
104 B. 3.58–62.
105 Hdt. I.85–91.

VI. TELLING STORIES

1 The exceptions to this generalisation are rare: Phrynichus' *Sack of Miletus* and Aeschylus' *Persians*; Pindar's *Paean* 2.
2 339.2–9.
3 N. 1.69–72.

4   Anders B. Drachmann (ed.), *Scholia vetera in Pindari carmina*, (Leipzig, 1927), vol. III, p. 19.
5   Ibid., vol. II, pp. 171–2.
6   N. 4.34–8. Conway's translation preserves the sea-going metaphor and translates *katabainein* in its sense of 'come to shore', rather than 'enter the contest': 'Our ship all eyes shall see, riding in the broad light of day, victorious over the foe, safely to shore.'
7   Drachmann (ed.), *Scholia vetera*, vol. III, pp. 74–5. In the scholiast's line numbering, which differs from the modern, the reference is to Nemean 4.60b.
8   Both quoted in Adolf Köhnken, *Die Funktion des Mythos bei Pindar* (Berlin, 1971), p. 227ff.
9   Maurice Bowra, *Pindar* (Oxford, 1964), p. 288.
10 Ibid., p. 296.
11 P. 11.38–9.
12 The use of prophecy is particularly prevalent in the Paeans.
13 N. 3.20–31.
14 P. 3.15–27.
15 P. 3.86–91.
16 As was already noted in Chapter 2, p. 45.
17 P. 9.51–2.
18 P. 9.67–9. See also Pa. 6.137–40 and Basil L. Gildersleeve, *Selections from 'Brief Mention'* (Baltimore, 1930), p. 164.
19 The passage is quoted at length in Chapter 4, pp. 94–5.
20 As Simon Hornblower points out in *Thucydides and Pindar: Historical Narrative and the World of Epinikian Poetry* (Oxford, 2004), p. 283, it is employed by Thucydides too.
21 N. 10.60–1.
22 N. 10.69–70.
23 N. 4.50–8.
24 N. 4.62–5.
25 N. 4.66–8.
26 O. 10.23–9.
27 See also Gretchen Kromer, 'The value of time in Pindar's *Olympian* 10', *Hermes* 104 (1976), pp. 420–36. Kromer shows that exact truth manifests itself with the passing of time, and thus makes praise incontrovertible: 'By recreating his own experience, the poet causes the victor to live on as he was at the time of his triumph.'
28 Herodotus 4.147–58.
29 For example at O. 6.17–18.
30 O. 1.52.
31 The argument is in the main that of Adolf Köhnken in 'Pindar as Innovator'.
32 N. 8.22–7.
33 Fr. 90–2.
34 See William Bedell Stanford, *The Ulysses Theme* (Oxford, 1963), pp. 81–117.

35 Richard Stoneman, 'Pindar and the mythological tradition', *Philologus* 125 (1981), pp. 44–63.
36 Pa. 7b.11–14.
37 I. 8.31–48 is the fullest narrative.
38 A well-known example is Dvořak's opera *Rusalka*.
39 Richard Stoneman, 'Pindar and the mythological tradition', pp. 50–1.
40 Apollodorus, *Bibliotheca* III. 6.4.
41 Fr. 192.
42 It is also the theme of H.D.'s long poem *Helen in Egypt* (1961).
43 Fr. 193.
44 A fragment of Simonides also refers to a Sogenes: 591.166 in Campbell.
45 For further bibliography, see Richard Stoneman, *Pindar: The Odes and Fragments*, re-edition of translation by Geoffrey S. Conway (London, 1997), p. 233. Aesop is another protecting hero who was murdered by the ancestors of those he now protects at Delphi.
46 Pa. 6.121.
47 N. 7.32–49.
48 Race's translation of *proxenia* as 'my host's hospitality' obscures the point.
49 Or perhaps to Argos, the head of the League of Apollo Pythaieus, as suggested in Thomas Figueira, *Aegina: Society and Politics* (New York, 1981). See also Ian Rutherford, *Pindar's Paeans: A Reading of the Fragments with a Survey of the Genre* (Oxford, 2001), p. 331, suggesting the Delphic Theoxenia.
50 Bruno Currie, *Pindar and the Cult of Heroes* (Oxford, 2005), p. 340.
51 Currie, *Cult of Heroes*, p. 311.
52 Burnett, *Pindar's Songs*, pp. 179–202.
53 N. 7.102–6.
54 Lloyd-Jones, 'Modern interpretation' p. 135 = 1990, 150; 'treat with unyielding words', as a periphrasis for 'praise' is a rather free translation of ουκ ελκύσαι, 'not to have mauled'. Cf. Ian Rutherford, *Pindar's Paeans: A Reading of the Fragments with a Survey of the Genre* (Oxford, 2001), p. 322f.
55 Currie, *Cult of Heroes*, p. 318f.
56 O. 2.68–79.
57 Nancy Demand, *Thebes in the Fifth Century* (London, 1982).

VII. RECEPTION

1 Dim echoes of epinician form appear in the epigrams of Posidippus for equestrian victors (71–88); but they concentrate mainly on the horses, though 74 ends with the programmatic details – which could, however, be borrowed from earlier epigram rather than from Pindar. Numbers 78, 79 and 82 for Berenice's victory focus on the lady herself, but they lack Pindar's subtlety (and everything else, too): 'The royal maiden, yes it is she! Berenice in her chariot winning at once every single harness garland in your contests, O Nemean Zeus!' (79, 1–3).

2   *Id.*18, 'Epithalamium for Helen', probably follows the *topoi* of Sappho's lost wedding-songs.
3   Trans. Robert Wells (Manchester, 1988).
4   115–17.
5   'Whoever attempts to emulate Pindar'.
6   Trans. Philip Francis.
7   T. P. Wiseman, *Unwritten Rome* (Exeter, 2008).
8   Richard F. Thomas, *Horace, Odes Book IV and Carmen Saeculare* (Cambridge, 2011), 150, ad. ll. 73–6.
9   Eduard Fraenkel, *Horace* (Oxford, 1957), p. 426ff. argues that it echoed *Paean* 6 in considerable detail.
10 Thomas, *Horace*, p. 197.
11 Fraenkel, *Horace*, p. 432.
12 See, for example, C. 1.33 and C. 4.3.
13 'Of what great man do you think you should sing?'
14 Trans. Diana Robin.
15 See Carol Maddison, *Apollo and the Nine: A History of the Ode* (London, 1960), pp. 105–99.
16 'Like one who takes up a cup, the sole honour of his treasure, and pours for each of the company in turn the wine that is laughing in the gold, so pouring the draught, with which my tongue is watered, upon the race of the Valois. In its sweet nectar I drench the King, most mighty whether in arms or in laws.'
17 *Odes* II.1 similarly echoes the opening of O. 6, and *Odes* I.22 echoes P. 1; *Odes* 16 echoes the metaphor of poem as merchandise in N. 5. In *Odes* II.2 (and commonly thereafter) the model is Horace.
18 'The good poet instructed by his own native wit... Those rhymesters who have learnt their craft with effort, toil and cunning.'
19 'They, compared to my fine songs, resemble the crows that cackle among the leaves against two eagles that stand guard beside the throne of their King.'
20 Epode 2. 'Having taken [the Muse] for my guide with the unfamiliar strain of my lute, I have come where the flowing Loire ripples against the luxuriant fields of your fortunate ancestors.'
21 William Fitzgerald, *Agonistic Poetry: The Pindaric Mode in Pindar, Horace, Hölderlin, and the English Ode* (Berkeley, 1987), p. 22.
22 Lines 65–74.
23 Preface to Cowley's translation of *Olympia* 2 (London, 1668). The quotation continues with the passage given on p. 166.
24 'The Resurrection', 4.1–4.
25 Maddison, *Apollo*, p. 339.
26 Lines 93–6; 107–8.
27 West, preface, p. v.
28 West, vol. I, p. xii.
29 Lines 112–23.
30 I have argued that the metonymy is misconceived: see Chapter 5, p. 118.

31 Humphrey Trevelyan, *Goethe and the Greeks* (Cambridge, 1941), p. 54.
32 Hellingrath, *Pindarübertragungen*, p. 47f., quoted in Maurice B. Benn, *Hölderlin and Pindar* (The Hague, 1962), p. 108, trans. Richard Stoneman.
33 Fitzgerald, *Agnostic Poetry*, pp. 37–8.
34 Michael Hamburger (trans.), *Hölderlin, Poems and Fragments*, 3rd edition (London, 1994), p. 397.
35 Benn, *Hölderlin*, p. 70.
36 Ibid., p. 63.
37 Hamburger (trans.), *Hölderlin*, p. 409.
38 Ibid., p. 395. See Albrecht Seifert, *Untersuchingen zu Hölderlins Pindar-Rezeption* (Munich, 1982), pp. 126ff.
39 My translation.
40 David Constantine, *Hölderlin* (Oxford, 1988), p. 240.
41 See Richard Stoneman, '"A Crazy Enterprise": German Translators of Sophocles, from Opitz to Boeckh', in Jasper Griffin (ed.), *Sophocles Revisited* (Oxford, 1999), pp. 307–29.
42 Quoted in Basil L. Gildersleeve, *Selections from 'Brief Mention'* (Baltimore, 1930), p. 120; one is reminded of Bernard Shaw's remark on Wagner, that he contains 'wonderful moments, but awful quarters of an hour'. I don't agree, of course, in either case.
43 Fr. 124.

BIBLIOGRAPHY

Asheri, David, 'Sicily 478–431 BC', in David M. Lewis, John Boardman, J.K. David and M. Ostwald (eds), *Cambridge Ancient History*, 2nd edition (Cambridge, 1992), vol. V, pp. 147–70.

Athanassaki, Lucia and Bowie, Ewen (eds), *Archaic and Classical Choral Song: Performance, Politics and Dissemination* (Berlin, 2011).

Avery, Peter, *The Collected Lyrics of Hafiz of Shiraz* (Cambridge, 2007).

Barron, John P., 'Ibycus: *Gorgias* and other poems', *Bulletin of the Institute of Classical Studies* 31 (1984), pp. 13–24.

Benn, Maurice B., *Hölderlin and Pindar* (The Hague, 1962).

Bernardini, Paola Angeli, 'L'"aquila tebana" vola ancora', *QUCC* 26 (1977), pp. 121–6.

Boardman, John and Donna Kurtz, *Greek Burial Customs* (London, 1971).

Boedeker, Deborah and David Sider, *The New Simonides: Contexts of Praise and Desire* (New York, 2001).

Bowra, C. Maurice, *Pindar* (Oxford, 1964).

Brophy, Robert H. and Mary Brophy, 'Death in the Panhellenic Games II', *AJP* 106 (1985), pp. 171–98.

Bulman, Patricia, *Phthonos in Pindar* (California, 1992).

Bundy, Elroy L, *Studia Pindarica* (California, 1986; first published 1962).

Burnett, Anne Pippin, *Pindar's Songs for Young Athletes of Aigina* (Oxford, 2005).

Burrow, John Anthony, *The Poetry of Praise* (Cambridge, 2008).

Calame, Claude, *Choruses of Young Women in Ancient Greece* (Lanham, MD, 2001).

Campbell, David, *Greek Lyric*, 5 volumes (Cambridge, MA, 1982–93).

Carey, Chris, 'Pindar's Eighth Nemean Ode', *PCPS* 22 (1976), pp. 26–41.

——'Prosopographica Pindarica', *CQ* 39 (1989), pp. 1–9.

Carson, Anne, 'Wedding at noon in Pindar's Ninth Pythian', *GRBS* 23 (1982), pp. 121–8.

Constantine, David, *Hölderlin* (Oxford, 1988).

Crotty, Kevin, *Song and Action: The Victory Odes of Pindar* (Baltimore, 1982).

Crowther, Nigel B., 'Male beauty contests in Greece: the Euandria and Euexia', *L'Antiquité Classique* 54 (1985), pp. 285–91.

Currie, Bruno, *Pindar and the Cult of Heroes* (Oxford, 2005).

Demand, Nancy, *Thebes in the Fifth Century* (London, 1982).

Deneken, Friedrich, *De Theoxeniis* (diss. Berlin, 1881).

Dougherty, Carol, *The Poetics of Colonization* (Oxford, 1994).

Drachmann, Anders B., *Scholia vetera in Pindari carmina*, vols I–III (Leipzig, 1903, 1910, 1927).

Ebert, Joachim, *Griechische Epigramme auf Sieger an gymnischen und hippischen Agonen* (Berlin, 1972).

Fearn, David W., *Bacchylides: Politics, Performance, Poetic Tradition* (Oxford, 2007).

——(ed.), *Aegina: Contexts for Choral Lyric Poetry: Myth, History, and Identity in the Fifth Century BC* (Oxford, 2011).

Figueira, Thomas, *Aegina: Society and Politics* (New York, 1981).

Finley, Moses I., *Aspects of Antiquity* (Harmondsworth, 1968).

Fitzgerald, William, *Agonistic Poetry: The Pindaric Mode in Pindar, Horace, Hölderlin, and the English Ode* (Berkeley, 1987).

Fraenkel, Eduard, *Horace* (Oxford, 1957).

Freeman, Edward Augustus, *The History of Sicily from the Earliest Times*, 4 volumes (Oxford, 1891–4).

Gallo, Italo (ed.), *POxy 2438* (Salerno, 1968).

Gildersleeve, Basil L., *Selections from 'Brief Mention'* (Baltimore, 1930).

Golden, Mark, *Greek Sport and Social Status* (Austin, 2008).

Hamburger, Michael, *Hölderlin, Poems and Fragments*, 3rd edition (London, 1994).

Hornblower, Simon, *Thucydides and Pindar: Historical Narrative and the World of Epinikian Poetry* (Oxford, 2004).

Hornblower, Simon and Catherine Morgan (eds), *Pindar's Poetry: Patrons and Festivals* (Oxford, 2007).

Hubbard, Thomas, 'Hieron and the Ape in Pi. P. 2.72–73'. *TAPA* 120 (1990), pp. 73–83.

Hunter, Richard and Ian Rutherford (eds), *Wandering Poets in Ancient Greek Culture* (Cambridge, 2009).

Instone, Stephen, 'Pythian 11: Did Pindar err?', *CQ* 36 (1986), pp. 86–94.

Köhnken, Adolf, 'Pindar as Innovator: Poseidon Hippios and the relevance of the Pelops story in *Olympian* 1', *CQ* 24 (1974), pp. 199–206.

——'Gods and descendants of Aiakos in Pindar's Eighth Isthmian Ode', *BICS* 22 (1975), pp. 25–36.

——*Die Funktion des Mythos bei Pindar* (Berlin, 1971).

Kromer, Gretchen, 'The value of time in Pindar's *Olympian* 10', *Hermes* 104 (1976), pp. 420–36.

Kurke, Leslie, 'Pindar's Sixth Pythian and the Tradition of Archaic Poetry', *TAPA* 120 (1990), pp. 85–107.

——*The Traffic in Praise: Pindar and the Poetics of Social Economy* (Ithaca, 1991).

Lane Fox, Robin, *Travelling Heroes: Greeks and Their Myths in the Epic Age of Homer* (London, 2008).

Lawler, Lillian B., *The Dance in Ancient Greece* (London, 1964).

Lee, Hugh M., 'The terma and the javelin in Pindar, *Nemean* vii 70–3, and Greek athletics', *JHS* 96 (1976), pp. 70–9.

Lefkowitz, Mary, 'ΤΩ ΚΑΙ ΕΓΩ: the first person in Pindar', *HSCP* 67 (1963), pp. 177–253.

——*The Victory Ode* (New Jersey, 1976).

——'Pindar's *Pythian* 8', *CJ* 72 (1977), pp. 209–21.

——*The Lives of the Greek Poets* (London, 1981).

——'Pindar's *Pythian* 5', *Pindare, Entretiens sur l'antiquité classique* (Geneva, 1985), vol. 31, pp. 33–58.

——'Who sang Pindar's Victory Odes?', *AJP* 109 (1988), pp. 1–11; also in Lefkowitz, *First Person Fictions*, pp. 191–201.

——*First Person Fictions: Pindar's Poetic 'I'* (Oxford, 1991).

Lloyd, Geoffrey Ernest Richard Lloyd, *Polarity and Analogy: Two Types of Argumentation in Early Greek Thought* (Cambridge, 1966).

——*The Ambitions of Curiosity: Understanding the World in Ancient Greece and China* (Cambridge, 2002).

Lloyd-Jones, Hugh, 'Pindar Fr. 169', *Harvard Studies in Classical Philology* 76 (1972), pp. 45–56 = Lloyd-Jones, *Greek Epic*, pp. 154–65.

———'Pindar and the afterlife', *Entretiens Hardt* 17 (1985), pp. 245–83 = Lloyd-Jones, *Greek Epic*, pp. 80–109.

———'Modern interpretation of Pindar: The second Pythian and seventh Nemean odes'. *JHS* 93 (1973), pp. 109–137 = Lloyd-Jones, *Greek Epic*, pp. 110–15.

———*Greek Epic, Lyric and Tragedy: Academic Papers* (Oxford, 1990).

Mackie, C.J., (ed.) *Oral Performance and Its Context* (Leiden, 2004).

Maddison, Carol, *Apollo and the Nine: A History of the Ode* (London, 1960).

Miller, Stephen G., *Ancient Greek Athletics* (New Haven, CT, 2004).

Mueller, Carl Otfried, *Aegineticorum liber* (Berlin, 1817).

Mullen, William, *Choreia: Pindar and Dance* (Princeton, NJ, 1982).

Naerebout, Frits G., *Attractive Performances: Ancient Greek Dance: Three Preliminary Studies* (Amsterdam, 1997).

Nagy, Gregory, *Pindar's Homer: The Lyric Possession of an Epic Past* (Baltimore, 1990).

Negri, Monica, *Eustazio di Tessalonica: introduzione al commentario a Pindaro* (Brescia, 2000).

———*Pindaro ad Alessandria: le edizioni e gli editori* (Brescia, 2004).

Nilsson, Martin P., *Griechische Feste* (Leipzig, 1906).

Page, Denys L., *Further Greek Epigrams* (Cambridge, 1981).

Parke, Herbert W., *Festivals of the Athenians* (London, 1977).

Parker, Robert, *On Greek Religion* (Ithaca, 2011).

Power, Timothy, *The Culture of Kitharodia* (Washington, DC, 2010).

Pfeijffer, Ilya, 'The images of the eagle in Pindar and Bacchylides', *Classical Philology* 89 (1994), pp. 305–17.

———'Athletic age categories in victory odes', *Nikephoros* 11 (1998), pp. 21–38.

———*Three Aeginetan Odes of Pindar: A Commentary on Nemean V, Nemean III and Pythian VIII* (Leiden, 1999).

Privitera, G. Aurelio, 'Pindaro, *Nem.* III 1–5 e l'acqua di Egina', *QUCC* 58 (1988).

Race, William H., 'Pindaric encomium and Isocrates' *Evagoras*', *TAPA* 117 (1987), pp. 131–55.

———*Pindar*, 2 volumes (Cambridge, MA, 1997).

Renault, Mary, *The Praise Singer* (London, 1978).

Russell, Donald Andrew and Wilson, N.G., *Menander Rhetor* (Oxford, 1981).

Rutherford, Ian, *Pindar's Paeans: A Reading of the Fragments with a Survey of the Genre* (Oxford, 2001).

Sansone, David, *Greek Athletics and the Genesis of Sport* (Berkeley, 1988).

Scanlon, Thomas F., *Eros and Greek Athletics* (New York, 2002).

Schachter, Albert, *Cults of Boeotia* (London, 1981).

Schadewaldt, Wolfgang, *Der Aufbau des pindarischen Epinikion* (Tübingen, 1966).

Schapera, Isaac, *Praise Poems of Tswana Chiefs* (Oxford, 1965).

Seaford, Richard, 'The "hyporchema" of Pratinas', *Maia* 29–30 (1977–8), pp. 81–94.

——*Money and the Early Greek Mind* (Cambridge, 2004).

Schmid, Erasmus, *Pindarou periodos, hoc est Pindari Lyricorum Principis... Olympionikai, Pythionikai, Nemeonikai, Isthmionikai* (Sumptibus Zachariae Schureri, 1616).

Seifert, Albrecht, *Untersuchungen zu Hölderlins Pindar-Rezeption* (Munich, 1982).

Stehle, Eva, *Performance and Gender in Ancient Greece: Non-Dramatic Poetry in Its Setting* (Princeton, NJ, 1997).

Stoneman, Richard, 'The "Theban Eagle"', *CQ* 26 (1976), pp. 188–97.

——'Pindar and the mythological tradition', *Philologus* 125 (1981), pp. 44–63.

——'Ploughing a garland: Metaphor and metonymy in Pindar', *Maia* 33 (1981), pp. 125–36.

——'The ideal courtier: Pindar and Hieron in *Pythian* 2', CQ 34 (1984), pp. 43–9.

——*Palmyra and Its Empire: Zenobia's Revolt against Rome* (Ann Arbor, MI, 1994).

——*Pindar: The Odes and Fragments*, re-edition of translation by Geoffrey S. Conway (London, 1997).

——'"A crazy enterprise": German translators of Sophocles, from Opitz to Boeckh', in Jasper Griffin (ed.), *Sophocles Revisited* (Oxford, 1999), pp. 307–29.

Swift, Laura, *The Hidden Chorus* (Oxford, 2010).

Thomas, Richard F., *Horace, Odes Book IV and Carmen Saeculare* (Cambridge, 2011).

Trevelyan, Humphrey, *Goethe and the Greeks* (Cambridge, 1941).

Tuve, Rosemond, *Elizabethan and Metaphysical Imagery* (Chicago, 1947).

Von der Mühll, Peter, 'Persönliche Verliebtheit des Dichters?' *Museum Helveticum* 21 (1964), pp. 168–72.

Walcot, Peter, *Envy and the Greeks* (Warminster, 1978).

West, M.L. *The Epic Cycle. A Commentary on the Lost Troy Epics* (Oxford UP, 2013).

Wilamowitz-Moellendorff, Ulrich von, *Pindaros* (Berlin, 1922).

——*History of Classical Scholarship* (Baltimore, MD, 1982).

Willcock, Malcolm M., 'Second reading of Pindar: "The Fourth Nemean"', *Greece and Rome* 29 (1982), pp. 1–10.

Wilson, John R., 'Kairos as "due measure"', *Glotta* 58 (1980), pp. 177–204.

Wilson, Peter, *The Athenian Institution of the Khoregia* (Cambridge, 2000).

Woodbury, Leonard, 'Pindar and the mercenary muse: *Isthm*. 2.1–13. *TAPA* 99 (1968), pp. 368–75.

——'Cyrene and the *Teleuta* of marriage in Pindar's Ninth Pythian Ode' *TAPA* 112 (1982), pp. 245–58.

Young, David C., *Three Odes of Pindar* (Leiden, 1968).

——*The Olympic Myth of Greek Amateur Athletics* (Chicago, 1984).

INDEX

Living persons mentioned in Pindar's odes (victors and their relatives) are marked with *.